tadt
Shopping
Neumarkt
St. Aposteln
Römerturm
Stadtmuseum
Friesenviertel

Lauren Dierickx, Laura Muyldermans, Olivier Goethals, Sander Rutgers, 'Building Application. 6 Urbanist Imaginations for Ghent and Brussels', exhibition in 019, Ghent, 2025/ Lauren Dierickx, Laura Muyldermans, Olivier Goethals, Sander Rutgers, 'Bouwaanvraag. 6 Stedenbouwkundige verbeeldingen voor Gent en Brussel', tentoonstelling in 019, Gent, 2025

Contemporary Settings for Brokering Quality

Maarten Liefooghe, Susan Holden, Elsbeth Ronner and Maarten Van Den Driessche

Architectural production is no longer simply understood as an interplay between clients, designers, builders and users. Today, a wide array of so-called 'quality mediators' operate both in the everyday practice of architecture and within the cultural forums that shape the architecture discourse. It is precisely this dual embeddedness that often proves decisive in determining the quality of outcomes. Some actors – such as the Dutch *welstandscommissies* (advisory design review committees) or the *Rijksbouwmeester* (Chief Government Architect) – have a longstanding tradition and a recognised institutional role. Yet these mediators are regularly challenged by shifting political and administrative frameworks, evolving design agendas and the emergence of new 'quality settings', all of which demand a continual redefinition of their roles.

The 2009 book *Mooi Europa: Ruimtelijke kwaliteitszorg in Europa* (Beautiful Europe: Spatial Quality in Europe) gives concrete form to an evolving discourse on quality.[1] Initiated by the Nederlandse Federatie Welstandstoezicht (Dutch Federation for Design Review), the book deliberately eschews the somewhat dated term *welstand* – a Dutch notion that relates both to aesthetic beauty and to the idea of being 'well-standing' or well-suited – in favour of 'beauty' and 'spatial quality'. However, the tension between these two concepts remains pertinent. As editors Nico Nelissen and Flip ten Cate wrote at the time:

> The term 'spatial quality' is actually a successor to the term *welstand*, which has lost popularity for several reasons. . . . Spatial quality is viewed as a less technical and legal term, one which moreover emphasises that it is not only about the quality of a building itself, but also about the quality of the space in which it is situated.[2]

The concept was thus broader and fundamentally different from 'architectural quality', typically understood as the degree to which a building adheres to the principles of good architectural design.[3] Ten Cate would later identify further conceptual developments, including 'environmental quality' (*omgevingskwaliteit*) and 'high-quality building culture'.[4]

The book examined the policies and institutional frameworks for spatial quality in seven Western European countries – the Netherlands, Belgium, France, Germany, Switzerland, Spain and England. It demonstrated that spatial quality is promoted differently in each country, shaped by unique administrative structures and building cultures that have evolved over time. This comparison and knowledge exchange aimed to foster critical development of quality assurance practices not only nationally but across Europe.

Mooi Europa concluded with a speculative, Black Mirror-esque vision of Europe in 2025, projecting 2009's local dynamics into the future. Today, this imagined future seems both amusing and outdated – a caricature of cultural stereotypes overtaken by the complexities of contemporary culture wars. Belgium, Spain and England were forecast to fare particularly poorly

1 Nico Nelissen and Flip ten Cate, *Mooi Europa: Ruimtelijke kwaliteitszorg in Europa* (Nijmegen: Sun, 2009).

2 Ibid., 12.

3 Ibid.

4 Flip ten Cate, 'Bouwcultuur: Elke ruimtelijke ingreep is een culturele daad', *Archined*, 3 February 2020, archined.nl/2020/02/bouwcultuur-elke-ruimtelijke-ingreep-is-een-culturele-daad/.

Hedendaagse omgevingen voor kwaliteitsbemiddeling

Maarten Liefooghe, Susan Holden, Elsbeth Ronner en Maarten Van Den Driessche

Architectuurproductie is al lang niet meer louter een samenspel tussen opdrachtgevers, ontwerpers, bouwers en gebruikers. Er zijn tegenwoordig meer actoren bij betrokken, bijvoorbeeld allerlei zogenaamde 'kwaliteitsborgers'. Ze opereren zowel in het dagelijkse architectuurbedrijf als op de fora van de architectuurcultuur, en precies die dubbele inbedding maakt vaak het verschil. Sommige instanties, zoals de Nederlandse welstandscommissies of het Rijksbouwmeesterschap hebben een eerbiedwaardige traditie en een gevestigde rol. Soms wordt hun aanpak ook ter discussie gesteld, bijvoorbeeld door wijzigende bestuurlijke regimes waardoor ze hun plaats opnieuw moeten verdedigen of heruitvinden, de accenten anders worden gelegd, bestuurlijke agenda's evolueren of andere typen 'kwaliteitskamers' in opkomst zijn.

Het in 2009 verschenen boek *Mooi Europa: Ruimtelijke kwaliteitszorg in Europa* maakte evoluties in het kwaliteitsdiscours kenbaar[1], een initiatief van de Nederlandse Federatie Welstandstoezicht. Maar niet dat wat oubollig klinkende kwaliteitsbegrip 'welstand' kreeg een plaats in de titel, wel de begrippen 'schoonheid' en 'ruimtelijke kwaliteit'. Niettemin ging er ook daartussen al een conceptuele spanning schuil die relevant blijft.' Zo schreven samenstellers Nico Nelissen en Flip ten Cate toen:

> Het begrip 'ruimtelijke kwaliteit' is eigenlijk een opvolger van het begrip 'welstand', dat om meerdere redenen aan populariteit heeft ingeboet. (...) Ruimtelijke kwaliteit wordt gezien als een minder technische en juridische term, die bovendien meer benadrukt dat het niet alleen gaat om de kwaliteit van een gebouw op zich, maar om de totale ruimte die ermee gemoeid is.[2]

Daarom was het concept ook fundamenteel breder, meer divers dan wat onder 'architectonische kwaliteit' begrepen kon worden: 'in hoeverre een gebouw beantwoordt aan criteria die te maken hebben met de basisprincipes van een goed architectonisch ontwerp'.[3] In Nederland zou Ten Cate later nog meer conceptuele verbredingen aanwijzen met de noties 'omgevingskwaliteit', en vervolgens 'kwaliteitsvolle bouwcultuur'.[4]

In het boek zelf werd het kwaliteitsbeleid van zeven West-Europese landen – Nederland, België, Frankrijk, Duitsland, Zwitserland, Spanje en Engeland – met elkaar vergeleken. Deze vergelijking liet zien hoe kwaliteitszorg er door verschillende instanties wordt gewaarborgd, hoezeer de beleidstradities ook lokaal verankerd zijn, en het beleid dus onlosmakelijk verbonden is met verschillende bouw- en bestuursculturen die daar door de tijd heen tot stand zijn gekomen. Die vergelijking en de wederzijdse kennisuitwisseling ging samen met een kritische oproep om kwaliteitszorg in elk van deze landen of regio's, en op Europees niveau, verder uit te bouwen.

Mooi Europa eindigde zowaar met een toekomstbeeld van Europa in 2025, op basis van een extrapolatie van de lokale dynamiek in 2009. Dit toekomstbeeld komt nu zowel vermakelijk als interessant achterhaald over. Het lijkt wel een parodie van culturele stereotypen die vandaag nog

1 Nico Nelissen en Flip ten Cate, *Mooi Europa: Ruimtelijke kwaliteitszorg in Europa* (Nijmegen: Sun, 2009).

2 Ibid, 12.

3 Ibid.

4 Flip ten Cate, 'Bouwcultuur: Elke ruimtelijke ingreep is een culturele daad', *Archined*, 3 februari 2020. https://www.archined.nl/2020/02/bouwcultuur-elke-ruimtelijke-ingreep-is-een-culturele-daad/

by 2025: 'Champions of spatial quality are taking early retirement, and the influx of skilled professionals is stagnating. In Belgium, "Gammadorpen" [DIY-store-builder villages] are emerging; in Spain, the "Costa d'Espagna" is deteriorating; and in England, "Coronation Streets" are proliferating.'[5] In contrast, Germany and France were imagined to have resisted the pressures of economic and populist forces, maintaining vital aspects of their quality systems.[6] Switzerland and the Netherlands, the exemplary 'guiding countries' of 2009, were depicted as having further solidified their leadership, thanks to policy decisions that preserved their quality management structures.[7]

Beyond the actual historical developments in these countries in the past 15 years, what stands out today is the growing intensity of cross-border exchanges of best practices. Quality has become an acknowledged concern at the European policy level. At the same time, it is increasingly cities and regions that drive the institutionalisation of design governance.[8] Two examples illustrate this dual dynamic. From the top down, former European Commission President Ursula von der Leyen unexpectedly launched the New European Bauhaus initiative, aligning architecture, design and art with the European Green Deal. This programme links cultural innovation with digital transformation and sustainability. From the bottom up, Newcastle's Urban Room – a collaboration between the Farrell Centre and Newcastle University – offers workshops for citizens, including children, to engage with urban development. These examples illustrate the multiplicity of roles that such initiatives play: offering inspiration, guiding commissioning practices, influencing spatial planning and opening up

5 Nelissen and Ten Cate, *Mooi Europa*, op. cit. (note 1), 218-219.

6 Ibid., 221.

7 Ibid., 223.

8 Mathew Carmona, Joao Bento and Tommaso Gabrieli, *Urban Design Governance: Soft Powers and the European Experience* (London: UCL Press, 2023).

'Beautiful Europe'. In 2009, Nelissen and Ten Cate discussed spatial quality as a matter of national frameworks and policies/ 'Mooi Europa'. In 2009 bediscussieerden Nelissen en Ten Cate ruimtelijke kwaliteit als een zaak van nationale kaders en beleid

pregnanter zijn door de werkelijkheid van cultuuroorlogen. België, Spanje en Engeland zouden er in 2025 veel slechter voorstaan dan in 2009: 'De voorvechters van kwaliteitszorg zijn met (vervroegd) pensioen en de nieuwe instroom van bekwame professionals op dit gebied stagneert. In België ontstaan "Gammadorpen", in Spanje verloedert de "Costa d'Espagna" en in Engeland rijgen de "Coronation Streets" zich aan elkaar.'[5] In Duitsland en Frankrijk zou 'men, ondanks de druk van economie en populisme, kans gezien [hebben] om belangrijke onderdelen van het stelsel van ruimtelijke kwaliteitszorg te behouden'.[6] De benijdenswaardige gidslanden anno 2009 zouden nog meer tot bakens van voorbeeldigheid uitgegroeid zijn. 'In een paar landen van Europa is men zo verstandig geweest om van ruimtelijke kwaliteitszorg een speerpunt van beleid te maken,' in Zwitserland en in Nederland met name, 'waar men op het laatste moment toch heeft afgezien van pogingen om het stelsel van ruimtelijke kwaliteitszorg te ontmantelen.'[7]

Los van de echte historische evoluties in elk van deze landen in de afgelopen 15 jaar moet vandaag vastgesteld worden hoe intens de uitwisseling van praktijken geworden is, dat kwaliteit op Europees beleidsniveau resoluut een thema werd, terwijl steden en regio's de echte aanjagers zijn geweest van de ontplooiing van (bestuurlijke) instellingen voor ontwerpcultuur.[8] Twee voorbeelden illustreren die twee niveaus: binnen haar vorige mandaat als voorzitter van de Europese Commissie lanceerde Ursula von der Leyen nogal onverwacht een New European Bauhaus-programma dat een culturele agenda aan de Europese Green Deal wilde toevoegen, en architectuur, ontwerp en kunst in voorbeeldprojecten wilde combineren met vernieuwingen in digitalisering en verduurzaming van de economie. Een voorbeeld van onderop is de Urban Room in Newcastle waar het Farrell Centre als culturele instelling, samen met Newcastle University, met kinderen en stadsbewoners workshops inricht. We zien dus initiatieven die, soms tegelijkertijd, verschillende rollen vervullen, variërend van het geven van een voorbeeldfunctie, het inspireren van opdrachtgevers, ontwerpers en betrokkenen tot het stimuleren van goed opdrachtgeverschap en het sturen op ruimtelijke ordening. Ze stellen elk vanuit hun verschillende posities ten aanzien van formele structuren, met behulp van verschillende instrumenten en beïnvloeding, de productie van architectuur aan de orde.

Bij de hedendaagse verspreiding van kwaliteitsconcepten en bemiddelingsfora gaat het niet alleen om fundamentele vragen over wat goede kwaliteit is, maar over hoe we daarover beslissen, met welke expertise en binnen welke organisatorische omgeving. Deze vragen hebben rechtstreeks te maken met de manier waarop de ontwerppraktijk verandert. Of anders gezegd: we kunnen in de nadruk, die besturen leggen op de agenda's voor ontwerpkwaliteit, nieuwe configuraties en discussies over ontwerpexpertise en professionele praktijken zien. Zien we hier ook een sterkere prioritering van het publieke belang en een zoektocht naar nieuwe maatschappelijke en sociale verbeelding?

Onder de brede noemer *quality settings*, waarvoor we ook het Nederlandse woord *kwaliteitskamers* introduceren, staat dit *OASE*-nummer stil bij hedendaagse instanties waar de kwaliteit van architectuur en stedenbouw nagestreefd en bemiddeld wordt.[9] De in dit nummer verzamelde artikelen buigen zich over institutionele omgevingen en bestuurlijke processen die ruimte trachten vrij te maken om kwaliteit niet vooraf te definiëren in een standaard, norm of controleproces, maar die juist een openheid aan de dag leggen om kwaliteit te zoeken in altijd andere contexten en

5 Nelissen en Ten Cate, *Mooi Europa*, op. cit. (noot 1), 218-219.

6 Ibid, 221.

7 Ibid., 223.

8 Mathew Carmona, Joao Bento en Tommaso Gabrieli, *Urban Design Governance: Soft Powers and the European Experience* (Londen: UCL Press, 2023).

9 Hoewel de in België gangbare betekenis van kwaliteitskamer enger is (een *design review panel*, vaak op stedelijk niveau), hanteren we in dit nummer het begrip als een borger voor kwaliteit in de brede zin: zowel in formele zin, gerelateerd aan een instituut of overheidsinstelling met een juridisch mandaat, of als informele *settings* uit het middenveld.

new avenues for civic engagement. Each engages architectural production from a distinct position within formal structures, employing diverse tools and exerting varied forms of influence.

What is at stake in this proliferation of quality concepts and mediation frameworks are fundamental questions: What constitutes good quality? How is it decided? Whose expertise is considered, and in which settings? These are not peripheral concerns – they lie at the heart of how design practice is evolving. The increasing visibility of urban design quality agendas within governance structures marks a shift in the configuration, and at times the contestation, of design expertise and professional identity. Might this also signal a renewed emphasis on the public interest and a search for new civic and social imaginaries?

Under the umbrella of *quality settings* (for which we introduced the Dutch term *kwaliteitskamers*), this issue of *OASE* examines contemporary contexts in which architectural and urban design quality is pursued and mediated.[9] The articles focus on institutional structures and governance processes that make space for quality to be explored and negotiated, rather than predefined by standards, norms or technical controls. They demonstrate how, in changing circumstances, relative consensus can be forged – again and again – through collaboration between peer designers, disciplinary experts and engaged citizens. The active inclusion of lay stakeholders at the 'quality table' is never automatic; it must be pursued intentionally within each setting discussed. One persistent tension is between the knowledge held by quality guardians and the creative experimentation that may challenge established norms. The urgent demands of ecological transition underscore the relevance of both. They also compel quality mediators to integrate environmental metrics – such as lifecycle assessments and carbon targets – into qualitative discussions.

Focusing on settings does not mean ignoring quality statements or the realised material outcomes of ambition and skill. General concepts – like Vitruvius's *utilitas*, *firmitas* and *venustas*, and their many reinterpretations – remain relevant, but always in constellation with concrete design work. As with any meaningful design process, the task in quality evaluation is not to isolate qualities or merely tally strengths and weaknesses, but to assess how they interrelate. This requires a mode of judgement that transcends quantification. Quality settings thus depend not only on critical expertise and accumulated architectural insight, but also on institutional conditions where diverse perspectives can be brought together – and trusted. Such settings thrive within a broader administrative and democratic culture that enables legitimacy to be built, critical resistance to be voiced and quality to be made public.

To peer into the quality kitchen is also to reflect on the performative dimension of role-playing. Quality negotiations require their own theatres – arenas in which policymakers, stakeholders, designers, experts and mediators can interact. These are the spaces where ambitions, projects and questions of quality are aired, where shared attention can be cultivated and where architecture's value to the public can be demonstrated and debated.

9
Although the common meaning of *kwaliteitskamer* (literally: quality chamber) in Belgium is narrower (a design review panel, often at the urban level), in this issue we use the term for any broker of quality in the broad sense: both in the formal sense, for an institution or government agency with a legal mandate, as well as for more informal initiatives in civil society.

omstandigheden. Hoe kan er telkens opnieuw een vorm van consensus opgebouwd worden met vakgenoten uit de ontwerpwereld en andere disciplinaire experts, waarbij professionele expertise verbonden kan worden (liever dan geconfronteerd) met de inbreng van leken-actoren? Hun emancipatie en actieve betrokkenheid aan de 'kwaliteitstafel' is nooit vanzelfsprekend, maar een cruciaal streven in elk van de *settings*, die in de artikelen van dit nummer worden besproken. Er bestaat ook een onvermijdelijke spanning tussen enerzijds de kennisopbouw en expertise van borgende experts, en anderzijds het experiment dat gevestigde praktijken provoceert. De uitdaging bij de ecologische transitie maakt ze allebei belangrijker, en dwingt kwaliteitsborgers ook om bijvoorbeeld levenscyclus- en CO2-reductiedoelstellingen te kwantificeren en een plek te geven in kwalitatieve evaluaties.

Natuurlijk is het nooit mogelijk, en ook niet wenselijk om bij zo'n focus op de *settings*, de opvattingen over kwaliteit en de verwerkelijking van ambities en kunde in de uitvoering buiten beschouwing te laten. Het is een samenspel tussen veralgemenende concepten en criteria, zoals de Vitruviaanse trias *utilitas*, *firmitas* en *venustas*, met bijbehorende actualiseringen én concrete ontwerpen met inachtneming van de dan geldende beperkingen. Net als bij elk goed ontwerpproject gaat het er bij elke onderhandeling over kwaliteit immers om, kwaliteitsaspecten niet afzonderlijk te evalueren, of sterkte/zwakte-analyses uit te voeren, maar om kwaliteitsaspecten samenhangend te beschouwen. Het vergt een oordeel dat ontsnapt aan kwantificatie en het zelfs overstijgt. Kwaliteitskamers vragen niet alleen om het architectuurkritisch oordeelsvermogen van experts en betrokkenen, maar ook om de omstandigheden waar verschillende inzichten en expertises bijeen gelegd kunnen worden. Ze vergen uiteindelijk een bestuurlijke en democratische cultuur waar vertrouwen is in 'kwaliteitskamers' als een gewaardeerde publieke instelling, waar verantwoording wordt afgelegd, maar ook kritisch weerwerk mogelijk is.

Binnenkijken in de kwaliteitskeuken is altijd ook stilstaan bij zowel de relativiteit als de performatieve kracht van een rollenspel. Kwaliteitsonderhandeling heeft immers ook behoefte aan eigen theaters waar beleidsmakers en betrokkenen, ontwerpers en experts, of regisseurs hun spel kunnen spelen ten opzichte van elkaar. Een plek waar locaties en architectuurprojecten, ambities, kwaliteiten en kwesties opgevoerd kunnen worden, waar aandacht voor kwalitatieve evaluatie en discussie wordt gestimuleerd. Een omgeving waar kwaliteit ook publiek gemaakt kan worden.

Design Quality as a Matter of Governance and Culture: A Diptych

Susan Holden and Maarten Liefooghe

The setting of the European Commission seems a long way from the everyday practices that shape the quality of the built environment on the ground. Yet the speech of Commission President Ursula von der Leyen in April 2024 at the second New European Bauhaus Festival, celebrating the (contested) advances of her NEB initiative, exemplifies how design quality has become a subject of governance and of cultural policy with seeming high stakes. Quality is today being fostered in both high-level statements and in myriad daily settings where architects, urban designers, politicians, bureaucrats and citizens interact in a range of configurations. These practices are at the same time informed by longer histories of urban regulation, cultures of professional practice and broader concepts of building culture and heritage.

In the parallel articles of this diptych, we distinguish, explore and contrast two such paradigms that inform contemporary practices and discourses of quality: design quality as a matter of design governance versus quality as a matter of culture. To those broader discursive and political framings correspond different notions of what is a good place, qualitative design and responsible architectural practice. They also imply different distributions of responsibilities across actors and different settings to foster quality. Susan Holden's contribution to the diptych engages with design governance, centring on the now widely used instrument of design review boards, as this instrument can emblematize design governance's trust in projects over prescriptions as grounds for quality, and in professional expertise of architects and urban designers.
To illustrate a cultural approach to architectural quality, Maaren Liefooghe's contribution focusses on the notion of *Baukultur*. The 2018 Declaration of Davos on High-Quality Baukultur has brought this perspective to the fore, projecting cultural values of the built environment as a concern for all actors in society.

In sketching the genealogies and particularities of these two quality traditions, we observed commonalities between them, in their soft power strategies and public interest focus for instance. But also differing contextual development in relation to urban governance and cultural policy contexts; differing emphasis on a professional culture of expertise versus a concept of quotidian but rich building culture; and differing prioritisation of excellence agendas versus agendas for sociocultural inclusion.

Such differentiation between discursive signifiers of quality and concomitant design governance genealogies is a way to question the consensus-seeking and unifying notion of quality, and to ponder how different notions of quality are intertwined with developments in the governance of culture and the political economy. It also makes it possible to interrogate the very remit of design governance as a new setting of professional practice – its limits and vulnerabilities, its inherent tensions and paradoxes, and the risks of defining national building cultures or instrumentalising quality discourses.

Quality as a Matter of Governance: Design Review

Susan Holden

Today, quality no longer emanates from the classical canon, the diktat of a decision-maker or the mind of a so-called 'creative genius' . . . Good architecture should promote a good urban society, which is why architectural quality always requires a healthy debate. . . . The participants must take their responsibilities seriously . . . The conversation becomes a foundation, and architectural quality becomes a shared value.[1]

Soft Power City-Making

The governance of design, or the idea that design quality is a matter for governing, is not new.[2] However, it has taken on a new meaning in the wake of neoliberal reforms of government since the 1980s that have dramatically changed the agency of public-sector actors in shaping the built environment. In this context, the

1
Bouwmeester Maître Architecte, 'Quality', bma.brussels/en/why-we-do-it (accessed 17 February 2025).

2
See, for example, the following publications that explore how architecture and aesthetic aspects of urban regulation intersect with the political economy and with assemblages of governmentality as theorised by Michel Foucault: Daniel M. Abramson, Arindam Dutta, Timothy Hyde and Jonathan Massey (Aggregate Architectural History Collective), *Governing by Design: Architecture, Economy, and Politics in the Twentieth Century* (Pittsburgh: University of Pittsburgh Press, 2012); Jules Lubbock, *The Tyranny of Taste: The Politics of Architecture and Design in Britain 1550-1960* (New Haven/London: Yale University Press, 1995); and Alan Hunt, 'Governing the City: Liberalism and early modern modes of governance,' in: Andrew Barry, Thomas Osborne and Nikolas Rose (eds.), *Foucault and Political Reason* (London: UCL Press, 1996), 167-188.

Quality as a Matter of Culture: *Baukultur*

Maarten Liefooghe

How neatly, how safely, how trimly, how solidly, how seriously, how spotlessly, how consciously, how tastefully, how tidily, how thoroughly, how seriously and so on they build in this country.

Max Frisch[1]

Conceiving the quality of architecture as a matter of culture appears both self-evident and a position that is staunchly defended today, precisely because it is perceived to be under threat.[2] On the one hand, we are accustomed to architecture being part of the programming of cultural institutions, to architecture books appearing on shelves alongside art volumes, and to architecture occupying a place in cultural policy across many countries.[3] In this sense, architectural quality concerns its appreciation in relation to criteria specific

1
Max Frisch, *I'm Not Stiller* (London: Methuen, 1982), 213, as cited in: Irina Davidovici, *Forms of Practice: German-Swiss Architecture 1980-2000* (Zurich: gta Verlag, 2018), 243.

2
For instance: *de Architect* 3 (2024): 'Architectuur als culturele waarde: voorbij praktisch nut.'

3
In his overview of architecture policies in Europe, João Bento notes that in national, regional and European policy constellations architecture is sometimes dealt with primarily in cultural policy, sometimes in spatial policy or in the development and management of public patrimony by governments. Consequently, at the semi-annual European Conferences for Architectural Policies (ECAP), national representatives at times come from cultural, heritage or other administrations. João Bento, *Architecture Policies in Europe* (Brussels: Architects' Council of Europe, 2023).

The South Australian State Design Review Panel Chairs with the Government Architect, Kirsteen Mackay

to architecture as a cultural practice – rather than merely as a technical discipline or utilitarian concern. On the other hand, the urgent emphasis on sustainability and ecological issues has placed this cultural perspective on the defensive, or at least prompted its redefinition. Yet, the cultural foundations of architectural quality cannot be affirmed only in contrast to technical, economic, or energy-performance metrics. Equally important is the question: what architectural or building culture do we presume, and which one do we wish to foster?

This question is especially pertinent today, as the term and concept of 'building culture' have begun to feature prominently in European policy frameworks. It has become a key vector in what João Bento identifies as the current 'Europeanisation' of architectural policy, visible in the evolution of national cultural agendas across the continent.[4] In German-speaking Europe, *Baukultur* has long referred to the cultural dimension of buildings and the built environment, and has featured in various policy initiatives. It has perhaps become so deeply ingrained that the ideals associated with it were barely noticed. But when 33 European culture ministers signed the Davos Declaration in 2018 – tellingly entitled *Towards*

concept of design governance captures new ways of directing design expertise and new sociopolitical motives for quality. The public interest agendas for quality in contemporary design governance relate to a new 'political economy of place-making', and more recently, to an equitable environmental transition.[3]

The concept of 'soft power' sits at the heart of the way high quality outcomes are advanced through the 'technologies' of design governance.[4] Kristiaan Borret, Brussels Bouwmeester Maître Architecte (BMA) expresses it well:

> In cities we have regulations, planning laws and so on. They can help to avoid excesses and eliminate blunders, but they are not enough if we want to go for excellence. For that, we need 'soft power' mechanisms that promote interesting architecture and urban design in the cities.[5]

Borret made these remarks in the context of the Urban Maestro project that surveyed a range of design governance practices across Europe to understand how 'soft powers of state . . . can deliver better-designed places'.[6] Established in 2009, the BMA was a partner in this research project. Their work has also been showcased

3
Rob Imre and Emma Street, *Architectural Design and Regulation* (West Sussex: Wiley-Blackwell, 2011), 244. Imre and Street refer to David Harvey's spatial analysis of postmodernity in David Harvey, *Spaces of Capital: Toward a Critical Geography* (New York: Routledge, 2001).

4
Mitchell Dean, *Governmentality: Power and Rule in Modern Society* (London: Sage, 1999/2010), 202. Dean's understanding of the technologies of advanced liberal governments maps on to design governance practices to the extent that they make occasions for broad stakeholder engagement in the negotiation of quality outcomes, and in the way they claim authority through their moral (professional) and political (governance) conduct.

5
Kristiaan Borret, quoted in: United Nations Human Settlements Programme (UN-Habitat), Bouwmeester Maître Architecte (BMA), Bartlett School of Planning (UCL), *Urban Maestro, New Governance Strategies for Urban Design* (London: University College London, 2021), 2.

6
The Urban Maestro project is the work of three partners: UN Habitat, Bouwmeester Maître Architecte, and University College London. It commenced in 2019 and was funded by the European Union's Horizon 2020 programme. See: urbanmaestro.org.

a High-Quality Baukultur *for Europe* – the term and its ideals received renewed attention.[5]

Tracing a path from Davos, through other Swiss sites where the building-cultural discourse developed, and back to Davos again, we can begin to visualise some of the term's meanings, and consider the complexities tied to this 'quality' watchword.

Culture, not Art

The Swiss Federal Office of Culture seized the momentum of the 2018 European Year of Cultural Heritage to gather European counterparts in Davos, endorsing a wide-ranging cultural agenda to elevate the quality of the built environment – placing it on par with economic and environmental policy objectives. The opening lines of the conference's declaration mobilise concern around an alleged general decline in quality in the built environment that goes beyond tangible and intangible heritage losses:

> Aware of a trend towards a loss of quality in both the built environment and open landscapes all over Europe, evident in the trivialisation of construction, the lack of design values, including a lack of concern for sustainability, the growth of faceless

4
Ibid., 10.

5
Davos Declaration 2018: Towards a High-Quality Baukultur *for Europe*, adopted at the Conference of Ministers of Culture, 20-22 January 2018, in Davos Switzerland, davosdeclaration2018.ch/en/ (accessed 6 June 2024).

in the recent exhibition 'Soft Power: The Brussels Way of Making the City' at the Swiss Architecture Museum, Basel.[7] The exhibition presented a selection of projects that exemplify the contribution of the BMA to cultivating a 'high quality building culture' in Brussels, facilitated largely through their advisory services and design-focused 'open call' commissioning system.[8] Several notable reuse projects were featured, including the high-profile Brussels World Trade Centre redevelopment (51N4E, l'AUC and Jaspers-Eyers) and the Zinneke offices and workshops (Zinneke, Rotor and Ouest), equally innovative in their co-design strategies. The exhibition scenography by Asli Çiçek was dominated by a field of metal-framed plinths of different dimensions and heights that displayed models, drawings and photographs. The closely spaced legs of the plinths resonated as an understorey for the projects: an effective support structure not unlike the BMA itself.

Following Borret's formulation, soft power highlights the non-regulatory status of many design governance processes that exploit opportunities for informal and sometimes opportunistic interventions in planning and development processes, from project briefing and procurement to design and delivery. The expertise

'Soft Power: The Brussels Way of Making the City' showcased the work of the Brussels Bouwmeester Maître Architecte in S AM Swiss Architecture Museum, Basel. Exhibition key visual, 2024

> urban sprawl and irresponsible land use, the deterioration of historic fabric, and the loss of regional traditions and identities.[6]

It is a curious yet telling move that European culture ministers chose the World Economic Forum in Davos as the setting to commit themselves – together with representatives of UNESCO, the Architects' Council of Europe, Europa Nostra, and others – to asserting and developing the built environment as a legitimate cultural policy domain. This context signals the role of culture within both neoliberal governance frameworks and consensus-oriented politics.

The building culture concept promoted in the Davos Declaration adopts a very broad and inclusive conception of the (un)built environment, as well as of the stakeholders and actors who are being called to take building culture to heart:

> Baukultur embraces every human activity that changes the built environment. The whole built environment, including every designed and built asset that is embedded in and relates to the natural environment, is to be understood as a single entity. Baukultur encompasses existing

Quality criteria according to the Davos *Baukultur* Quality System, 2021

of architects and urban designers – such as Borret – remain crucial to achieving high-quality outcomes, but they are deployed to guide and influence in their roles as government architects, design advisers and advocates. In the logic of design governance, quality thus becomes something contingent on the negotiations between specific actors, as much as it is generated independently or located only in designs themselves. This suggests a new productive realm and new forms of design expertise that are expanding the identity of the architecture profession. As architecture critic Elias Baumgarten remarked in a review of the Soft Power exhibition: 'It seems to be precisely this role of neutral expert that enables Borret to steer urban development.'[9]

Beyond this understanding, soft power has a more freighted association, linking design governance discourse to the rise of 'third way' governments in the last decades of the twentieth century, and specifically to the endeavours of the UK Commission for Architecture and the Built Environment (CABE, 1999-2011). CABE was established in the wake of New Labour's historic election win in 1997 and was part of their wide-ranging social and economic policy reforms that included a focus on the creative and knowledge economies as

7
The exhibition ran from 19 October 2024 to 16 March 2025 and was curated by Roxane Le Grelle and Andreas Kofler in cooperation with the Bouwmeester Maître Architecte and the support of the Brussels Capital Region. Denoo Jan and Hedwig van der Linden, *Soft Power: 10 Years of Bouwmeester Maître Architecte in Brussels* (Cologne: Walther König, 2024).

8
SAM, 'Soft Power: The Brussels Way of Making the City', sam-basel.org/en/ausstellungen/aktuell (accessed 20 January 2025). Even though the work of the BMA is only advisory, they must be consulted on projects over 5000 m^2, according to the parameters of the Brussels Planning Legislation (Article 11/1 of the CoBAT/BWRO). However the review process is open for other projects as well. 'What We Do: Design Review,' Bouwmeester Maître Architecte, bma.brussels/en/what-we-do/#DESIGN%20REVIEW (accessed 17 February 2025).

9
Elias Baumgarten, 'Learning from Brussels', *World-Architects: For Quality in Architecture*, 4 November 2024, world-architects.com/en/architecture-news/insight/learning-from-brussels (accessed 20 January 2025).

> buildings, including monuments and other elements of cultural heritage, as well as the design and construction of contemporary buildings, infrastructure, public spaces and landscapes.[7]

At the very least, *Baukultur* is as much about the work of non-architects as it is about that of architects. Indeed, the word 'architect' does not appear even once in the Davos statement. This is not merely a case of *building culture* encompassing a narrower *architectural culture*, or a reiteration of familiar dichotomies between expert and popular culture, high and low art, or avant-garde and rear-garde – any more than architecture can be simply subsumed under *Baukunst*.[8] German German philosopher of art, Ludger Schwarte, for instance, contrasts two conceptions of architecture: one as a conformist *cultural* practice, and the other – *Baukunst* – as an exceptional art form. For Schwarte, 'an art of building is, like all art, the negation of culture . . . Art is not a cultural resource, but, as long as it functions as art, the opposite of culture'.[9] Despite the ambiguous position of the architect, *Baukultur*'s discourse on quality aspires both to high-quality design across buildings, infrastructure and landscapes, and to

6
Ibid., preamble.

7
Ibid., Article 4. A small anthology published / by the Swiss magazine *werk, bauen + wohnen* sketches the Swiss debate on *Baukultur* similarly: 'The self-image of architecture and urban planning as well as the work of the administration or expert commissions in the municipalities, building laws, standards and inventories must be reviewed for their suitability for the future, as must the transfer of knowledge and the organization of innovation, professional training opportunities and professional exchange.' Roland Züger et al., *7 Texte zur Baukultur, Werk, Debatte* (Zurich: Verlag Werk AG, 2022), 12.

8
Flip ten Cate outlines another broadening: 'In fact, the way Building Culture is described in the Davos Declaration is a superlative of our concept of "environmental quality" (*omgevingskwaliteit*) which in turn is an extension of "spatial quality" (*ruimtelijke kwaliteit*).' Flip ten Cate, 'Bouwcultuur: Elke ruimtelijke ingreep is een culturele daad,' *Archined*, 3 February 2020, archined.nl/2020/02/bouwcultuur-elke-ruimtelijke-ingreep-is-een-culturele-daad/ (accessed 11 March 2024).

9
Ludger Schwarte, 'Was ist Baukunst?', in: Daniel Martin Feige and Sandra Meireis (eds.), *Ästhetik und Architektur* (Bielefeld: transcript, 2023), 261.

new areas for growth and prosperity. Improving urban quality and vitality through an 'urban renaissance' was promoted as one way to propel economic reform.[10] As an executive non-departmental body that operated at arm's length from government, CABE had limited regulatory power. Its governance structure epitomised third-way policy strategies introduced by Labour's Prime Minister Tony Blair, as well as the more ubiquitous new public management reforms of the 1980s that sought a more efficient and service-oriented approach to public administration. Here, quality emerges as an extrinsic dimension that can be enhanced through management protocols and techniques, defining quality management as a specific domain of expertise.[11]

CABE has become a touchstone in design governance discourse through its theorisation by Matthew Carmona et al.[12] This theorisation of quality as a matter of governance parallels the broader uptake of a 'governance perspective', which British political scientist Gerry Stoker characterises as a 'stepping back of the state', a blurring of the 'boundaries between and within public and private sectors', and shifts in the way governments seek to exercise power and 'steer collective action'.[13] In these terms, soft power describes the

10
The Urban Design Task Force (Richard Rogers), *Towards an Urban Renaissance* (London: Routledge, 1999).

11
For a discussion on quality and new public management in the public health sector in the UK, see: Ross Millar, Justin Waring and Mirza Lalani, 'Quality and the NHS: Fair-Weather Friends or a Longstanding Relationship?', in: Martin Powell et al. (eds.), *The NHS at 75: The State of UK Health Policy* (Bristol University Press, 2023), 136-156.

12
Matthew Carmona, Claudio de Magalhaes and Lucy Natarajan, *Design Governance: The CABE Experiment* (New York/London: Routledge, 2017). For a discussion of the evolution of third way policies in relation to architecture, see: Helena Mattsson, *Architecture and Retrenchment:*

a high-quality building culture itself – conceived both as a precondition for, and an outcome of, meaningful living environments.

In the Learning Villa

Building culture is thus a value to be cultivated. This is not only the high-level ambition of the Davos Declaration, but also of other actors in Switzerland. The establishment of a 'public centre for building culture' in 2013 by the NGO Schweizer Heimatschutz reflects this drive while linking contemporary discourse to its historical roots. Founded in 1905, the association today defines its mission as encompassing the preservation of historic buildings, natural assets and good architecture. Structured into 25 cantonal sections, it engages in a range of activities, from publishing on architectural heritage to awarding the annual *Wakkerpreis* to municipalities with exemplary planning projects, and filing legal objections to safeguard heritage values.

Schweizer Heimatschutz established its headquarters in the restored and converted Villa Patumbah, a sumptuous 1885 residence near Zurich's botanical garden. The location was developed as a centre for building culture. The villa had long stood vacant and

Alfred Chiodera and Theophil Tschudy, Villa Patumbah, Zurich (Seefeld), 1885. Heimatschutzzentrum and seat of Schweizer Heimatschutz since 2013

distributed decision-making and consensus-seeking agendas of liberal democratic governments at the turn of the twenty-first century, and the interdependence of private and public sector actors in the making of the built environment. Moreover, it attributes a productive power to the myriad exchanges between designers and other stakeholders who can influence its quality including public authorities, property owners, politicians, investors, financiers, building users and communities, which nonetheless demand new forms of authority and conduct to manage competing interests.[14]

Design Review: Good Design and Good Governance

The theorisation of design governance as it was practiced by CABE and in the Urban Maestro survey emphasises a 'toolkit' approach, which answers a need of governments to benchmark their work and highlights the transferability and adaptability of practices across diverse regulatory contexts and professional cultures.[15] However, embedded in many design governance tools are forms of situated design review that epitomise the role of soft power in contemporary urban governance.[16] Often convened as part of public procurement or

Neoliberalization of The Swedish Model Across Aesthetics and Space, 1968-1994 (London: Bloomsbury, 2023). In the UK context, the concept is linked to the work of sociologist Anthony Giddens and his book *The Third Way: The Renewal of Social Democracy* (London: Polity, 1998).

13
Gerry Stoker, 'Governance as Theory: Five Propositions,' *International Social Science Journal* 50 (1998), 17, 19 and 21.

14
For a discussion of Foucault's concept of pastoral power in relation to design governance, see: John Macarthur and Susan Holden, 'Beauty in Urban Design Governance', *Islands: 40th Annual Conference of the Society of Architectural Historians o f Australia and New Zealand* (Brisbane: SAHANZ, 2024). Abstract available at: sahanz.net/publications/papers/beauty-in-urban-design-governance (accessed 20 January 2025).

15
Matthew Carmona, 'The Formal and Informal Tools of Design Governance', *Journal of Urban Design* 22/1 (2017), 1-36; Matthew Carmona, Joao Bento and Tommaso Gabrieli, *Urban Design Governance: Soft Powers and the European Experience* (London: UCL Press, 2023).

16
The Urban Maestro database features several examples of design review, including the work of the Baukollegium Zurich design advisory board, Q-Teams in the Netherlands, marketised design review in the UK, design advisory boards in Austria, and the BMA. See: urbanmaestro.org (accessed 24 June 2024).

faced demolition before it was protected and thoroughly restored – an effort in which Schweizer Heimatschutz played a decisive role. The architecture magazine *Hochparterre* called it *Die Baukulturlernvilla* – the 'building culture learning villa' – in a 2013 article praising the permanent exhibition and describing the villa itself as an experiential learning tool: 'Apart from the exhibition, the villa is of course in itself a lesson in building culture – and especially the culture of historical preservation.'[10]

The extent to which *Baukultur* has become the object of cultural reflection is also evident in its uptake as a pedagogical concept. In *Elemente einer baukulturellen Allgemeinbildung* (2021), pedagogue Roland Reichenbach outlines its goals: acquiring knowledge, refining perception, and developing critical judgement regarding the built environment. Building culture, he argues, should not merely be lived passively but engaged with reflectively.[11] The book compiles texts that address core knowledge for a 'general building culture education', asking: 'What should the empowered citizen know about building culture?'[12] The book is an initiative of Archijeunes, a civil society organisation dedicated since 2008 to building-cultural education for children and

10
Rahel Marti, 'Die Baukulturlernvilla', *Hochparterre online*, 26 August 2013.

11
Roland Reichenbach, 'Baukulturelle Allgemeinbildung: Eine bildungstheoretische Annäherung', in: Kathrin Siebert (ed.), *Elemente einer baukulturellen Allgemeinbildung* (Zurich: Park Books, 2021), 61.

12
Kathrin Siebert, 'Einleitung. Baukulturelle Bildung braucht Grundwissen', in: ibid., 11.

'Soft Power: The Brussels Way of Making the City' in S AM Swiss Architecture Museum, Basel

young people, including developing learning materials for schools.[13] The 16 chapters cover such knowledge domains, from the history of architecture and building technique to sociology, project development, historic preservation, traffic and landscape. The challenge is not to transmit fixed packages of disciplinary knowledge, but to foster cross-disciplinary dialogue in the 'integrative and connective' spirit of building culture.[14]

In the same book, Ákos Moravánszky remarks that the term *Baukultur* is appealing in its simultaneous elitist and democratic overtones.[15] Like the notion of culture itself, it is ambivalent: on one side, the high-minded ideal of *Bildung*, advocating an improved building culture through cultivated engagement; on the other, a descriptive relativism, akin to food or music culture, embracing all practices from vernacular methods to architectural publishing.

This being said, Moravánszky also points at the intrinsically defensive nature of *Baukultur*, although it is not always clear what exactly is to be defended: 'The identity of a region? The cohesive cityscape? In any case, historic preservation or *Heimatschutz* . . . is often mentioned as a primary task for Baukultur.'[16] Can *Baukultur* be limited to heritage, Moravanszky asks rhetorically?

'Bijou oder Bausünde. Über unseren Umgang mit *Baukultur*' (2022-2024): exhibition flyer with Triemli Tower in Zurich

Even if on many occasions and by many actors a both-and narrative of heritage and contemporary architecture is propagated, the building culture discourse tends to originate from a conservative reflex.

This is also apparent in the historical bedrock that helped shape the concept of *Baukultur*, as outlined by Moravanszky: from the ten-volume book series *Kulturarbeiten* in which Paul Schultze-Naumberg, protagonist of the German Heimatschutz movement, made the 'culture of the visible' and the 'physiognomy of the landscape' the subject of his critiques from 1901 onwards, its ills to be countered with sustained design attention; to the news magazine *Die Baukultur*, published in the 1930s by the Stuttgart architects' association Der Block, which had the Kochenhofsiedlung built as a heimatic countermodel to the Weissenhofsiedlung; and the way that the *Baukultur* discourse was rekindled in Switzerland in the 1970s, along with criticism of modernism and of the further encroaching urbanisation and environmental pollution, this time with concrete and the *Grossiedlung* as fundamental counterimages of *Baukultur*. Such a history prompts thought, reminiscent of the (evolving) ideological content of the concept. It is certainly worth noting that the

13
Archijeunes is funded through private donations and through financial support from the Swiss Society of Engineers and Architects (SIA) and the Bund Schweizer Architektinnen und Architecten (BSA).

14
Siebert, 'Einleitung. Baukulturelle Bildung braucht Grundwissen', op. cit. (note 12), 11. The Davos Declaration similarly considers interdisciplinarity as a prerequisite for high-quality building culture, mentioned in the same breath with cross-sectoral cooperation, and with the necessary participation from civil society and the role of an informed public. (art. 16) So when design competitions are highlighted as a key instrument for fostering high-quality *Baukultur*, it comes with the qualification of 'interdisciplinary and widely-debated' competitions.

15
Ákos Moravánszky, 'Wege zur Baukultur', in: Siebert (ed.), *Elemente einer baukulturellen Allgemeinbildung*, op. cit. (note 11), 38.

16
Moravánszky, 'Wege zur Baukultur', op. cit. (note 15), 37-38.

development assessment processes, design review boards or panels typically bring together a group of independent experts to evaluate the design quality of proposals in parallel with their regulatory approval, leveraging the expertise of panel members to advise, advocate and persuade. Design review panels thus reinforce the capacity of architects to make good judgements about design quality, and a concept of quality linked directly to professional expertise, even as panels increasingly include diverse and multidisciplinary participants.

Design review is by no means a new practice. It is foundational to the pedagogical and peer review traditions of the design disciplines and has a longer history as a governance tool. In the United States the incorporation of design review processes in planning emerged in the 1950s, evolving as a useful, if ad hoc, companion to zoning-ordinance systems of regulation. It legitimised the incorporation of aesthetic controls in urban governance that were otherwise limited in relation to constitutional property rights and rights to freedom of speech.[17] The 1992 International Conference on Design Review held in Cincinnati brought together participants from the United States, the UK, Germany, South Africa, Brazil and Australia, stimulating international knowledge

recent *Baukultur* discourse suppresses any nativism and embraces a plurality of building cultures.

Jewels and Sins

Today, brutalist concrete architecture is once again contested, but now as young heritage. The issue is not so much one of architectural-historical importance, or the appropriate criteria for heritage status, but beauty and the political significance of a generation of residential buildings and welfare facilities. From September 2022 until May 2024, the exhibition 'Bijou oder Bausünde? Über unseren Umgang mit Baukultur' (Jewel or building sin? About our dealings with building culture) was on view in Villa Patumbah, and not coincidentally, its poster featured Zurich's brutalist Triemli Tower (1966). The apartment building, designed by Esther and Rudolf Guyer, was chosen as Switzerland's ugliest building as recently as 2018 by readers of the free newspaper *20 Minuten*. Others defended the brutalist building legacy as testimony to 'social ambition, creativity and courageous optimism in the postwar period'.[17] It is one of the examples in the exhibition that pushes beyond philosophical consideration of architecture as a matter of culture and asks citizens to take a position

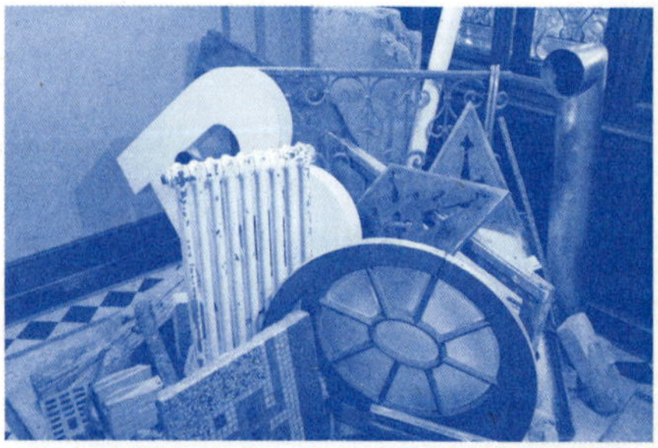

'Bijou oder Bausünde'. Display problematising waste

'Bijou oder Bausünde'. Speech bubbles with quotes about *Baukultur* and aesthetics

exchange on design review practices that was already underway.[18] In the book that followed this conference, Brenda Case Scheer astutely identified the intersecting challenges of design review to negotiate power, freedom, justice and aesthetics.[19] These terms continue to be at stake in design governance, if not explicit agendas of design review panels.

In the UK CABE continued design review practices established by its predecessor the Royal Fine Arts Commission (RFAC).[20] However, the development of design review under CABE marked a distinct shift in its scope and intention compared with previous forms of aesthetic control operating in the UK. Carmona et al. characterised this shift as a move 'away from . . . aesthetics to . . . urban design'.[21] It reflected a more explicit political interest in the design quality of cities, and the rise of urban design as an independent discipline, as well as the elevation of a concept of good design over the aesthetic category of beauty.

Design review became a key part of CABE's endeavour: a tangible way to prioritise a quality agenda within an otherwise weak discretionary planning system, and a vital nexus for its broader advocacy and advisory activities. CABE produced numerous documents to

17 John Delafons, *Aesthetic Control: A Report on Methods Used in the USA to Control the Design of Buildings* (Berkeley: University of California, 1990).

18 Brenda Case Scheer and Wolfgang F.E. Preiser (eds.), *Design Review: Challenging Urban Aesthetic Control* (London/New York: Chapman & Hall, 1994).

19 Brenda Case Scheer, 'Introduction: The Debate on Design Review', in: ibid., 4-9.

20 On the development of aesthetic control under the Royal Fine Arts Commission, see: John Punter, 'A History of Aesthetic Control: Part 1, 1909-1953: The Control of the External Appearance of Development in England and Wales', *The Town Planning Review* 57/4 (1986), 351-381; John Delafons, 'In Britain: the Enduring Ambivalence', in: Delafons, *Aesthetic Control*, op. cit. (note 17), 71-81; Matthew Carmona et al., 'The RFAC and Seventy-Five Years of English Design Review, 1924-1999', in: Carmona et al., *The CABE Experiment*, op. cit. (note 12), 69-87.

21 Carmona et. al., *The CABE Experiment*, op. cit. (note 12), 81.

on its quality: 'We can all contribute with our actions to the shaping of buildings and open space, argue about bijous and building sins, or advocate for valuable building ensembles.'[18] A pile of salvaged building fragments extracted from renovated buildings prompted the question: 'Can this go?', and was meant to elicit questions and reactions from visitors, as was a cloud of speech bubbles with quotes and comparative before-and-after images of demolished, relocated, restored, remodelled or replaced buildings. Such pairs of images fit into a tradition of propping up an architectural aesthetic-cum-moral discourse with contrasting 'good' and 'bad' examples, as in Pugin's *Contrasts* (1836) or Schultze-Naumberg's books already mentioned.[19] This time, however, the pairs of images were still offered primarily in question form – not as explicit, binary taste or ideological education. Aesthetic and practical judgment seemed to be left to the visitor.

The challenge to operationalise *Baukultur* as a cultural programme, then, is not only one of its definitions in relation to broader cultural concerns, but also its utility in relation to the specific social, economic, political and ecological circumstances in which buildings are made and maintained. In this sense, Villa

17 Karin Bürki on her website *Heartbrut*, June 2022, as cited in the exhibition 'Bijou oder Bausünde'. See also: heartbrut.com/compendium/triemlitower/.

18 Introductory wall text.

19 Augustus W. Pugin, *Contrasts: Or, a Parallel between the Noble Edifices of the Middle Ages and Corresponding Buildings of the Present Day* (Cambridge: Cambridge University Press, 2013). About Schultze-Naumberg's use of images, see: Matthias Noell, 'Kultur des Sichtbaren: Der fotografische Blick des Herrn Schultze', in: Hans-Rudolf Meier and Daniela Spiegel (eds.), *Kulturreformer, Rassenideologe, Hochschuldirektor: Der lange Schatten des Paul Schultze-Naumburg* (Heidelberg: Arthistoricum.net, 2018), 35.

CABE produced numerous publications and resources to support the improvement of built environment design quality including *The Value of Good Design* (2002) and *Design Review: Principles and Practice* (2013, 2019)

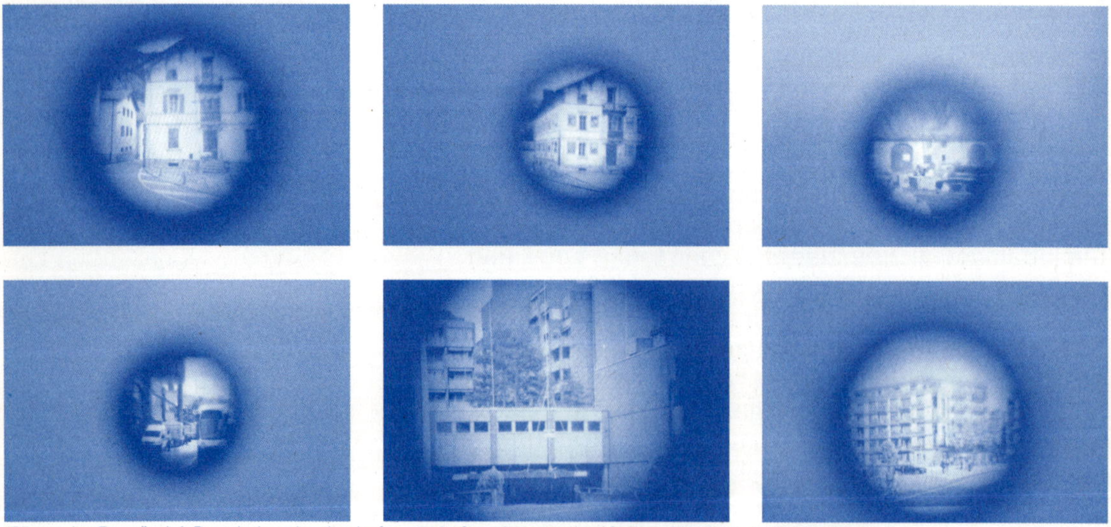

'Bijou oder Bausünde'. Peep holes showing before and after photographs of altered heritage in Switzerland

explain the role of design review panels in promoting good design. It's guidance documents provided criteria for what made a good project with reference to Vitruvius's triumvirate of commodity, firmness and delight, but also highlighted the role of design review processes in prioritising design quality over conformity or compliance with planning regulation.[22] It stated that: 'Design is a creative activity, and definitions of quality in design are elusive. It cannot be reduced to codes and prescriptions. . . . the best examples often break or transcend the rules.'[23] A subsequent CABE publication *The Value Handbook*, placed design quality within a more pervasive quality management ecosystem and at the same time declared more objective criteria, stating:

> By good design we mean design that is fit for purpose, sustainable, efficient, coherent, flexible, responsive to context, good looking and a clear expression of the requirements of the brief. We believe that assessing quality is to a large extent an objective process. Ultimately, of course, some questions come down to matters of individual taste and preference. It is not often, however, that questions of this kind are important in deciding whether a project, judged in the round, is a good one. What matters is quality, not style.[24]

22 Commission for Architecture and the Built Environment, *Design Review: How CABE Evaluates Quality in Architecture and Urban Design* (London: CABE, 2006), 14. This guide was first published in 2001 and revised in 2006.

23 Ibid., 5.

24 Commission for Architecture and the Built Environment, *The Value Handbook: Getting the Most from Your Buildings and Spaces* (London: CABE, 2006), 5.

Patumbah itself is both *Bijou* and *Bausünde*. Since the summer of 2020, a small parallel exhibition has been on view in the villa's demi-sous-sol: 'Patumbah Is a Place in Sumatra' situates the villa as colonial heritage.[20] The show does not engage with the architecture's combination of an Italianate neo-renaissance villa with aspects of a Chinese courtyard house, or with the exoticising ornamentation from the dragon-shaped gargoyles protruding from the classical façades to the (real and fake) Chinese inscriptions in interiors of the second floor; it documents the colonial reality of Sumatra's plantations that generated the fortunes that went in this villa. Its builder, Carl Fürchtegott Grob, was one of the Swiss who had made his fortune in the plantation economy in the Dutch East Indies. Between 1871 and 1889, together with a Bavarian business partner, he ran one of the biggest tobacco plantations on the north-east coast of Sumatra, operating the colonial system in which indentured labourers brought over from Java and China, among other places, were exploited, and the land use and social organisation of the local Batak and Malays were replaced. On returning to Zurich, Grob built the sumptuous villa with coach house and landscaped garden. A gilded inscription

20 'Switzerland is one of the most globalized countries in the world. The traditional image of an island in the middle of the European political construct bears little resemblance to reality – neither today nor in the past. . . . The recognition that Switzerland was engaged in colonialism even without colonies of its own is gradually taking hold in contemporary historiography.' Judith Schubiger, Karin Artho and Céline Hug, Heimatschutzzentrum, *Patumbah liegt auf Sumatra* (Zurich: Schweizer Heimatschutz, 2022), 57.

The tension between regulation and judgement that can nonetheless surface in design review processes, is not necessarily unique to the evaluation of design, but a feature of governing. As historian of sciences and author of the book *Rules: A Short History of What We Live By* Lorraine Daston points out, rules always contain exceptions, and any kind of performance evaluation requires a degree of qualitative judgement. Who has the power to decide exceptions is not only ever-present in the activity of design review, but it is also the crux of the political economy.[25] Such occasions where rules, regulations and standards can be tempered by expert judgement and experience remain a crucial part of governing that is potentially threatened by quality management regimes that seek to limit them. Design review panels speak to this qualitative dimension of governing, and what is at stake in it. While most design review panels legitimise the evaluation of good design with accompanying design guidelines or principles, they also materialise the work and value of negotiated and situated judgement, and at best, protect the idea of quality without a fixed or pre-determined standard.

CABE prided itself on making its design advice public, to cultivate confidence in the design review

'Patumbah is a place in Sumatra', cabinet exhibition. Floor map and displayed book *Schweizer Verein Deli-Sumatra* (Zurich, 1936)

process, and enshrine its pillars of transparency and accountability.[26] This attention to the process itself became a focus in later CABE publications, moving the discourse beyond discussions of what is good design to what is a good governance. In this respect, design review is as much a setting as a tool, in the way it makes a space for reflection, deliberation, and constructive conversation.

The proliferation of design review illustrates its continued evolution as a prominent form of design governance.[27] Its evolution in Australia also highlights the legacy of CABE after its demise in the UK. In Australia design review panels have become a core function of the offices of State and Territory Government Architects that replaced colonial era government architect positions and public works departments.[28] The CABE design review model was initially licenced by the South Australian Government in 2011 at a time when CABE was being incorporated into the Design Council UK and seeking to marketise its design review services.[29] Kirsteen Mackay, formerly CABE's Head of Design Review joined the Office for Design and Architecture South Australia, becoming South Australia's Government Architect in 2015 and Chair of its Design Review Panel.

25
Lorraine Daston, *Rules: A Short History of What We Live By* (Princeton/ Oxford: Princeton University Press, 2022), 256.

26
CABE articulated ten principles to guide the process of design review, stating that panels should be: independent, expert, multidisciplinary, accountable, transparent, proportionate, timely, advisory, objective and accessible. Design Council UK, *Design Review: Principles and Practice* (London: Design Council, 2019 [2013]).

27
John Punter has documented the wide adoption of design review in both regulatory and discretionary planning systems internationally. John Punter, 'Developing Urban Design as Public Policy: Best Practice Principles for Design Review and Development Management', *Journal of Urban Design* 12/2 (2007), 167-202.

28
Susan Holden and Kirsty Volz, 'The Value of Architects in Government: Research Dossier', *Architecture Australia* 112/2 (2023), 53-69.

29
Office for Design and Architecture South Australia, *State Design Review in South Australia* (Adelaide: Government of South Australia, 2021).

refers to the place Patumbak, turning the villa into more than mere 'transactional architecture': a stirring cultural testimony to European extractive colonialism and its propagandist monumentalisation.[21] The Villa is a continuing reminder – provided that a critical reading is sufficiently developed through, for example, an exhibition such as that in the sous-sol – not to cut loose building culture from wider politico-ecological perspectives and concerns.[22]

Demonstrative Design

One of the settings for the World Economic Forum itself, the Kirchner Museum is another instance when architecture can be understood as providing a situated lesson in *Baukultur*. The former sanatorium and current ski and conference resort of Davos in the canton of Grisons (Graubünden) is not only known as the venue for the annual WEF, but also the site of the Kirchner Museum, which has achieved some fame in the architectural world since its opening in 1992. This early project by Annette Gigon and Mike Guyer broke with postmodernist museum architecture. With its constructive grammar, pared-down and non-hierarchical plan structure, and a reduced formal language

21
'Transactional architecture' is the title of a thematic dossier in issue 24 (2024) of *ABE Journal – Architecture beyond Europe*. In 'I Will Burn Tuan's House: Tobacco, Opium, and the Villa Patumbah', Will Davis proposes to read the Villa Patumbah as more than transactional architecture: as a European metamorphosis of the plantation itself, and as a site of colonial encounter where 'conditions of tropical violence were required for visitors to comprehend a tropics of material indulgence'.

22
Joan Ockman, 'Toward a Political Ecology of Architecture', *Places Journal* (March 2022).

Simulaa, *Design Standards* (2022) in the foreground of the Civic Architecture display, in the exhibition 'Melbourne Now' at The Ian Potter Centre, National Gallery of Victoria, Melbourne, 2023

that brings its crystalline materiality and atmospheric qualities to the fore, the building could exemplify the most important theoretical discussions of that time in Switzerland, as well as an idea of (Swiss) architectural quality *tout court* (however problematic such a generalisation is).[23] In a 2019 campaign to raise awareness about recent architectural heritage, the Kirchner Museum was promoted by the cantonal heritage society Bündner Heimatschutz as one the 52 best post-war buildings in Graubünden, 'buildings with high claims to building art (*von hohem baukünstlerischem Anspruch*), which shape our identity just as much as the monuments of earlier eras'.[24]

How might the architectural quality of this building in Davos be understood in relation to the *Baukultur* ideal proclaimed in the Davos Declaration, issued three decades later? Here, Irina Davidovici's analysis of German-Swiss architecture in the final two decades of the twentieth century proves both instructive and thought-provoking. She interprets the qualities of singular projects such as the Kirchner Museum in relation to broader Swiss conditions that enabled their production. These include, firstly, aspects of Swiss culture such as a Protestant ethos of work and capital, a strong

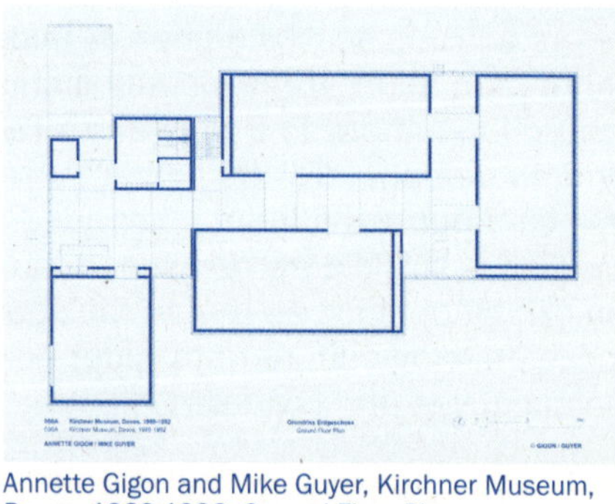

Annette Gigon and Mike Guyer, Kirchner Museum, Davos, 1989-1992. Ground Floor Plan

democratic organisation with considerable municipal autonomy, and a territorial self-image shaped by the juxtaposition of alpine villages and dense urban infrastructure. Secondly, she highlights a background of international architectural theory – shaped significantly by ETH Zurich – which promoted ideals of architectural autonomy. Thirdly, she points to a professional culture in which architects were closely involved in the act of building, further characterised by a tightly regulated Swiss competition system that offered opportunities to emerging practices like Gigon/Guyer, and by exceptionally high standards of construction quality.[25] Each of these generalisations is, as Davidovici notes, subject to qualification; she is careful, for example, to distinguish particularities of building culture in the canton of Grisons.[26]

Davidovici interprets the pronounced design investment in constructive grammar, and the aestheticisation – and even moralisation – of the well-crafted building detail within Swiss architectural culture at the end of the twentieth century, as a defensive reaction. This response emerged as the division between design architects and those specialising in construction

23
Irina Davidovici and Laurent Stalder have each retrospectively pointed at this exemplarity. Davidovici, *Forms of Practice,* op. cit. (note 1), 122-141; Laurent Stalder, 'Um 1990: Ein Bau und Viele Texte', in: Katharina Beisiegel (ed.), *GIGON/GUYER Kirchner Museum revisited* (Munich: Hirmer Verlag, 2022), 61-65.

24
Bündner Heimatschutz, *52 Beste Bauten: Baukultur Graubünden 1950-2000: Jede Woche ein neuer Blick* (2020), 52bestebauten.ch/idee-konzept/ (accessed 1 February 2025).

25
'Davidovici, *Forms of Practice*, op. cit. (note 1), 246.

26
'Graubünden architecture is not illustrative of the wider conditions of Swiss praxis. It operates as a system within a system. . . . What attracts attention is the responsiveness of this rural, mainly conservative canton to radical contemporary architecture. This rapport can be explained in two ways. Firstly, building quality constitutes a common ground that mediates between architects and the communities they serve. Secondly, as a consequence of its dominant tourist industry, Graubünden's character displays inherent urban traits.' Ibid., 247.

Design review is now embedded in South Australia for state significant projects and shepherds a quality agenda across dispersed public agencies and authorities. CABE's design review methodology and principles of good governance have influenced the practice of design review more widely across Australia, even as panels are guided by principles of good design that accommodate local definitions of place, character, and form.[30] In doing so design review panels have made a new setting for professional expertise to influence the design of the public realm.

A New Form of Civic Design

Writing in 1990, John Delafons saw the rise of design quality agendas in urban governance as 'redolent of an older tradition of civic design'.[31] We can now recognise the neoliberal context that seeded the design governance practices that proliferate today, and be alive to their interests and contradictions, and the limits of governing quality. We can also see beyond that moment, to new concepts of civic design that are shaping contemporary quality discourses. But can contemporary design governance – understood as a re-regulation of design quality in urban governance

Davos, with Grandhotel Belvédère and Kirchner Museum during World Economic Forum

after the demise of the welfare state and nation-building policy frameworks – also make space for a situated critique of the social and environmental effects of neoliberalism?

The 'Civic Architecture' exhibition that was part of the National Gallery of Victoria's 2023 'Melbourne Now' show presented a new perspective on civic design. It took the question of quality out of its projective guise, as it is often cast in the realm of design governance, bringing it back to the substance of the city itself.[32] Curated by Timothy Moore, it presented a collection of recent Melbourne-based projects that have used the opportunities of public design briefs – for libraries, transit infrastructure, university buildings – to advance new images of the city as a civic domain: as the place of citizenship ceremonies, service work, learning and play. The projects were realised through a range of procurement and delivery models that increasingly involve design review processes, reflecting the expansion of design governance practices in Victoria under the banner of 'Government as Smart Client'.[33] Another component of the exhibition was 'Design Standards' (2022) a display vitrine containing scale models of urban furniture situated around the featured projects,

30
Emma Appleton, 'The State of Play in Design', in: John Byrne, Bill Chandler and Bruce Echberg (eds.), *Urban Voices: Celebrating Urban Design in Australia* (Melbourne: Urban Design Forum, 2013), 109-112; Susan Holden and John Macarthur, 'Soft-Power and Design Review: The CABE Legacy in Australia', *Australian Planner* 180/2 (2025), forthcoming. Examples of good design guides include the Queensland Government's *Q Design Manual* (2018), which guides the State Urban Design and Places Panel and foregrounds subtropical design; and *101 Design Ideas from 5 Years of the NSW State Design Review Panel* (2023) published by the Government Architect of New South Wales that foregrounds the principle of designing with Country.

31
Delafons, *Aesthetic Control: A Report*, op. cit. (note 17), 38.

32
Melbourne Now ran from 24 March to 20 August 2023. National Gallery of Victoria, 'Civic Architecture', ngv.vic.gov.au/melbourne-now/projects/civic-architecture (accessed 20 January 2025).

33
Office of the Victorian Government Architect, *Government as Smart Client* (Melbourne: State Government of Victoria, 2024 [2013]).

management began to take hold in Switzerland too, prompted by a globalising construction economy:

> Rigour is thus not simply culturally conditioned; it is a statement of authorship, a kind of defence mechanism. Constructional precision articulates a resistance to changing global conditions. Swiss architecture at the close of the twentieth century is not a seamless continuation of earlier construction or cultural traditions, but represents the architects' response to a worldwide threat to these traditions.[27]

Such a focus on the role of architects as professional experts may initially appear to contrast with the inclusive, all-actor perspective championed by the *Baukultur* discourse. Yet Davidovici also shows how this role itself is shaped and redefined by broader shifts in the building economy. One might even draw an analogy here: the Swiss-European promotion of high-quality *Baukultur* could likewise be seen as a response to the multidisciplinary fragmentation and growing quantification of quality perceptions and assurance processes in the first decades of the twenty-first century. For the time being, the appeal of the Davos Declaration – its call for

27
Ibid., 246.

The South Australian State Design Review Panel in action. Office of Design and Architecture SA, Government of South Australia. CC BY 3.0 AU

52 Beste Bauten: Baukultur Graubünden 1950-2000, 2020, including the Kirchner Museum in Davos

but made across a longer time period. These ubiquitous objects are a material reality of the cityscape that is often overlooked as resulting from both design and governance, but one that can nonetheless qualitatively affect our experience of the built environment, and our conception of design quality itself. Based on the research work of architecture practice Simulaa, the models of streetlights, benches, rubbish bins and bike racks were rendered in a uniform white resin. Seeing them in an intimate array highlights the diversity of design outcomes in what we might expect to be standard objects, but also their associations with making the public realm welcoming and comfortable. It is an apt illustration of the gambit of contemporary design governance: that good design can be an expression of social and civic values, as it also aims to tangibly improve the quality of individual lives.

integrality and its affirmation of the built environment as a cultural matter – along with the examples of Swiss architecture from the past four decades, carries more persuasive force than the quality system developed in its wake to operationalise this meta-policy.[28] The enumeration of eight quality criteria in the Davos Quality System – including not only context and beauty, but also governance – gives the system a bureaucratic and administrative character that may, in the end, stand at odds with the promise of a building-cultural allure.

28 Swiss Federal Office of Culture, *The Davos Baukultur Quality System* (Berne: Swiss Federal Office of Culture, 2021), bak.admin.ch/bak/en/home/baukultur/qualitaet/davos-qualitaetssystem-baukultur.html (accessed 11 March 2024).

Ontwerpkwaliteit als kwestie van bestuur en cultuur: Een tweeluik

Susan Holden en Maarten Liefooghe

De omgeving waarin de Europese Commissie haar werk doet, lijkt ver af te staan van de alledaagse activiteiten die de kwaliteit van de gebouwde omgeving bepalen.

Toch illustreerde de toespraak van Commissievoorzitter Ursula von der Leyen op het tweede New European Bauhaus Festival in april 2024 (dat de – overigens betwiste – vooruitgang van haar NEB-initiatief vierde) dat 'ontwerpkwaliteit' tegenwoordig een onderwerp is dat bij zowel bestuurders als cultuurbeleidsmakers een zekere voorrang heeft bemachtigd. Kwaliteit wordt tegenwoordig nagejaagd zowel in beleidsverklaringen op hoog niveau als op talrijke plekken waar architecten, stedenbouwkundigen, politici, bureaucraten en burgers in uiteenlopende configuraties samenwerken. Deze praktijken liggen ook wel in het verlengde van langere tradities van stedenbouwkundige regelgeving en verbredende beroepscultuur, terwijl ze ook aansluiten bij bredere opvattingen over bouwcultuur en erfgoed.

In de parallelle artikelen van dit tweeluik onderscheiden, verkennen en vergelijken we twee denkmodellen die in de hedendaagse kwaliteitsdebatten en -praktijken hun neerslag vinden: ontwerpkwaliteit als een kwestie van ontwerpend besturen (design governance) versus ontwerpkwaliteit als een kwestie van cultuur. Met deze twee ruimere discursieve en politieke kaders stemmen andere opvattingen overeen over wat een goede plek is, een hoogwaardig ontwerp of een verantwoorde architectuurpraktijk. Ze impliceren ook een verschillende verspreiding van verantwoordelijkheden over actoren en omgevingen om kwaliteit te bevorderen. Het deel van het tweeluik dat geschreven is door Susan Holden, dat over design governance gaat, spitst zich meer bepaald toe op het tegenwoordig veelgebruikte instrument van de ontwerpbeoordelingscommissie. Dit instrument kan als symbool fungeren voor het gegeven dat bij ontwerpend besturen eerder vertrouwen wordt gesteld in ontwerpprojecten – die eerder als basis voor

kwaliteit worden gezien dan allerlei voorschriften – en tevens in de professionele deskundigheid van architecten en stedenbouwkundigen. In het deel van het tweeluik geschreven door Maarten Liefooghe is ervoor gekozen de culturele benadering van architectonische kwaliteit te illustreren aan de hand van het begrip *Baukultur*. De Verklaring van Davos uit 2018, over hoogkwalitatieve *Baukultur*, bracht dit perspectief op de voorgrond en vatte de culturele waarden van de gebouwde omgeving op, als iets wat iedereen in de samenleving aangaat.

Terwijl we de genealogieën en bijzonderheden van deze twee tradities van kwaliteit schetsten, viel ons een aantal overeenkomsten op, bijvoorbeeld het feit dat ze allebei 'zachte' strategieën gebruiken, of dat ze het algemeen belang benadrukken. Maar we zien ook verschillende ontwikkelingen in relatie tot stedelijk bestuur en cultureel beleid. Met een andere nadruk op professionele expertise dan wel op een alledaagse maar rijke bouwtraditie, en met een verschillend idee en agenda over de prioriteit van excellentie versus sociaal-culturele inclusiviteit.

Het articuleren van de verschillen tussen kwaliteitswoorden en de bijbehorende bestuurlijke genealogieën is een manier om het streven naar consensus onder de verenigende kwaliteitsvlag aan de orde te stellen. Het is ook een aanleiding om te reflecteren op de manier waarop verschillende noties van kwaliteit verweven zijn met ontwikkelingen in cultuurbeleid en politieke economie. Het maakt het tevens mogelijk om vraagtekens te plaatsen bij het eigenlijke mandaat van ontwerpend besturen als nieuwe verschijningsvorm van een beroepspraktijk – de grenzen en kwetsbaarheden ervan, de inherente spanningen en paradoxen. En niet te vergeten de risico's bij het definiëren van een nationale bouwcultuur of het instrumentaliseren van de discussie over kwaliteit.

Vertaling: InOtherWords, Maria van Tol

Kwaliteit als een kwestie van *governance*: Ontwerpbeoordeling

Susan Holden

Tegenwoordig is kwaliteit niet langer iets dat voortkomt uit de klassieke canon, een dictaat van een besluitvormer of de geest van een zogenaamd 'creatief genie' (...) Goede architectuur is bedoeld om de goede stedelijke samenleving te bevorderen en daarom vereist architectonische kwaliteit altijd een gezond debat. (...) De deelnemers moeten hun verantwoordelijkheid serieus nemen (...) Dan wordt het gesprek een fundament, en architectonische kwaliteit een gedeelde waarde.[1]

Een 'zachte' manier van stadmaken

Ontwerpend besturen (*design governance*), het idee dat ontwerpkwaliteit een zaak is van besturen, is niet nieuw.[2] Het begrip heeft echter in het kielzog van de neoliberale hervormingen van de overheid sinds de jaren 1980 een nieuwe betekenis gekregen, waardoor de rol van actoren

1 Bouwmeester Maître Architecte, 'Quality', bma.brussels/en/why-we-do-it (geraadpleegd 17 februari 2025).

2 Zie bijvoorbeeld de volgende publicaties, waarin het raakvlak tussen architectuur en de esthetische aspecten van stedelijke regulering, en de politieke economie en bestuurlijke constructen zoals die te vinden zijn in de theorieën van Michel Foucault, wordt verkend: Daniel M. Abramson et al., (Aggregate Architectural History Collective), *Governing by Design: Architecture, Economy, and Politics in the Twentieth Century* (Pittsburgh: University of Pittsburgh Press, 2012); Jules Lubbock, *The Tyranny of Taste: The Politics of Architecture and Design in Britain 1550-1960* (New Haven/Londen: Yale University Press, 1995); Alan Hunt,

Kwaliteit als een kwestie van cultuur: *Baukultur*

Maarten Liefooghe

Wat bouwen ze toch keurig, veilig, verzorgd, solide, serieus, vlekkeloos, bewust, smaakvol, netjes, grondig, serieus, enzovoort, in dit land.

Max Frisch[1]

De kwaliteit van architectuur beschouwen als een kwestie van cultuur lijkt vanzelfsprekend, maar het is ook een standpunt dat tegenwoordig krachtig wordt verdedigd, omdat het als bedreigd wordt ervaren.[2] Enerzijds zijn we eraan gewend dat architectuur onderdeel is van de programmering van culturele instellingen, dat de architectuurboeken in de buurt van de kunstboeken op de plank staan en dat architectuur in veel landen een plaats heeft in het cultuurbeleid.[3] Architectonische kwaliteit heeft dus betrekking op de waardering ervan in relatie tot ijkpunten en criteria

in de publieke sector bij het vormgeven van de gebouwde omgeving ingrijpend is veranderd. Zo omvat het concept 'ontwerpend besturen' nieuwe manieren om ontwerpexpertise, en nieuwe sociaal-politieke redenen om kwaliteit te realiseren, te stimuleren. Het huidige ontwerpend besturen is erop gericht om, in het algemeen belang, kwaliteit te realiseren, als een nieuwe 'politieke economie van plaatsmaken' en een rechtvaardige ecologische transitie.[3]

De notie van *soft power* staat centraal in de manier waarop hoogwaardige resultaten worden gestimuleerd via de 'technologieën' van het ontwerpbestuur.[4] Kristiaan Borret, Bouwmeester / Maître Architecte (BMA) van het Brussel Hoofdstedelijk Gewest, verwoordt het goed:

> In steden hebben we verordeningen, planningswetten, enzovoort. Ze kunnen ons helpen om excessen te vermijden en blunders te elimineren, maar ze volstaan niet als we uitmuntendheid willen bereiken. Daarvoor hebben we de technieken van *soft power* nodig, die interessante architectuur en stedenbouw bevorderen.[5]

Borret zei dit in het kader van het Urban Maestro-project, waarbinnen een reeks praktijken op het gebied

'Governing the City: Liberalism and Early Modern Modes of Governance', in: Andrew Barry, Thomas Osborne en Nikolas Rose (red.), *Foucault and Political Reason* (Londen: UCL Press, 1996) 167-188.

3
Rob Imre en Emma Street, *Architectural Design and Regulation* (West Sussex: Wiley-Blackwell, 2011), 244. Imre en Street verwijzen naar David Harvey's ruimtelijke analyse van postmoderniteit in: David Harvey, *Spaces of Capital: Toward a Critical Geography* (New York: Routledge, 2001).

4
Mitchell Dean, *Governmentality: Power and Rule in Modern Society* (Londen: Sage, 1999/2010), 202. Dean's opvatting van de technologieën van geavanceerde liberale regeringen sluit aan bij de ontwerpbestuurspraktijk in die zin, dat ze ruimte maken voor een bredere betrokkenheid van belanghebbenden bij de onderhandeling over hoogwaardige resultaten en dat ze gezag opeisen door hun morele (professionele) en politieke (bestuurlijke) gedrag.

5
Kristiaan Borret, geciteerd in: United Nations Human Settlements Programme (UN-Habitat), Bouwmeester Maître Architecte (BMA), Bartlett School of Planning (UCL), *Urban Maestro, New Governance Strategies for Urban Design* (Londen: University College London, 2021), 2.

die specifiek zijn voor de architectuur als een culturele praktijk, en dus niet louter als een technische discipline of een kwestie van nuttigheid. Anderzijds heeft een groeiende focus op duurzaamheid, ecologie en systeemdenken juist dit culturele perspectief in het defensief gedrukt, of in ieder geval: aangedrongen op een herdefiniëring. Maar een culturele pijler van architectonische kwaliteit kan niet alleen worden bevestigd als tegenwicht voor puur bouwtechnische, economische of energieprestatiemaatregelen. Minstens zo belangrijk is de vraag van welke architectonische of bouwcultuur we uitgaan – of willen uitgaan?

Deze vraag is actueel, omdat de term en het concept 'bouwcultuur' de laatste jaren zelfbewust hun intrede doen in de Europese beleidskaders. Het is zelfs een van de prominente vectoren in de huidige 'Europeanisering' van het architectuurbeleid, die João Bento waarneemt in de evolutie van nationale culturele beleidsagenda's in heel Europa.[4] In Duitstalig Europa is de term *Baukultur* al lange tijd in gebruik om te verwijzen naar de culturele dimensie van gebouwen en de gebouwde omgeving, en het onderwerp van verschillende beleidsinitiatieven. Het is er misschien wel zó ingebakken dat de culturele idealen die ermee verbonden

1
Max Frisch, *I'm Not Stiller* (Londen: Methuen, 1982), 213, geciteerd in: Irina Davidovici, *Forms of Practice: German-Swiss Architecture 1980-2000* (Zürich: GTA Verlag, 2018), 243.

2
Zie ook: *de Architect* 3 (2024): 'Architectuur als culturele waarde: voorbij praktisch nut.'

3
In zijn overzicht van het architectuurbeleid in Europa merkt João Bento op dat het onderwerp 'architectuur' in nationaal, regionaal en Europees beleid dan weer vooral aan bod komt als onderdeel van het cultuurbeleid, en dan vooral in het ruimtelijk beleid of in de ontwikkeling en het beheer van het openbaar gebouwenpark door overheden. Op de halfjaarlijkse Europese conferenties voor architectuurbeleid (ECAP) zijn nationale vertegenwoordigers in voorkomende gevallen dan ook verbonden aan culturele, erfgoed- of andere instanties. João Bento, *Architecture Policies in Europe* (Brussel: Architects' Council of Europe, 2023).

4
Ibid., 10.

De voorzitters van het South Australian State Design Review Panel met de bouwmeester van deze staat, Kirsteen Mackay

zijn, nauwelijks nog waarneembaar zijn. Maar sinds 33 Europese cultuurministers in 2018 de Verklaring van Davos ondertekenden, die de resolute titel *Towards a High-Quality* Baukultur *for Europe* droeg, wekken de term en het gepropageerde ideaal opnieuw de aandacht.[5]

Via een hink-stap-sprong – van Davos, langs andere Zwitserse plaatsen waar het bouwculturele discours is ontwikkeld en weer terug naar Davos – kunnen we aspecten van de betekenis ervan in beeld brengen en nadenken over de verwikkelingen die het signaalwoord 'kwaliteit' met zich meebrengt.

Cultuur, geen kunst

Het Zwitserse Federale Cultuurbureau greep in 2018 het momentum van het Europese Jaar van het Cultureel Erfgoed aan om zijn Europese collega's in Davos bijeen te roepen om een brede culturele doelstelling te valideren en de kwaliteit van de gebouwde omgeving even belangrijk te maken als initiatieven op het vlak van economie en milieubeleid. De openingswoorden van de eindverklaring van de conferentie draaien om de urgentie van een zogenaamd algemeen kwaliteitsverlies in de gebouwde omgeving, dat verder zou gaan dan de teloorgang van materieel en immaterieel erfgoed:

van ontwerpend besturen in heel Europa werd onderzocht, om te begrijpen hoe 'zachte staatsmacht (...) voor beter ontworpen plaatsen kan zorgen'.[6] Het in 2009 opgerichte instituut BMA was partner in dit onderzoeksproject. Het werk van het BMA was ook te zien tijdens de recente tentoonstelling 'Soft Power: The Brussels Way of Making the City' die plaatsvond in het Zwitserse Architectuurmuseum in Bazel.[7] De tentoonstelling bevatte een aantal projecten dat illustratief was voor de manier waarop het BMA bijdroeg aan een 'hoogwaardige bouwcultuur' in Brussel. Deze projecten waren merendeels mogelijk gemaakt door de adviesdiensten van het BMA en door een ontwerpgericht aanbestedingssysteem dat gebruik maakt van 'open oproepen'.[8] Er waren verschillende opmerkelijke herbestemmingsprojecten te zien, waaronder het spraakmakende, herontwikkelde Brussels World Trade Centre (51N4E, l'AUC en Jaspers-Eyers) en de kantoren en ateliers van Zinneke (Zinneke, Rotor en Ouest); in beide gevallen werd gebruik gemaakt van innovatieve co-designstrategieën. In het tentoonstellingsontwerp van Asli Çiçek domineerde een veld met metaalomlijste sokkels van verschillende afmetingen en hoogten waarop maquettes, tekeningen en foto's te zien waren. De dicht bij

6
Het Urban Maestro-project is het werk van drie partners: de UN Habitat, BMA en het University College London. Het project begon in 2019 en werd gefinancierd door het Horizon 2020-programma van de Europese Unie. Zie: urbanmaestro.org.

7
De tentoonstelling liep van 19 oktober 2024 tot 16 maart 2025 en werd samengesteld door Roxane Le Grelle en Andreas Kofler in samenwerking met de BMA en met steun van het Brussels Hoofdstedelijk Gewest. Jan Denoo en Hedwig van der Linden, *Soft Power: 10 Years of Bouwmeester Maître Architecte in Brussels* (Keulen: Walther König, 2024).

8
SAM, 'Soft Power: The Brussels Way of Making the City', sam-basel.org/en/ausstellungen/aktuell (geraadpleegd 20 januari 2025). Hoewel het BMA slechts adviserend optreedt, moet de organisatie worden geraadpleegd bij projecten van meer dan 5.000 m², volgens de richtlijnen van de Brusselse wetgeving inzake de ruimtelijke ordening (art.11/1 van het CoBAT/BWRO). Het beoordelingsproces staat ook open voor andere projecten. BMA, 'What We Do: Design Review', bma.brussels/en/what-we-do/#DESIGN%20REVIEW (geraadpleegd 17 februari 2025).

> Bewust van een trend richting kwaliteitsverlies in de gebouwde omgeving zowel als open landschappen in heel Europa, die zich manifesteert in de trivialisering van de bouw, een gebrek aan ontwerpwaarden, inclusief een gebrek aan aandacht voor duurzaamheid, de toename van gezichtsloze verstedelijking en onverantwoordelijk landgebruik, de teloorgang van historisch erfgoed en het verlies van regionale tradities en identiteiten.[6]

Het is een merkwaardige maar veelbetekenende stap dat deze conferentie van de Europese ministers van Cultuur het World Economic Forum in Davos koos als de achtergrond waartegen zij zich wilden verplichten – samen met vertegenwoordigers van de UNESCO, de Raad van Architecten Europa, Europa Nostra en andere organisaties – om de gebouwde omgeving te claimen en te ontwikkelen als een domein van het cultuurbeleid. Deze achtergrond suggereert dat cultuur belangrijk is in zowel het neoliberaal bestuur als in de consensuszoekende politiek.

Het bouwcultuurconcept dat wordt gepromoot in de Verklaring van Davos, hanteert een zeer brede en inclusieve opvatting van de (on)gebouwde omgeving,

5
Davos Declaration 2018: Towards a High-Quality Baukultur for Europe, aangenomen tijdens de conferentie van ministers van cultuur, 20-22 januari 2018, in Davos, Zwitserland, https://davosdeclaration2018.ch/en (geraadpleegd 6 juni 2024).

6
Ibid., voorwoord.

elkaar geplaatste poten van de sokkels leken wel wat op een onderverdieping: een effectieve dragende structuur, net als het BMA zelf.

In de formulering van Borret belicht 'zachte macht' de niet-regelgevende status van veel ontwerpbestuurlijke processen die kansen benutten voor informele en soms opportunistische interventies in plannings- en ontwikkelingsprocessen, van projectadvisering en -aanbesteding tot ontwerp en uitvoering. De expertise van architecten en stedenbouwkundigen, zoals Borret, is cruciaal voor het realiseren van hoogwaardige resultaten, maar zij worden in hun rol van overheidsarchitect, ontwerpadviseur en pleitbezorger ingezet om te sturen en te beïnvloeden. Volgens de logica van ontwerpend besturen wordt kwaliteit zoiets dat net zo afhankelijk is van onderhandelingen tussen specifieke actoren, dan dat het onafhankelijk wordt gegenereerd of alleen in de ontwerpen zelf zit. Dit suggereert het bestaan van een nieuw productief domein en van nieuwe vormen van ontwerpexpertise die de identiteit van het architectenberoep uitbreiden. Zoals de architectuurcriticus Elias Baumgarten opmerkte in een recensie van de 'Soft Power'-tentoonstelling: 'Het lijkt

'Soft Power: The Brussels Way of Making the City' toonde het werk van de Brusselse Bouwmeester/ Maître Architecte in S AM Swiss Architecture Museum, Bazel. Campagnebeeld, 2024

evenals van de belanghebbenden en actoren die worden opgeroepen om de bouwcultuur serieus te nemen:

> *Baukultur* omvat elke menselijke activiteit die ingrijpt in de gebouwde omgeving. De gebouwde omgeving, inclusief elk ontworpen en gebouwd object dat is ingebed in en gerelateerd aan de natuurlijke omgeving, moet als één geheel worden gezien. *Baukultur* omvat bestaande gebouwen, inclusief monumenten en ander cultureel erfgoed, maar ook het ontwerp en de bouw van hedendaagse gebouwen, infrastructuur, openbare ruimten en landschappen.[7]

'Bouwcultuur' heeft op zijn minst evenveel betrekking op het werk van andere actoren als op dat van architecten. In de verklaring van Davos komt het woord 'architect' zelfs helemaal niet voor. Dit duidt echter niet simpelweg op een algemene 'bouwcultuur', met daarbinnen een specifiekere categorie 'architectuurcultuur', of op het opnieuw inzetten van de bekende scheidslijnen tussen deskundigen en leken, hoge en lage kunstvormen, voorhoede en achterhoede, net zo min als architectuur alleen maar 'bouwkunst' zou zijn.[8] De Duitse estheticus Ludger Schwarte, bijvoorbeeld, die de laatste twee

Kwaliteitscriteria volgens het Davos *Baukultur* Quality System, 2021

juist deze rol van neutrale expert te zijn die Borret in staat stelt om de stedenbouw aan te sturen.'[9]

Behalve deze opvatting heeft 'zachte macht' een nog beladener associatie, die het discours over ontwerpend besturen verbindt met de opkomst van 'derdeweg'-regeringen in de laatste decennia van de twintigste eeuw. Dit geldt in het bijzonder voor de inspanningen van de Britse Commission for Architecture and the Built Environment (CABE, 1999-2011). CABE werd in 1997 door New Labour opgericht in het kielzog van haar historische verkiezingsoverwinning, en speelde een rol bij New Labour's brede maatschappelijke en economische beleidshervormingen. Deze waren onder andere gericht op de creatieve economie en de kenniseconomie, die werden gezien als nieuwe domeinen voor groei en welvaart. Het verbeteren van de kwaliteit en vitaliteit van de stad door middel van een 'stedelijke renaissance' werd gepromoot als een manier om economische hervormingen te stimuleren.[10] Als een niet-departementaal uitvoerend orgaan dat onafhankelijk van de regering opereerde, had CABE een beperkte regelgevende bevoegdheid. De bestuursvorm van CABE stond niet alleen symbool voor het derdeweg-beleid, dat op initiatief van Labour-premier Tony Blair was geïntroduceerd, maar ook

9
Elias Baumgarten, 'Learning from Brussels', *World-Architects: For Quality in Architecture*, 4 november 2024, world-architects.com/en/architecture-news/insight/learning-from-brussels (geraadpleegd 20 januari 2025).

10
The Urban Design Task Force (Richard Rogers), *Towards an Urban Renaissance* (Londen: Routledge, 1999).

opvattingen over architectuur tegenover elkaar heeft geplaatst, beschouwt architectuur vooral als een conformerende *culturele* praktijk, en slechts bij uitzondering als *Baukunst:* 'Bouwkunst is, net als alle kunst, de ontkenning van cultuur (...) Kunst is geen culturele grondstof maar, zolang ze als kunst functioneert, het tegenovergestelde van cultuur.'[9] Ondanks de dubbelzinnige positie van de architect streeft het kwaliteitsdiscours van de *Baukultur* zowel naar hoogwaardige ontwerpen van gebouwen, infrastructuur, landschappen of plaatsen in het algemeen, als meer specifiek naar een hoogwaardige bouwcultuur als voorwaarde voor het behoud en de productie van kwalitatieve leefomgevingen, maar ook als een doel op zich.

In de leervilla

Bouwcultuur is het dus waard om te cultiveren, en dit is niet alleen het hoogwaardige doel van de Verklaring van Davos, maar ook dat van andere Zwitserse actoren. De oprichting van een 'openbaar centrum voor bouwcultuur' in 2013 door de ngo Schweizer Heimatschutz is een voorbeeld van deze impuls en verbindt tegelijkertijd het recente discours over *Baukultur* met zijn lange traditie. De in 1905 opgerichte vereniging Schweizer

7
Ibid., artikel 4. Een kleine bloemlezing gepubliceerd door het Zwitserse tijdschrift *werk, bauen + wohnen* schetst het Zwitserse debat over *Baukultur* op dezelfde manier: 'Het zelfbeeld van architectuur en stedenbouw maar ook het werk van administraties en commissies van deskundigen in gemeenten, bouwwetten, standaarden en inventarissen moeten geëvalueerd worden met het oog op hun geschiktheid voor de toekomst, net als ook de kennisoverdracht en de organisatie van innovatie, gelegenheden voor professionele vorming en uitwisseling.' Roland Züger et al., *7 Texte zur Baukultur, werk, Debatte* (Zürich: Verlag Werk AG, 2022), 12.

8
Flip ten Cate schetst een andere veralgemening: 'Feitelijk is de manier waarop Bouwcultuur in de verklaring van Davos beschreven wordt een overtreffende trap van ons begrip "omgevingskwaliteit", dat weer een uitbreiding is van "ruimtelijke kwaliteit".' Flip ten Cate, 'Bouwcultuur: Elke ruimtelijke ingreep is een culturele daad,' *Archined*, 3 februari 2020, archined.nl/2020/02/bouwcultuurelke-ruimtelijke-ingreep-is-een-culturele-daad (geraadpleegd 11 maart 2024).

9
Ludger Schwarte, 'Was ist Baukunst?', in: Daniel Martin Feige en Sandra Meireis (red.), *Ästhetik und Architektur* (Bielefeld: transcript, 2023), 261.

voor de breder verspreide hervormingen van het *new public management* van de jaren 1980, die waren gericht op een efficiëntere en meer servicegerichte benadering van het openbaar bestuur. Kwaliteit komt hier naar voren als een extrinsieke dimensie die kan worden verbeterd door middel van managementprotocollen en -technieken, waarbij kwaliteitsmanagement als een specifiek domein van expertise wordt gedefinieerd.[11]

CABE is uitgegroeid tot een toetssteen in het discours over ontwerpend besturen, grotendeels dankzij de theorieën van Matthew Carmona en collega-onderzoekers.[12] De theorievorming over kwaliteit als een kwestie van (aan)sturen verliep parallel met de algemenere invoering van een '*governance* perspectief'. Dit perspectief is door de Britse politicoloog Gerry Stoker gekarakteriseerd als een 'stap terug door de staat', als een verwatering van de 'grenzen tussen – en binnen – de publieke en private sector' en als een verschuiving in de manier waarop overheden macht proberen uit te oefenen en 'collectieve actie proberen aan te sturen'.[13] In deze zin beschrijft zachte macht de verspreide besluitvormende en consensuszoekende ideeën van de liberaal-democratische regeringen uit het begin van de eenentwintigste eeuw en de onderlinge afhankelijkheid

11 Zie voor een discussie over kwaliteit en nieuw openbaar beheer in de openbare gezondheidszorg in Groot-Brittannië: Ross Millar, Justin Waring en Mirza Lalani, 'Quality and the NHS: Fair-Weather Friends or a Longstanding Relationship?', in: Martin Powell et al. (red.), *The NHS at 75: The State of UK Health Policy* (Bristol: Bristol University Press, 2023), 136-156.

12 Matthew Carmona, Claudio de Magalhaes en Lucy Natarajan, *Design Governance: The CABE Experiment* (New York/Londen: Routledge, 2017). Zie voor een bespreking van de evolutie van het derdeweg-beleid in relatie tot de architectuur: Helena Mattsson, *Architecture and Retrenchment: Neoliberalization of The Swedish Model Across Aesthetics and Space, 1968-1994* (Londen: Bloomsbury,

Heimatschutz omschrijft haar missie tegenwoordig als het behoud van historische gebouwen, natuurlijke rijkdommen en goede architectuur. Deze ledenvereniging is georganiseerd in 25 kantonnale afdelingen. De activiteiten variëren van publicaties over architectonisch erfgoed tot de jaarlijkse toekenning van de Wakkerpreis voor een voorbeeldig planningsproject aan een gemeente en het indienen van bezwaren om erfgoedwaarden te beschermen.

Het hoofdkwartier van de Schweizer Heimatschutz bevindt zich in de gerestaureerde en herbestemde exuberante Villa Patumbah, aan de rand van Zürich in de buurt van de botanische tuin. De organisatie ontwikkelde de locatie als een centrum voor bouwcultuur. De villa uit 1885 stond al jaren leeg en dreigde gesloopt te worden, voordat men overging tot bescherming van villa en aangrenzend park, en een uitgebreide restauratie, een reddingsoperatie waarin Schweizer Heimatschutz zelf een grote rol speelde. Het nieuwe doel van de historische villa werd enthousiast beschreven in een artikel uit 2013 in het architectuurtijdschrift *Hochparterre,* getiteld 'Die Baukulturlernvilla' ('bouwcultuurleervilla'). De permanente tentoonstelling waarmee het centrum opende, werd 'fijnzinnig' genoemd en de villa zelf werd

Alfred Chiodera en Theophil Tschudy, Villa Patumbah, Zürich (Seefeld), 1885. Heimatschutzzentrum en bestuurszetel van Schweizer Heimatschutz sinds 2013

van actoren uit de private en publieke sector bij de totstandkoming van de gebouwde omgeving. Bovendien kent het concept een productieve kracht toe aan de talloze uitwisselingen tussen ontwerpers en andere belanghebbenden die de kwaliteit van de gebouwde omgeving kunnen beïnvloeden, zoals overheden, vastgoedeigenaren, politici, investeerders, financiers, de gebruikers van gebouwen en gemeenschappen – die niettemin nieuwe vormen van zeggenschap en gedrag vereisen, om hun concurrerende belangen te beheren.[14]

Ontwerpbeoordeling: Goed ontwerp en goed bestuur

De theorievorming over ontwerpend besturen zoals die door CABE en in het Urban Maestro-onderzoek in praktijk is gebracht, legt de nadruk op een 'gereedschapkist'-achtige benadering, die beantwoordt aan de behoefte van overheden om hun werk te ijken, en die de overdraagbaarheid en aanpasbaarheid van praktijken onderstreept door verschillende regelomgevingen en beroepsculturen heen.[15] In veel ontwerpbestuurlijke instrumenten liggen echter vormen van contextuele ontwerpbeoordeling verscholen die de rol van 'zachte macht' in het hedendaagse stedelijke bestuur

2023). In de Britse context wordt het concept geassocieerd met het werk van socioloog Anthony Giddens en zijn boek *The Third Way: The Renewal of Social Democracy* (Londen: Polity, 1998).

13
Gerry Stoker, 'Governance as Theory: Five Propositions', *International Social Science Journal* 50 (1998), 17, 19, 21.

14
Zie voor een bespreking van Foucault's concept van pastorale macht in relatie tot ontwerpbestuur: John Macarthur en Susan Holden, 'Beauty in Urban Design Governance', *Islands: 40th Annual Conference of the Society of Architectural Historians of Australia and New Zealand* (Brisbane: SAHANZ, 2024). Uittreksel online: sahanz.net/publications/papers/beauty-in-urban-design-governance (geraadpleegd 20 januari 2025).

15
Matthew Carmona, 'The Formal and Informal Tools of Design Governance', *Journal of Urban Design* 22/1 (2017), 1-36; Matthew Carmona, Joao Bento en Tommaso Gabrieli, *Urban Design Governance: Soft Powers and the European Experience* (Londen: UCL Press, 2023).

geprezen als op ervaring gericht lesmateriaal: 'Los van de tentoonstelling is de villa natuurlijk op zichzelf al een les in bouwcultuur – en in het bijzonder de cultuur van het erfgoedbehoud.'[10]

De mate waarin *Baukultur* het onderwerp is geworden van toegewijde culturele reflectie blijkt ook duidelijk uit de acceptatie ervan als pedagogisch concept. In *Elemente einer baukulturellen Allgemeinbildung* (2021), vat pedagoog Roland Reichenbach het als volgt samen: 'Algemene bouwcultuureducatie gaat over (1) het verwerven van kennis, (2) het verfijnen van de waarneming en (3) het ontwikkelen van beoordelingsvaardigheden met betrekking tot artefacten die deel uitmaken van de leefomgeving.' Dat wil zeggen dat mensen niet alleen deel uitmaken van de bouwcultuur, maar ook een reflectieve relatie tot de bouwcultuur kunnen ontwikkelen.[11] Het boek bestaat uit teksten waarin de benodigde basiskennis voor een 'algemene bouwcultuureducatie' te vinden is op basis van het criterium: 'Wat moet de mondige burger over bouwcultuur weten?'[12] Het boek is een initiatief van Archijeunes, een maatschappelijke organisatie die zich sinds 2008 inzet voor bouwcultuureducatie voor kinderen en jongeren en die onder meer lesmateriaal voor scholen

10
Rahel Marti, 'Die Baukulturlernvilla', *Hochparterre online* (26 augustus 2013).

11
Roland Reichenbach, 'Baukulturelle Allgemeinbildung: Eine bildungstheoretische Annäherung', in: Kathrin Siebert (red.), *Elemente einer baukulturellen Allgemeinbildung* (Zürich: Park Books, 2021), 61.

12
Kathrin Siebert, 'Einleitung. Baukulturelle Bildung braucht Grundwissen', in: ibid., 11.

‘Soft Power: The Brussels Way of Making the City’ in S AM Swiss Architecture Museum, Bazel

ontwikkelt.[13] De 16 hoofdstukken gaan over kennisgebieden als architectuurgeschiedenis, bouwtechniek, sociologie, projectontwikkeling, monumentenzorg, verkeer en landschap. In de inleiding wordt opgemerkt dat de uitdaging niet ligt in het simpelweg overbrengen van bundels disciplinaire kennis, maar eerder in het – in de ‘integratieve en verbindende’ geest van de bouwcultuur – openstellen van disciplines ten behoeve van uitwisseling.[14]

In hetzelfde boek merkt Ákos Moravánszky op dat het woord *Baukultur* aantrekkelijk is, omdat het zowel elitair als democratisch klinkt.[15] ‘Bouwcultuur’ reproduceert onvermijdelijk de ambivalentie van een cultuurbegrip en dat heeft zowel een normatieve, beoordelende als een beschrijvende, cultuurrelativistische betekenis. Het gaat enerzijds om de *Kultur* die we kennen van het hooggestemde ideaal van de *Bildung*, die een imperatief voor een betere bouwcultuur impliceert dankzij de cultivering van alle betrokken actoren, zowel als een onderscheidende culturele productie. Aan de andere kant heeft het betrekking op cultuur zoals begrepen in antropologie, archeologie of culturele studies – bouwcultuur omvat dan gewoon alle cultuur, hoog en laag, van het bouwen en de gebouwde omgeving, net zoals er ook eetcultuur

‘Bijou oder Bausünde. Über unseren Umgang mit *Baukultur*’ (2022-2024): tentoonstellingsflyer met de Triemlitoren in Zürich

of muziekcultuur bestaat, van lokale bouwmethoden tot de architectonische publicatiecultuur.

Dit neemt niet weg dat Moravánszky ook op de intrinsiek defensieve aard van *Baukultur* wijst, hoewel het niet altijd duidelijk is wat er precies verdedigd moet worden: 'De identiteit van een regio? Het samenhangende stadsgezicht? In ieder geval wordt erfgoedbehoud of *Heimatschutz* (...) vaak genoemd als een primaire taak van de *Baukultur*.'[16] 'Kan *Baukultur* beperkt worden tot erfgoed?' vraagt Moravánszky zich retorisch af. Ook al propageren veel betrokkenen bij veel gelegenheden een en-en-verhaal over erfgoed en hedendaagse architectuur, het bouwcultuurdiscours is en blijft gebaseerd op een conservatieve reflex.

Dit blijkt ook uit het historische fundament waarop het concept *Baukultur* – zoals Moravánszky dat schetst – mede is opgetrokken. Denk aan de tiendelige boekenreeks *Kulturarbeiten* waarin Paul Schultze-Naumberg, protagonist van de Duitse Heimatschutz-beweging, vanaf 1901 de 'cultuur van het zichtbare' en de 'fysionomie van het landschap' tot onderwerp van zijn kritiek maakte – de eruit voorvloeiende kwalen moesten worden bestreden met voortdurende aandacht voor het ontwerp. En ook aan het nieuwsmagazine *Die*

13
Archijeunes wordt gefinancierd door particuliere donoren en krijgt financiële steun van de Swiss Society of Engineers and Architects (SIA) en de Bund Schweizer Architektinnen und Architecten (BSA).

14
Siebert, 'Einleitung. Baukulturelle Bildung braucht Grundwissen', op. cit. (noot 12), 11. De Verklaring van Davos beschouwt interdisciplinariteit ook als een voorwaarde voor een hoogwaardige bouwcultuur en dit wordt in één adem genoemd met sectoroverschrijdende samenwerking en met de noodzakelijke deelname van het maatschappelijk middenveld en de rol van een geïnformeerd publiek (art. 16). Dus wanneer de prijsvraag wordt aangewezen als een belangrijk instrument voor het bevorderen van een hoogwaardige *Baukultur*, dan staat daar de kwalificatie 'interdisciplinaire en breed bediscussieerde' prijsvraag bij.

15
Akos Moravánszky, 'Wege zur Baukultur', in: Siebert, *Elemente einer baukulturellen Allgemeinbildung*, op. cit. (noot 11), 38.

16
Moravánszky, 'Wege zur Baukultur', op. cit. (noot 15), 37-38.

symboliseren.[16] Commissies of panels om ontwerpen te beoordelen, die vaak worden bijeengeroepen bij een openbare aanbesteding of ontwikkelingsproject, bestaan doorgaans uit een aantal onafhankelijke experts. Deze beoordelen de ontwerpkwaliteit van voorstellen, parallel aan de wettelijke goedkeuring ervan. De expertise van de panelleden wordt ingezet om te adviseren, te bepleiten en te overtuigen. De panels versterken zodoende het vermogen van architecten om een goed oordeel te vellen over de ontwerpkwaliteit; de notie van kwaliteit wordt direct gekoppeld aan professionele expertise, zelfs wanneer de commissies steeds vaker diverse en multidisciplinaire deelnemers opnemen.

Ontwerpbeoordeling is helemaal geen nieuwe praktijk. Het is een basiselement in de pedagogische traditie en collegiale beoordeling van de ontwerpdisciplines en wordt al lange tijd als bestuurlijk middel toegepast. In de Verenigde Staten, in de jaren 1950, kwam er een integratie tussen ontwerpbeoordeling en planning tot stand en dit ontwikkelde zich tot een nuttige, zij het ad hoc aanvulling op regelgeving via bestemmingsplannen. Het legitimeerde het gebruik van esthetische controle door stadsbesturen, die anderszins beperkt was vanwege grondwettelijke eigendomsrechten en het

Baukultur, dat in de jaren 1930 werd uitgegeven door de architectenvereniging Der Block uit Stuttgart, die de Kochenhofsiedlung liet bouwen als *heimatisch* tegenmodel van de Weissenhofsiedlung. Verder aan de manier waarop in Zwitserland in de jaren 1970 het *Baukultur*-discours opnieuw werd aangezwengeld, dit naast de kritiek op het modernisme en de verder oprukkende verstedelijking en milieuvervuiling, met beton en de *Grossiedlung* als fundamentele tegenbeelden van *Baukultur*. Een dergelijke geschiedenis zet aan tot peinzen en doet denken aan de (evoluerende) ideologische inhoud van het concept. Het is zeker de moeite waard om op te merken dat het recente *Baukultur*-discours elk nativisme onderdrukt en een veelheid aan bouwculturen omarmt.

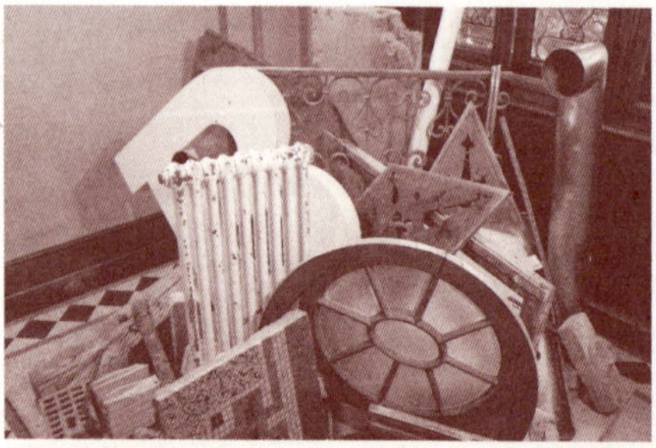

'Bijou oder Bausünde': presentatie die bouwafval problematiseert

'Bijou oder Bausünde'. Tekstballonnen met citaten over *Baukultur* en esthetiek

Juwelen en zonden

Tegenwoordig is de brutalistische betonarchitectuur opnieuw onderwerp van discussie, maar nu als jong erfgoed, en de kwestie is er niet zozeer een van architectuurhistorisch belang en gaat niet over de juiste criteria voor erfgoedstatus, maar over schoonheid en de politieke betekenis van een generatie woongebouwen en welzijnsinstellingen. Van september 2022 tot mei

recht op vrijheid van meningsuiting.[17] De International Conference on Design Review, die in 1992 in Cincinnati werd gehouden, bracht deelnemers uit de Verenigde Staten, Groot-Brittannië, Duitsland, Zuid-Afrika, Brazilië en Australië bij elkaar om de al in gang gezette internationale kennisuitwisseling over manieren van ontwerpbeoordeling verder te stimuleren.[18] In het boek dat na de conferentie werd gepubliceerd, benoemde Brenda Case Scheer op scherpzinnige wijze de uitdagingen waarmee een ontwerpbeoordeling te maken krijgt tijdens het onderhandelen over macht, vrijheid, rechtvaardigheid en esthetiek.[19] Deze spelen nog steeds een rol in het ontwerpend besturen, als ze niet al de expliciete agenda van die ontwerpbeoordelingscommissies uitmaken.

In Groot-Brittannië zette CABE de ontwerpbeoordelingspraktijk voort die haar voorganger, de Royal Fine Arts Commission (RFAC), had ingesteld.[20] Maar de ontwerpbeoordeling onder de CABE ging vergeleken met eerdere vormen van esthetische controle duidelijk verder qua reikwijdte en intentie. Carmona et al. karakteriseerden dit als een verschuiving 'weg van (...) de esthetiek en richting (...) stadsontwerp'.[21] Het weerspiegelde een explicietere politieke interesse in de ontwerpkwaliteit van steden, de opgang van stadsontwerp als onafhankelijke

16
De Urban Maestro-database bevat verschillende voorbeelden van ontwerpbeoordelingscommissies, waaronder het werk van het Baukollegium Zürich, de Nederlandse Q-Teams, vermarkte ontwerpbeoordeling in Groot-Brittannië, ontwerpbeoordelingscommissies in Oostenrijk, en de BMA. Zie: urbanmaestro.org (geraadpleegd 24 juni 2024).

17
John Delafons, *Aesthetic Control: A Report on Methods Used in the USA to Control the Design of Buildings* (Berkeley: University of California, 1990).

18
Brenda Case Scheer en Wolfgang F.E. Preiser (red.), *Design Review: Challenging Urban Aesthetic Control* (Londen/ New York: Chapman & Hall, 1994).

19
Brenda Case Scheer, 'Introduction: The Debate on Design Review', in: ibid., 4-9.

20
Zie voor meer informatie over de ontwikkeling van esthetische controle onder de Royal Fine Arts Commission: John Punter, 'A History of Aesthetic Control: Part 1, 1909-1953: The Control of the External Appearance of Development in England and Wales', *The Town Planning Review* 57/4 (1986), 351-381; John Delafons, 'In Britain: the Enduring Ambivalence', in: Delafons, *Aesthetic Control*, op. cit. (noot 17), 71-81; Matthew Carmona et al., 'The RFAC and Seventy-Five Years of English Design Review, 1924-1999', in: Carmona et al., *The CABE Experiment*, op. cit. (noot 12), 69-87.

21
Carmona et al., *The CABE Experiment*, op. cit. (noot 12), 8

2024 was in Villa Patumbah de tentoonstelling 'Bijou oder Bausünde? Über unseren Umgang mit Baukultur' ('Juweel of bouwzonde? Over onze omgang met bouwcultuur') te zien. Het is niet toevallig dat juist de brutalistische Zürichse Triemli-woontoren op het affiche staat afgebeeld. Dit door Esther en Rudolf Guyer ontworpen flatgebouw uit 1966 werd in 2018 nog door lezers van de gratis krant *20 Minuten* tot het lelijkste gebouw van Zwitserland verkozen. Anderen verdedigden het brutalistische bouwerfgoed als getuigend van 'maatschappelijke ambitie, creativiteit en moedig optimisme in de naoorlogse periode'.[17] Het is een van de voorbeelden in de tentoonstelling die de filosofische beschouwing van de architectuur als een kwestie van cultuur overstijgt en burgers vraagt om een standpunt in te nemen over de kwaliteit ervan: 'We kunnen, door wat we doen, allemaal bijdragen aan de vormgeving van gebouwen en de openbare ruimte, discussiëren over juwelen en bouwzonden en pleiten voor het behoud van waardevolle gebouwensembles.'[18] Een partij uit gerenoveerde gebouwen gewonnen, gedemonteerde bouwelementen die de vraag: 'Kan dit weg?' opriep, was bedoeld om vragen en reacties van bezoekers uit te lokken; een wolk van tekstballonnen met citaten en

17
Karin Bürki op haar website *Heartbrut*, juni 2022, geciteerd in de tentoonstelling 'Bijou oder Bausünde'. Zie ook: heartbrut.com/compendium/triemlitower.

18
Inleidende muurtekst.

CABE vervaardigde talrijke publicaties en hulpmiddelen om de kwaliteit van de gebouwde omgeving te verbeteren, zoals *The Value of Good Design (2002) en Design Review: Principles and Practice* (2013, 2019)

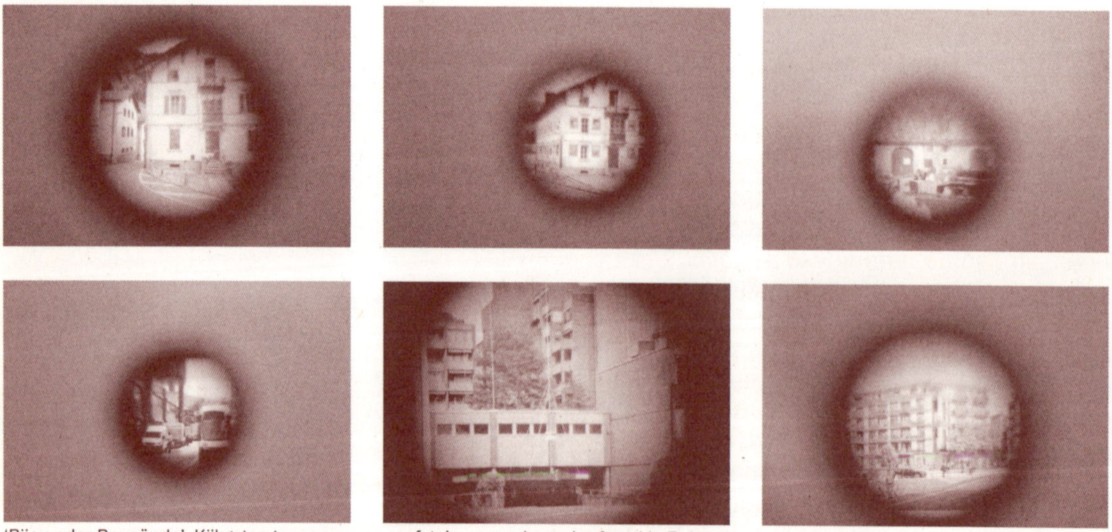

'Bijou oder Bausünde'. Kijkgaten tonen voor en na foto's van verbouwd erfgoed in Zwitserland

discipline en de verheffing van het concept 'goed ontwerp' boven de esthetische categorie 'schoonheid'.

Ontwerpbeoordeling werd een sleutelonderdeel van CABE's opzet: een tastbare werkwijze om noties over kwaliteit binnen een voor het overige zwak discretionair planningssysteem voorrang te geven; het bleek een vitale schakel bij CABE-taken als algemene bewustmaking en het geven van advies. CABE produceerde talloze documenten om de rol van ontwerpbeoordelingscommissies bij het bevorderen van goed ontwerp uit te leggen. Deze leidraden voorzagen in criteria voor wat een goed project was en verwezen daarbij enerzijds naar Vitruvius' drietal *firmitas, utilitas en venustas*, maar benadrukten anderzijds ook de rol van ontwerpbeoordeling bij het prioriteren van ontwerpkwaliteit boven conformiteit of naleving van planningsvoorschriften.[22] Men stelde: 'Ontwerpen is een creatieve activiteit en definities van ontwerpkwaliteit zijn ongrijpbaar. Ontwerpkwaliteit kan niet worden gereduceerd tot regels en voorschriften. (...) de beste voorbeelden breken vaak met de regels of stijgen er bovenuit.'[23] Een latere CABE-publicatie, *The Value Handbook*, plaatste ontwerpkwaliteit binnen een meer alomvattend ecosysteem van kwaliteitsbeheer en presenteerde tegelijkertijd objectievere criteria, met de woorden:

22 Commission for Architecture and the Built Environment, *Design Review: How CABE Evaluates Quality in Architecture and Urban Design* (Londen: CABE, 2006), 14. Deze gids werd voor het eerst gepubliceerd in 2001 en herzien in 2006.

23 Ibid., 5.

vergelijkende voor- en na-afbeeldingen van gesloopte, verplaatste, gerestaureerde, verbouwde of vervangen gebouwen diende hetzelfde doel. Dergelijke beeldparen passen in een traditie van het ondersteunen van het architectonisch esthetisch-moreel discours met contrasterende 'goede' en 'slechte' voorbeelden, zoals in Pugin's *Contrasts* (1836) of de al genoemde boeken van Schultze-Naumberg.[19] In dit geval werden de beeldparen echter nog voornamelijk in de vorm van vragen gepresenteerd – niet als expliciete, binaire smaak- of ideologielessen. Het esthetische en praktische oordeel leek aan de bezoeker te worden overgelaten.

De uitdaging om de *Baukultur* te operationaliseren als een cultureel programma, schuilt dus niet alleen in het articuleren van haar relatie tot bredere culturele kwesties, maar is er ook een van haar nut in relatie tot de specifieke maatschappelijke, economische, politieke en ecologische omstandigheden waarin gebouwen worden gemaakt en onderhouden. In dat opzicht blijkt de Villa Patumbah zelf een geladen *Bijou* of *Bausünde* te zijn. Sinds de zomer van 2020 is er in het ondergrondse deel van de villa een kleine paralleltentoonstelling te zien, 'Patumbah liegt auf Sumatra' (Patumbah ligt op Sumatra), waarin de villa geduid en

19 Augustus W. Pugin, *Contrasts: Or, a Parallel between the Noble Edifices of the Middle Ages and Corresponding Buildings of the Present Day* (Cambridge: Cambridge University Press, 2013). Zie voor meer informatie over Schultze-Naumberg's gebruik van afbeeldingen: Matthias Noell, 'Kultur des Sichtbaren: Der fotografische Blick des Herrn Schultze', in: Hans-Rudolf Meier en Daniela Spiegel (red.), *Kulturreformer, Rassenideologe, Hochschuldirektor: Der lange Schatten des Paul Schultze-Naumburg* (Heidelberg: Arthistoricum.net, 2018), 35.

> Onder goed ontwerp verstaan we een ontwerp dat geschikt is voor het beoogde doel, duurzaam, efficiënt, samenhangend, flexibel, dat inspeelt op de context, er goed uitziet en een duidelijke uitdrukking is van de eisen van de opdracht. Wij geloven dat het beoordelen van kwaliteit in grote mate een objectief proces is. Uiteindelijk komen sommige kwesties natuurlijk neer op individuele smaak en voorkeur. Het komt echter niet vaak voor dat dit soort kwesties van belang zijn om te bepalen of een project, alles welbeschouwd, een goed project is. Wat telt is kwaliteit, niet stijl.[24]

De spanning tussen regelgeving en oordeel die desondanks bij *design review* van ontwerpen kan opduiken, is niet noodzakelijk uniek voor de beoordeling van ontwerpen, maar eerder een kenmerk van het besturen. Wetenschapshistoricus Lorraine Daston, en auteur van het boek *Rules: A Short History of What We Live By*, wijst erop dat er altijd uitzonderingen op de regel zijn en dat elke vorm van prestatiebeoordeling in zekere zin ook kwalitatieve beoordeling vereist. De vraag wie de macht heeft om over de uitzonderingen te beslissen, speelt niet alleen een rol in de activiteit van het

'Patumbah ligt op Sumatra', een kabinettentoonstelling in Villa Patumbah, 2020. Vloerkaart en tentoongesteld boek *Schweizer Verein Deli-Sumatra* (Zürich, 1936)

ontwerp beoordelen, maar dit is ook de crux van de politieke economie.[25] Gelegenheden waarbij regels, voorschriften en standaarden kunnen worden getemperd door het oordeel en de ervaring van experts, blijven een cruciaal onderdeel van besturen, hoewel mogelijk bedreigd door vormen van kwaliteitsbeheer die juist deze situaties aan banden proberen te leggen. De commissies die ontwerpen beoordelen, houden zich bezig met deze kwalitatieve dimensie van besturen en wat daarbij op het spel staat. Hoewel de meeste commissies de evaluatie van een goed ontwerp legitimeren met begeleidende ontwerprichtlijnen of -principes, houden ze zich ook bezig met het werk en de waarde van een onderhandeld en gesitueerd oordeel, en beschermen ze in het beste geval het idee van kwaliteit zonder een vaste of vooraf bepaalde maatstaf.

CABE ging er prat op dat ze haar ontwerpadviezen openbaar maakte om vertrouwen in het beoordelingsproces te kweken en haar pijlers, transparantie en verantwoording, te verankeren.[26] Deze aandacht voor het proces zelf werd een aandachtspunt in latere CABE-publicaties, waardoor het discours verschoof van discussies over wat goed ontwerp is, naar discussies over wat goed bestuur is. In dit opzicht is ontwerpbeoordeling

24 Commission for Architecture and the Built Environment, *The Value Handbook: Getting the Most from Your Buildings and Spaces* (Londen: CABE, 2006), 5.

25 Lorraine Daston, *Rules: A Short History of What We Live By* (Princeton/Oxford: Princeton University Press, 2022), 256.

26 CABE heeft als leidraad voor het ontwerpbeoordelingsproces tien principes geformuleerd en stelde dat de panels onafhankelijk, deskundig, multidisciplinair, verantwoordelijkheid nemend, transparant, proportioneel, tijdgevoelig, adviserend, objectief en toegankelijk moesten zijn. Design Council UK, *Design Review: Principles and Practice* (Londen: Design Council, 2019 [2013]).

gesitueerd wordt als koloniaal erfgoed.[20] Deze tentoonstelling houdt zich niet bezig met de gecombineerde architectuur van deze Italiaanse neorenaissancevilla met aspecten van een Chinese binnenhofwoning, of met de exotiserende ornamenten – van draakvormige waterspuwers die uit de klassieke gevels steken tot (echte en valse) Chinese inscripties in de interieurs van de tweede verdieping. De tentoonstelling documenteert in plaats daarvan de koloniale realiteit van de Sumatraanse plantages die het kapitaal genereerden dat deze villa mogelijk maakte. De bouwer, Carl Fürchtegott Grob, was een Zwitser die fortuin had gemaakt in de plantage-economie van Nederlands-Indië. Tussen 1871 en 1889 dreef hij samen met een Beierse zakenpartner een van de grootste tabaksplantages aan de noordoostkust van Sumatra. Hij hanteerde het koloniale systeem waarbij contractarbeiders van onder andere Java en uit China werden uitgebuit, en het landgebruik en de sociale organisatie van de lokale Batak en Maleiers werden vervangen. Eenmaal terug in Zürich liet Grob de somptueuze villa met koetshuis bouwen en de landschapstuin aanleggen. Een vergulde inscriptie verwijst naar de plaats Patumbak, waardoor de villa meer wordt dan louter 'transactiearchitectuur', maar een roerende culturele

20 'Zwitserland is een van de meest geglobaliseerde landen in de wereld. Het traditionele beeld van een eiland midden in de Europese politieke constructie heeft weinig gelijkenis met de werkelijkheid – noch vandaag, noch in het verleden (...) De erkenning dat Zwitserland deelnam aan kolonialisme zelfs zonder eigen kolonies wordt steeds meer gevestigd in hedendaagse historiografie.' Judith Schubiger, Karin Artho en Céline Hug, Heimatschutzzentrum, *Patumbah liegt auf Sumatra* (Zürich: Schweizer Heimatschutz, 2022), 57.

Simulaa, *Design Standards* (2022) op de voorgrond van de sectie Civic Architecture, in de tentoonstelling 'Melbourne Now' in het Ian Potter Centre, National Gallery of Victoria, Melbourne, 2023

getuige van het Europese plunderende kolonialisme èn van de propagandistische monumentalisering ervan.[21] En – mits een kritische lectuur voldoende wordt ontwikkeld, door bijvoorbeeld een tentoonstelling zoals die in het souterrain – is de Villa ook een blijvende aanmaning om de bouwcultuur niet los te koppelen van bredere politiek-ecologische perspectieven en kwesties.[22]

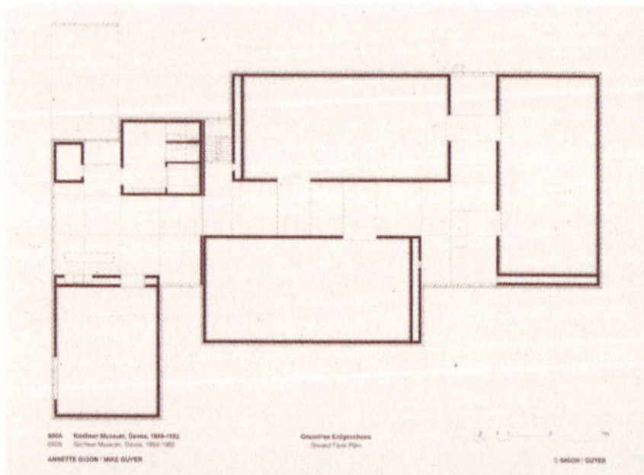

Annette Gigon en Mike Guyer, Kirchner Museum, Davos, 1989-1992. Plattegrond begane grond

Demonstratief ontwerp

Het Kirchner Museum, een van de plaatsen waar het World Economic Forum plaatsvindt, is een ander voorbeeld van architectuur die kan worden opgevat als een plaatsgebonden les in *Baukultur*. Het voormalige sanatorium en huidige ski- en conferentieoord Davos in het kanton Graubünden is niet alleen bekend als plek waar het jaarlijkse WEF plaatsvindt, het is ook de locatie van het Kirchner Museum, dat sinds de opening in 1992 enige bekendheid heeft verworven in de architectuurwereld. In dit vroege project braken Annette Gigon en Mike Guyer met de postmodernistische museumarchitectuur. Met zijn constructieve grammatica, zijn minimale en niet-hiërarchische plattegrond en een gereduceerde vormentaal die de kristallijne materialiteit en atmosferische kwaliteiten van het museum

op de voorgrond plaatst, kan het gebouw de belangrijkste architectuurtheoretische discussies belichamen die destijds in Zwitserland speelden – en misschien zelfs ook het idee van (Zwitserse) architectonische kwaliteit in het algemeen (hoe problematisch zo'n veralgemenisering ook is).[23] In een campagne uit 2019, die was bedoeld om het bewustzijn van recent architectonisch erfgoed te vergroten, werd het Kirchner Museum door de kantonnale erfgoedvereniging Bündner Heimatschutz gepromoot als een van de 52 beste naoorlogse gebouwen in Graubünden. Het ging daarbij om 'gebouwen die er zeker aanspraak op zouden kunnen maken, bouwkunst te zijn (*von hohem baukünstlerischem Anspruch*), die onze identiteit net zozeer vormgeven als de monumenten uit vroegere tijdperken'.[24]

Hoe kan de architectonische kwaliteit van dit object in Davos worden begrepen in relatie tot het *Baukultur*-ideaal dat in de Verklaring van Davos van drie decennia later werd afgekondigd? In deze context blijkt Irina Davidovici's analyse van de Duits-Zwitserse architectuur van de laatste twee decennia van de twintigste eeuw leerzaam en tot nadenken stemmend. Davidovici interpreteert de eigenschappen van unieke projecten zoals het Kirchner Museum in relatie tot

21
'Transactional Architecture' is de titel van een thematisch dossier in nummer 24 (2021) van *ABE Journal – Architecture beyond Europe*. In 'I Will Burn Tuan's House: Tobacco, Opium, and the Villa Patumbah' stelt Will Davis voor om Villa Patumbah niet op te vatten als transactionele architectuur, maar als een Europese metamorfose van de plantage zelf en als een plek van koloniale ontmoeting waar 'omstandigheden van tropisch geweld nodig waren om bezoekers de materiële overvloed van de tropen te laten begrijpen.'

22
Joan Ockman, 'Toward a Political Ecology of Architecture,' *Places Journal* (maart 2022).

23
Irina Davidovici en Laurent Stalder hebben achteraf allebei op dit voorbeeld gewezen. Davidovici, *Forms of Practice,* op. cit. (noot 1), 122-141; Laurent Stalder, 'Um 1990: Ein Bau und Viele Texte', in: Katharina Beisiegel (red.), *GIGON/GUYER Kirchner Museum revisited* (München: Hirmer Verlag, 2022), 61-65.

24
Bündner Heimatschutz, *52 Beste Bauten: Baukultur Graubünden 1950-2000: Jede Woche ein neuer Blick* (2020), 52bestebauten.ch/idee-konzept (geraadpleegd 1 februari 2025).

evenzeer een omgeving als een instrument, doordat het ruimte schept voor reflectie, overleg en constructieve gesprekken.

De proliferatie van de ontwerpbeoordeling illustreert de voortdurende evolutie ervan als een prominente vorm van ontwerpend besturen.[27] Deze evolutie in Australië houdt de nalatenschap van CABE in ere, na de ondergang van de organisatie in Groot-Brittannië. In Australië zijn ontwerpbeoordelingspanels een kerntaak geworden van de bureaus van de staats- en territoriale rijksbouwmeesters die in de plaats zijn gekomen van de overheidsarchitecten en afdelingen Openbare Werken uit het koloniale tijdperk.[28] Het ontwerpbeoordelingsmodel van CABE werd in eerste instantie in 2011 in licentie gegeven aan de Zuid-Australische regering, toen CABE opging in de Design Council UK en haar adviesdiensten te gelde wilde maken.[29] Kirsteen Mackay, voorheen chef Design Review bij CABE, trad in dienst bij het Office for Design and Architecture South Australia en werd in 2015 bouwmeester van Zuid-Australië zowel als voorzitter van het Design Review Panel van die staat. In Zuid-Australië is ontwerpbeoordeling nu gebruikelijk bij belangrijke staatsprojecten en dit heeft geleid tot een op kwaliteit gerichte agenda voor verscheidene openbare

Davos, met het Grandhotel Belvédère en het Kirchner Museum tijdens het World Economic Forum

organisaties en overheden. De methoden en degelijke bestuurlijke principes van CABE hebben de praktijk om ontwerpen te beoordelen in heel Australië beïnvloed, zelfs al laten de commissies zich leiden door principes van goed ontwerp die ruimte maken voor lokale definities van plaats, karakter en vorm.[30] Op die manier heeft de praktijk van ontwerpbeoordeling een nieuwe omgeving gecreëerd waar professionele deskundigheid het ontwerp van de openbare ruimte kan beïnvloeden.

Een nieuwe vorm van civiel ontwerp

In 1990 beschreef John Delafons de opkomst van ideeën over ontwerpkwaliteit bij stadsbesturen als 'voortbordurend op een oudere traditie van civiel ontwerp'.[31] We zijn nu in staat de neoliberale context die ten grondslag ligt aan de ontwerpbestuurlijke praktijken die tegenwoordig wijdverspreid zijn, te herkennen – en we zijn ons bewust van belangen en tegenstrijdigheden en van de grenzen van het kwaliteitsbeheer. We zijn ook in staat verder te kijken dan dat ene moment, naar nieuwe concepten van civiel ontwerp die het hedendaagse kwaliteitsdiscours vormgeven. Maar kan het tegenwoordige ontwerpend besturen, opgevat als de herregulering van ontwerpkwaliteit in het besturen van steden

27
John Punter heeft gedocumenteerd dat ontwerpbeoordelingen internationaal op grote schaal worden toegepast in zowel regulerende als discretionaire planningssystemen. John Punter, 'Developing Urban Design as Public Policy: Best Practice Principles for Design Review and Development Management', *Journal of Urban Design* 12/2 (2007), 167-202.

28
Susan Holden en Kirsty Volz, 'The Value of Architects in Government: Research Dossier,' *Architecture Australia* 112/2 (2023), 53-69.

29
Office for Design and Architecture South Australia, *State Design Review in South Australia* (Adelaide: Government of South Australia, 2021).

30
Emma Appleton, 'The State of Play in Design,' in: John Byrne, Bill Chandler en Bruce Echberg (red.), *Urban Voices: Celebrating Urban Design in Australia* (Melbourne: Urban Design Forum, 2013), 109-112; Susan Holden en John Macarthur, 'Soft-Power and Design Review: The CABE Legacy in Australia', *Australian Planner* 180/2 (2025), binnenkort te verschijnen. Voorbeelden van gidsen voor goed ontwerp zijn de *Q Design Manual* (2018) van de regering van Queensland, die als leidraad dient voor het State Urban Design and Places Panel en subtropische ontwerpen benadrukt en *101 Design Ideas from 5 Years of the NSW State Design Review Panel* (2023), gepubliceerd door de Government Architect van New South Wales, die het principe van ontwerpen met *Country* benadrukt.

31
Delafons, *Aesthetic Control: A Report*, op. cit. (noot 17), 38.

bredere (toenmalige) Zwitserse condities die de productie ervan mogelijk maakten, met name op drie punten. Het gaat daarbij om aspecten van de Zwitserse cultuur zoals een protestants werk- en kapitaalethos, een sterke democratische organisatie met grote gemeentelijke autonomie, of het territoriale zelfbeeld van dorpen in berglandschappen versus geconcentreerde steden en hightech infrastructuur. Daarnaast op aspecten als een achtergrond van (internationale) theorievorming die, grotendeels vanuit de dominante ETH Zürich, het ideaal van een architecturale autonomie cultiveerde. En tenslotte om een beroepscultuur waarin architecten zeer nauw betrokken waren bij het bouwen, met het strak gereguleerde Zwitserse competitiesysteem dat destijds ook kansen kon bieden aan jonge architecten zoals Gigon/Guyer, en met hoge productiewaarden in de bouw.[25] Bij elk van deze generalisaties plaatst Davidovici niettemin ook kanttekeningen, zoals wanneer ze de specifieke kenmerken van de bouwcultuur in het kanton Graubünden uitlicht.[26]

Davidovici interpreteert de nadrukkelijke ontwerpinvestering in een bouwgrammatica, en de esthetisering en zelfs moralisering van het goede bouwdetail binnen de Zwitserse architectuurcultuur aan het einde van de

25
Davidovici, *Forms of Practice*, op. cit. (noot 1), 246.

26
'De architectuur in Graubünden is niet representatief voor de bredere condities van de praktijk in Zwitserland. Het werkt als een systeem binnen een systeem. (...) Opzienbarend is de ontvankelijkheid van dit landelijke, hoofdzakelijk conservatieve kanton voor radicaal hedendaagse architectuur. Deze verbinding kan op twee manieren uitgelegd worden. Ten eerste vormt bouwkwaliteit een gedeelde grond die bemiddelt tussen architecten en de gemeenschappen die ze dienen. Ten tweede vertoont het karakter van Graubünden inherent stedelijke trekken, ten gevolge van zijn dominante toeristische industrie.' Ibid., 247.

Het South Australian State Design Review Panel in actie

52 Beste Bauten: Baukultur Graubünden 1950-2000, 2020, waaronder het Kirchner Museum in Davos

na de teloorgang van de verzorgingsstaat en natievormende beleidskaders, ook ruimte maken voor een gesitueerde kritiek op de maatschappelijke en ecologische effecten van het neoliberalisme?

De tentoonstelling 'Civic Architecture', die deel uitmaakte van de 'Melbourne Now'- show die in 2023 werd gehouden in de National Gallery of Victoria, presenteerde een nieuw perspectief op het onderwerp. Deze tentoonstelling ontdeed de kwaliteitsvraag van de projectieve vermomming die het in het ontwerpbestuurlijke domein vaak aanneemt en herleidt de vraag naar de substantie van de stad zelf.[32] In de door Timothy Moore samengestelde tentoonstelling was een verzameling recente Melbournse projecten te zien waar de mogelijkheden van ontwerpopdrachten voor openbare gebouwen – bibliotheken, vervoersinfrastructuur, universiteitsgebouwen – waren gebruikt om nieuwe beelden van de stad als civiel domein te presenteren: van een plaats voor burgerschapsceremonieën, gemeenschapstaken, leren en spelen. Deze projecten waren gerealiseerd via een waaier aan aanbestedings- en opleveringsprocedures die steeds vaker ook een ontwerpbeoordeling omvatten, wat een weerspiegeling is van de toename van ontwerpbestuurlijke praktijken in Victoria onder

32 'Melbourne Now' liep van 24 maart tot 20 augustus 2023. National Gallery of Victoria, 'Civic Architecture', ngv.vic.gov.au/melbourne-now/projects/civic-architecture (geraadpleegd 20 januari 2025).

twintigste eeuw, als een defensieve reactie. Het gaat om een reactie tegen de opdeling van architecten, in zij die ontwerpen maakten en zij die het bouwmanagement op zich namen, die ook in Zwitserland een hoge vlucht begon te nemen als gevolg van de mondialiserende bouweconomie. Ze stelde:

> Strengheid is dus niet simpelweg cultureel geconditioneerd; het is een verklaring van auteurschap, een soort verdedigingsmechanisme. Bouwkundige precisie articuleert verzet tegen veranderende mondiale omstandigheden. De Zwitserse architectuur van het einde van de twintigste eeuw is geen naadloze voortzetting van eerdere bouw- of culturele tradities, maar vertegenwoordigt het antwoord van de architect op een wereldwijde bedreiging van deze tradities.[27]

Een dergelijke focus op de rol van de architect als professionele expert lijkt op het eerste gezicht in tegenspraak met de alle-actoren-nadruk van het bouwcultuurdiscours, maar Davidovici verruimde tegelijk ook de blik als ze erop wijst hoe rollen veranderden naar aanleiding van bredere economische verschuivingen in de bouw. Misschien kan zelfs de volgende vergelijking worden

27 Ibid., 246.

de noemer 'Government as Smart Client'.[33] Een ander onderdeel van de tentoonstelling, 'Design Standards' (2022), bestond uit een vitrine met schaalmodellen van het stadsmeubilair dat rond de getoonde projecten stond, maar die over een langere periode waren vervaardigd. Deze objecten zijn een tastbare realiteit van het stadslandschap die vaak over het hoofd worden gezien in zowel het ontwerp als het bestuur, maar die niettemin onze ervaring van de gebouwde omgeving en onze opvattingen over ontwerpkwaliteit positief kunnen beïnvloeden. De schaalmodellen van straatlantaarns, bankjes, vuilnisbakken en fietsenrekken steunden op onderzoekswerk van architectenbureau Simulaa en waren uitgevoerd in een uniforme witte hars. Zo allemaal intiem bij elkaar uitgestald, wordt niet alleen de diversiteit van de ontwerpen – waar we standaardobjecten konden verwachten – kenbaar gemaakt, maar ook de associaties met het uitnodigend en comfortabel inrichten van de openbare ruimte. Het is een mooie illustratie van het gambiet aan hedendaags ontwerpend besturen: dat goed ontwerp maatschappelijke en civiele waarden kan uitdrukken, terwijl goed ontwerp ook de kwaliteit van individuele levens daadwerkelijk wil verbeteren.

Vertaling: InOtherWords, Maria van Tol

33 Office of the Victorian Government Architect, *Government as Smart Client* (Melbourne: State Government of Victoria, 2024 [2013]).

gemaakt: de Zwitsers-Europese doelstelling om een hoogwaardige *Baukultur* te realiseren, kan ook een reactie zijn geweest op een multidisciplinaire fragmentatie en een kwantificering van kwaliteitspercepties en borgingsprocessen in de eerste decennia van de eenentwintigste eeuw. Vooralsnog gaat er meer zeggingskracht uit van het appèl van de Verklaring van Davos op integraliteit en haar validatie van de gebouwde omgeving als een culturele aangelegenheid, en van de voorbeelden van Zwitserse architectuur uit de afgelopen vier decennia, dan van het kwaliteitssysteem dat in het kielzog van de Verklaring werd ontwikkeld om dit metabeleid te operationaliseren.[28] De opsomming van acht kwaliteitscriteria in het Davos Quality System – waaronder niet alleen context en schoonheid, maar ook bestuur – geeft het kwaliteitssysteem een bureaucratische en bestuurlijke kleur die misschien uiteindelijk haaks staat op de belofte van een bouwculturele allure.

Vertaling: InOtherWords, Maria van Tol

28 Swiss Federal Office of Culture, *The Davos Baukultur Quality System* (Bern: Swiss Federal Office of Culture, 2021), bak.admin.ch/bak/en/home/baukultur/qualitaet/davos-qualitaets-system-baukultur.html (geraadpleegd 11 maart 2024).

Justification, Negotiation and Mediation: Instituting Architectural Quality

Maarten Van Den Driessche

In 2012, Team Flemish Government Architect inaugurated the Atelier Bouwmeester as their dedicated space in the heart of Brussels. As a government body, the role of the Flemish Government Architect is to promote architectural quality throughout the Flemish region. While the word 'atelier' suggests a makerspace, Atelier Bouwmeester is primarily an institutional environment that could also be described as a Quality Setting. It is a place for Team Flemish Government Architect to meet and host workshops, exhibitions, lectures and juries. One of the first events held here was the *Assembly (Going Public)* focused on *Thing 001359* by Agency, an initiative by artist Kobe Matthys.[1] The photos show, seated on a temporary stage, the panel of experts to whom the legal conflict surrounding the demolition of the Chico Mendez Mural Garden in New York was submitted for discussion: one of the numerous files from the archives at the heart of Agency's practice.

In 2011, the art cell of Team Flemish Government Architect invited Agency to contribute to the publication *Openbaarheid* (Publicity). On the occasion of this commission, Agency was invited to the Atelier, where they moderated a so-called 'Samenkomst – Assembly – Assemblée – Versammlung – Asamblea – Batzar'. For the publication, Agency made a text highlighting and discussing the legal controversy surrounding the demolition of the garden as a case study.[2]

Around 2000, American artist Ron English had filed a lawsuit against property developer BFC&R to protect the Chico Mendez Mural Garden from demolition. The site of this community garden was originally public land owned by the City of New York. In the 1970s, activists protesting against land speculation, high real estate pressure and the lack of open space had illegally occupied the vacant lot and turned it into a community garden. Next, an artists' collective developed the garden by adding plants and graffiti art. However, under the neoliberal mayoralty of Rudy Guilliani, this and many similar community gardens were earmarked for privatisation to make way for new property development and social housing. To prevent its destruction, Ron English invoked the copyright of the artists' collective that had created the graffiti on the garden's walls.

In response to the art cell's invitation, the artist proposed installing a replica of the New York community garden's fence around the Lapperfort forest. This forest, located on the outskirts of Bruges, frequently appeared in the media between 2002 and 2012 as environmentalists occupied its treetops to protect the ecological habitat. This proposal brought the legal conflict, which had been settled in New York City at the end of the twentieth century, to Belgium, lending a sense of local relevance and immediacy to the overseas conflict.

In this text, I draw on the compelling analogy between Agency's art project and the work of the Flemish Government Architect to outline, through a theoretical lens, a series of operations that underpin quality mediation processes. Reflecting on both situations allows us to describe

1 Agency was founded in 1992 by Kobe Matthys, who died in 2023. For a brief biographical sketch, see: Wim Cuyvers, 'Kobe Matthys (1970-2023)', *De Witte Raaf* 224 (2023).

2 Kobe Matthys, 'Ding 001359 (Chico Mendez Mural Garden)', in: Katrien Laenen et al. (eds.), *Cahier #3 Openbaarheid: Over publiek domein, planning en restruimte* (Brussels: Vlaams Bouwmeester, 2011), 22-30.

Verantwoording, Onderhandeling, Bemiddeling: Architectuurkwaliteit instellen

Maarten Van Den Driessche

In 2012 werd het Atelier Bouwmeester, als de representatieve ruimte van het Team Vlaams Bouwmeester, feestelijk geopend in het centrum van Brussel. Als overheidsinstantie heeft de Vlaams Bouwmeester de opdracht de architectuurkwaliteit in de Vlaamse regio te bevorderen. Terwijl het woord atelier een maakplek suggereert, gaat het hier toch vooral om een institutionele omgeving die we ook als een *Quality Setting* kunnen omschrijven. Het is een plek waar het Team Vlaams Bouwmeester vergadert, workshops houdt, tentoonstellingen, lezingen en jury's organiseert. Eén van de eerste activiteiten in deze ruimte was de *Vergadering (Openbaarheid)* rondom *Ding 001359* van Agentschap, een initiatief van de kunstenaar Kobe Matthys.[1] Op foto's zien we in het midden van een tijdelijke tribune een panel van experts aan wie het juridisch geschil rondom de sloop van de *Chico Mendez Mural Garden* in New York ter discussie voorlegt: één van de talloze dossiers uit het archief dat de kern vormt van Agentschap's praktijk.

Agentschap werd in 2011 door de kunstcel van Team Vlaams Bouwmeester uitgenodigd om een bijdrage te leveren aan het cahier *Openbaarheid*. Naar aanleiding hiervan was Agentschap ook in het atelier te gast en modereerde Matthys er een 'Samenkomst – Assembly – Assemblée – Versammlung – Asamblea – Batzar'. Voor het cahier maakte Agentschap een tekst waarin de juridische controverse rond de sloop van de tuin als zaak werd uitgelicht.[2]

Tegen 2000 had de Amerikaanse kunstenaar Ron English een juridisch geding tegen vastgoedontwikkelaar BFC&R aangespannen, opdat de *Chico Mendez Mural Garden* van sloop zou worden gevrijwaard. De grond onder deze gemeenschapstuin was oorspronkelijk publiek eigendom van de stad New York. Als protest tegen de grondspeculatie, de hoge vastgoeddruk en de schaarse open ruimte was het braakliggend perceel sinds de jaren 1970 door activisten illegaal als gemeenschapstuin in gebruik genomen. Een collectief van kunstenaars had zich de tuin met beplanting en graffitikunst toegeëigend. Onder het neoliberale burgemeesterschap van Rudy Giuliani zou de gemeenschapstuin net als vele andere kavels echter geprivatiseerd worden, om plaats te maken voor nieuwe projectontwikkeling en sociale woningen. Om de tuin van sloop te redden deed Ron English beroep op het auteursrecht van het collectief dat de schilderingen op de muren van de tuin vervaardigde.

Als antwoord op de vraag van de kunstcel deed de kunstenaar het voorstel om een replica van de omheining van de New Yorkse gemeenschapstuin rondom het Lapperfortbos te plaatsen. Dat bosterrein aan de rand van Brugge kwam tussen 2002 en 2012 regelmatig in de media terecht, omdat milieuactivisten zich in de toppen van de bomen hadden verschanst om de ecologische habitat in bescherming te nemen. Dit voorstel bracht het juridische geschil dat op het einde van de vorige eeuw in de stad New York werd beslecht naar België, waardoor het overzeese conflict ook lokaal de nodige urgentie en actualiteit verkreeg.

1 Agentschap werd in 1992 opgericht door Kobe Matthys, die in 2023 is overleden. Voor een korte biografische schets zie: Wim Cuyvers. 'Kobe Matthys (1970-2023)', *De Witte Raaf* 224 (2023).

2 Kobe Matthys, 'Ding 001359 (Chico Mendez Mural Garden)', in: Katrien Laenen et al. (red.), *Cahier #3 Openbaarheid: Over publiek domein, planning en restruimte* (Brussel: Vlaams Bouwmeester, 2011), 22-30.

architectural quality assessment as three institutional operations that interact and significantly influence each other. These operations include: Justification – establishing the criteria that serve as the foundation for decision-making; Negotiation – bringing together expertise and facilitating debate among diverse stakeholders to arrive at (or not) a shared judgement; and finally, Mediation – defining the object of consensus and the tools employed by various actors to achieve this goal.[3]

Discursive Justification

Agency developed an investigative artistic practice in which legal conflicts over intellectual property (copyrights, patents, trademarks) were subjected to scrutiny, filed in an expanding archive and discussed during performative gatherings. The standardisation and uniformisation inherent in the legal system form the cornerstone of the modern capitalist model, but, according to Agency, fail to appreciate the embedding of artistic practices in a wider ecosystem.[4] Agency's mission statement argues that:

> The colonial concept of ownership relies upon the fundamental assumption of the split between culture and nature and consequently between: expressions and ideas, creations and facts, subjects and objects, humans and non-humans, originality and tradition, individuals and collectives, mind and body, etc . . . Each controversy, included on the list, witnesses a resistance in terms of these divisions.[5]

By reenacting previous intellectual property controversies, the different views and positions regarding the conflict are explained, giving new life to the hesitation that preceded the legal judgement. This is why Agency uses the term 'boundary things'.

In the case of *Thing 001359 (Chico Mendez Mural Garden)*, for example, the differences between private and public, temporary and permanent, legal and illegal, individual and collective are the subject of discussion. Linguistic conventions and jargon fuel legal controversy. Labelling graffiti as 'illegal' or calling it an 'artistic statement' are symbolic operations with real consequences. Agency contends that although legal criteria are not intrinsic properties of works of art, they do affect them. Recognising or not recognising the shared authorship of an ensemble of wall paintings, for example, could endorse the demolition of a community garden, or initiate legal protection resulting in the halting of building plans. Radically questioning the moment of *justification* is central to Agency's investigation into boundary things. Through reenactment, Agency questions the finality of previously pronounced legal rulings.

The notion of 'architectural quality' occupies a central position in today's architecture discourse. The built environment has quality when it is 'appropriate', 'sustainable', 'recognisable', 'socially inclusive', wheelchair accessible', 'safe', 'standards compliant', 'integrally designed', 'robust', 'iconic' and 'distinctive', to name but a few of the commonly used qualifiers. The generic term 'architectural quality' allows for the interpretation of properties that cannot be purely objectively determined or measured. Consequently, the above signifiers mediate the recognition of certain qualities in certain objects. Strictly speaking, the term 'quality' does not originate in architectural discourse, but is borrowed from management literature. It refers either to the assignment of 'value' to products themselves, or to the control of the process of creation in such a way as to ensure that quality guarantees are built into the production of the artefact. As the

3 The text builds on the principle of translation in actor-network theory as developed by Michel Serres, Bruno Latour and Michel Callon. Michel Callon, 'Some Elements of a Sociology of Translation', *The Sociological Review* 32 (1984), 196-233.

4 Kobe Matthys and Tom Van Imschoot, 'Een ecologie van kunstpraktijken', kunsten.be/nu-in-de-kunsten/een-ecologie-van-kunstpraktijken (accessed 20 May 2024).

5 Kobe Matthys's mission statement as found on Agentive.org (accessed 16 July 2024).

Agentschap, *Vergadering (Openbaarheid), over Ding 001359 (Chico Mendez Mural Garden)*, Atelier Bouwmeester, Brussel, 2012

Agency, *Assembly (Going Public), about Thing 001359 (Chico Mendez Mural Garden)*, Atelier Bouwmeester, Brussels, 2012

In deze tekst gebruik ik de fascinerende analogie tussen dit kunstproject en de werking van de Vlaams Bouwmeester om vanuit een theoretisch referentiekader een set operaties te articuleren die kwaliteitsbemiddelingsprocessen begeleiden. Door beide situaties te spiegelen kan de beoordeling van architectuurkwaliteit worden beschreven als drie institutionele acties die op elkaar ingrijpen en elkaar in belangrijke mate beïnvloeden: *Verantwoording* – de formulering van criteria die de basis vormen voor het nemen van beslissingen, *Onderhandeling* – het samenbrengen van expertise en het debat tussen verschillende betrokkenen om (al dan niet) tot een gedeeld oordeel te komen en ten slotte *Bemiddeling* – het voorwerp waarover overeenstemming wordt gezocht en de middelen die verschillende actoren hiertoe inzetten.[3]

Talige verantwoording

Agentschap heeft een onderzoekende artistieke praktijk ontwikkeld, waar juridische geschillen inzake intellectueel eigendom (copyrights, patenten, handelsmerken) worden onderzocht, gearchiveerd en tijdens performatieve samenkomsten aan nadere reflectie worden onderworpen. De standaardisatie en uniformisering, eigen aan de jurisdictie, zijn de hoeksteen van het moderne kapitalistische model, maar ze miskennen volgens Agentschap de inbedding van artistieke praktijken in een breder ecosysteem.[4] Agentschap's *mission statement* stelt:

> Het concept van intellectuele eigendom berust op de fundamentele uitgangspositie dat er een scheiding bestaat tussen natuur en cultuur, en bijgevolg ook tussen expressie en ideeën, creatie en feiten, subject en object, mens en niet-mens, originaliteit en traditie, individu en collectief, lichaam en geest, etc. Elke controverse op de lijst getuigt van een moment van twijfel over deze scheiding.[5]

Door eerdere controverses omtrent intellectueel eigendom opnieuw onder de loep te leggen, worden de verschillende zienswijzen en standpunten betreffende het geschil uiteengelegd, waardoor de aarzeling die voorafging aan het juridische oordeel opnieuw bestaansrecht krijgt. Agentschap spreekt daarom ook over 'grensgevallen'.

In het geval van *Ding 001359 (Chico Mendez Mural Garden)* vormen bijvoorbeeld de verschillen tussen privé en publiek, tijdelijk en permanent, legaal en illegaal, individueel en collectief het onderwerp van de discussie. Talige conventies en jargon voeden de juridische controverse. Graffiti als 'illegaal' bestempelen dan wel een 'artistiek statement' noemen, is een symbolische operatie met reële effecten. Juridische criteria zijn volgens Agentschap geen intrinsieke eigenschap van kunstwerken, maar beïnvloeden ze wel. Een al dan niet erkenning van het gedeeld auteurschap van een ensemble van muurschilderingen kon bijvoorbeeld zowel de sloop van een gemeenschapstuin in gang zetten, als een wettelijke bescherming inleiden met het stopzetten van de bouwplannen tot gevolg. Het radicaal ter discussie stellen van het moment van *Verantwoording* staat centraal in Agentschap's onderzoek naar grensgevallen. De reconstructie van het geschil stelt kanttekeningen bij het definitieve karakter van eerder uitgesproken juridische uitspraken.

Als notie neemt 'architectuurkwaliteit' vandaag een centrale plaats in het architectuurdebat in. De gebouwde omgeving is kwalitatief want 'gepast', 'duurzaam', 'herkenbaar', 'sociaal inclusief', 'rolstoeltoegankelijk', 'veilig', 'norm-conform', 'geïntegreerd ontworpen', 'robuust', 'iconisch',

3 De tekst bouwt voort op het principe van translatie in de *actor-network-theory* zoals ontwikkeld door Michel Serres, Bruno Latour en Michel Callon. Michel Callon, 'Some Elements of a Sociology of Translation', *The Sociological Review* 32 (1984), 196-233.

4 Kobe Matthys en Tom Van Imschoot, 'Een ecologie van kunstpraktijken,' kunsten.be/nu-in-de-kunsten/een-ecologie-van-kunstpraktijken/ (geraadpleegd 20 mei 2024).

5 Kobe Matthys' mission statement zoals terug te vinden op Agentive.org (geraadpleegd 16 juli 2024).

pursuit of architectural quality becomes central to policy documents, administrative protocols, tendering procedures, architecture competitions, consultations and recommendations of various committees, the term not only refers to a surplus symbolic value, but its use has significant practical consequences as well. Since the criteria serve as guidelines for both design and assessment processes, they shape considerations and direct actions. Much like intellectual property, the term is the cornerstone of a legal-administrative complex in which products and services are weighed against each other according to market logic.[6]

In their seminal work *De la Justification*, sociologist Luc Boltanski and economist Laurent Thévenot analyse this process of justification. Their key observation is that, in everyday situations requiring decision-making, people rarely rely on rigid protocols or a strict hierarchy of standards. Instead, they continually weigh a variety of considerations against each other. In both specialised and general contexts, different vocabularies are employed to justify actions and choices. These vocabularies draw on distinct frames of reference and, in turn, represent very different social worlds.[7] A community garden fosters residents' sense of identification with their city, while the development of social housing involves expanding the amenities of the welfare state. In contrast, a property developer such as BFC focuses on surplus value creation. This means that the decision to demolish or protect an urban space can be considered on the basis of different motives and underlying beliefs. Agency's reenactments demonstrate that the judgment in a legal case can vary depending on the perspective from which the case is considered. We can extrapolate these insights to a Quality Setting. Clearly, we engage with a different register when a project is part of an evolving body of work by an architect or artist collective, when financial profit, investment and maintenance costs are the primary considerations, or when the tourist potential of a site is at stake. Each of these registers of meaning refers to different qualities that can be attributed to architecture, but the premises from which architectural quality is interpreted vary significantly.

Rather than a neutral fact, architectural quality is an 'essentially contested concept'.[8] When urban design processes, architectural projects and spatial and landscape interventions are subjected to judgment, their value can be assessed from very different perspectives. Different logics can enter into dialogue with each other, but they can also contradict each other, so that the different interests must also be positioned in relation to each other. Therefore, it is not only important how the architectural object itself 'exists', but equally important from which value systems the architectural object is discussed. Legitimation demands ideological commitment, statements about the idea of 'good architecture' and continuous adjustments to the assessment process itself. Moreover, institutionally motivated justification does not occur solely in response to a single, idiosyncratic project; it must balance the specific expectations of a particular site with broader, more general ambitions and wishes that transcend the individual case. This requires the formulation of discursive statements that provide the initial elements of the motivation, even before there is in fact a project to be assessed.

Both the formulation of a commission and the actual assessment involve a symbolic act of interpretation. Not only institutions such as the Flemish Government Architect, but also bodies such as the Aesthetic Committee of a medium-sized city or a regional heritage commission

6 Luc Boltanski and Eve Chiappello, *Le Nouvel Esprit du Capitalisme* (Paris: Edition Gallimard, 1999).

7 Luc Boltanski and Laurent Thévenot, *De la justification* (Paris: Editions Gallimard, 1991). The French thinkers distinguish between six *cités*, each of which they link to a major thinker: the inspired world (St Augustine), the domestic world (Bossuet), the world of fame and glory (Hobbes), the world of social wellbeing (Rousseau), the market (Adam Smith) and the industrial world (Saint-Simon).

8 Walter Bryce Gallie, 'Essentially Contested Concepts', *Proceedings of the Aristotelian Society* 56 (1956), 167-198.

'onderscheidend', om maar een reeks veelvoorkomende kwalificaties op te lijsten. De generische term 'architectuurkwaliteit' laat toe om eigenschappen te duiden die niet louter objectief te bepalen of te meten zijn. Via bovenvermelde betekenaars worden in voorwerpen bijgevolg bepaalde kwaliteiten onderkend. De term 'kwaliteit' komt *strictu sensu* niet uit het architectuurdiscours, maar is afkomstig uit de managementliteratuur. Het is een manier om de producten ofwel zelf 'waarde' toe te kennen, ofwel het ontstaansproces zodanig te monitoren, dat er bij de totstandkoming van het artefact kwaliteitsgaranties worden ingebouwd. Omdat het streven naar architectuurkwaliteit centraal komt te staan in beleidsnota's, administratieve protocollen en aanbestedingsprocedures, bij architectuurprijsvragen, raadplegingen en adviezen van allerhande commissies, wijst de term niet alleen op een surplus-symboolwaarde, maar kent het gebruik ervan ook zeer uitgesproken uitwerkingen. Aangezien de criteria zowel in het ontwerp- als beoordelingsproces als richtsnoer dienen, bepalen ze overwegingen en sturen ze het handelen. Net zoals intellectueel eigendom vormt de term de hoeksteen van een juridisch-administratief complex waarbij producten en diensten, in een vrije marktlogica, ten opzichte van elkaar worden afgewogen.[6]

De socioloog Luc Boltanksi en econoom Laurent Thévenot hebben in hun sleutelwerk *De la Justification* dit proces van verantwoording geanalyseerd. In dagelijkse situaties waar beslissingen moeten worden genomen, worden zelden zeer strikte protocollen of een hiërarchische set maatstaven gehanteerd, aldus Boltanski en Thévenot, maar wordt steeds opnieuw een waaier aan overwegingen tegen elkaar uitgespeeld. Zowel in gespecialiseerde als minder gespecialiseerde contexten worden er verschillende *vocabulaires* gehanteerd om handelingen en keuzes te rechtvaardigen. Deze vocabularia verwijzen naar andere referentiekaders en vertegenwoordigen op hun beurt zeer verschillende sociale werelden.[7] Een gemeenschapstuin zorgt voor de identificatie van de bewoners met hun stad. Bij het realiseren van sociale woningen worden de voorzieningen van de verzorgingsstaat uitgebouwd, terwijl een vastgoedontwikkelaar zoals BFC vooral meerwaardecreatie voor ogen heeft. De overweging om tot sloop dan wel bescherming over te gaan, kan dus vanuit verschillende motieven en overtuigingen worden bekeken. Agentschap's reconstructie demonstreert dat het oordeel in een juridische zaak kan verschillen naar gelang de lens van waaruit deze wordt bekeken. We kunnen deze inzichten extrapoleren naar een *Quality Setting*. Het mag duidelijk zijn dat een ander register wordt aangesneden, wanneer een project wordt gesitueerd in een zich ontwikkelend oeuvre van een architect of een kunstenaarscollectief, dan wel wanneer financiële winst, investerings- en onderhoudskosten als eerste criterium worden opgevoerd, of wanneer we het toeristisch potentieel van een plek in ogenschouw nemen. Elk van deze betekenisregisters heeft betrekking op andere kwaliteiten die aan architectuur kunnen worden toegeschreven, alleen zijn de premisses van waaruit architectuurkwaliteit wordt geduid onderling zeer verschillend.

Architectuurkwaliteit is geen neutraal gegeven, maar een 'wezenlijk betwist begrip'.[8] Wanneer stedelijke planningsprocessen, architectuurprojecten, ruimtelijke en landschappelijke interventies aan een oordeel worden onderworpen, kan de waarde ervan vanuit zeer verschillende perspectieven worden beschouwd. De verschillende logica's treden met elkaar in dialoog, maar kunnen elkaar ook onderling tegenspreken, en

6
Luc Boltanski en Eve Chiappello, *Le Nouvel Esprit du Capitalisme* (Parijs: Éditions Gallimard, 1999)

7
Luc Boltanski en Laurent Thévenot, *De la justification* (Parijs: Éditions Gallimard, 1991). De Franse denkers maken onderscheid tussen zes 'cités' die ze telkens met een belangrijke denker verbinden: de geïnspireerde wereld (St. Augustinus), de domestieke wereld (Bossuet), de wereld van faam en roem (Hobbes), de wereld van het maatschappelijk welzijn (Rousseau), de markt (Adam Smith) en de industriële wereld (Saint-Simon).

8
Walter Bryce Gallie, 'Essentially contested concepts', *Proceedings of the Aristotelian Society* 56 (1956), 167-198.

create a discursive space in which priorities are set among a multitude of interests and criteria. When Flemish Government Architects give advice in the exercise of their mandate – such as in heritage cases – their perspective on architecture, informed by field expertise, professional experience, and personal architectural vision, inevitably influences their judgment. When initiating research by design, such as their Pilot projects (another tool of Team Flemish Government Architect), a framework of a few rules is established, in which certain environmental development criteria are put on hold and other dimensions take precedence.

Negotiation between Stakeholders

Public institutions such as the Flemish Government Architect create a democratic space for discussion. Negotiation involves the process of justification described above. To this end, the public body brings in not only those directly involved in the project in question – such as the commissioned architects and the commissioners – but also peers and external experts to oversee the 'quality' of the living environment. The stakeholders represent – and, in a sense, safeguard – the different value systems that inform and shape the judgement. In principle, public commissioners and competent administrations have the social interest – or: specific social interests – in mind. Politicians and local representatives likely represent the prestige or economic interests of their city; users and residents focus on the usability, identity and recognisability of their transforming living environment.

Opening of 'Atelier Bouwmeester', Ravensteingallery, Brussels, 2012/ Opening van 'Atelier Bouwmeester', Ravesteingalerie, Brussel, 2012

dus moeten de verschillende belangen ook ten opzichte van elkaar worden gepositioneerd. Het is dus niet alleen van belang hoe het architecturale voorwerp zelf 'bestaat', maar evenzeer vanuit welke waardesystemen er over deze architectuur wordt gesproken. De legitimatie vraagt ideologisch engagement, uitspraken met betrekking tot het idee van 'goede architectuur' én voortdurende bijstellingen aan het proces van de beoordeling zelf. Een institutioneel gemotiveerde verantwoording gebeurt daarenboven niet alleen in het licht van het ene idiosyncratische project, maar moet specifieke verwachtingen met betrekking tot die ene concrete plek balanceren met meer generieke ambities en betrachtingen die het particuliere geval overstijgen. Het noopt tot het formuleren van discursieve stellingen die de eerste elementen van de motivatie bevatten, zelfs nog voordat er effectief sprake is van een te beoordelen project.

Zowel in de formulering van een opdracht als de eigenlijke beoordeling vindt er een symbolische interpretatie-arbeid plaats. Instellingen zoals de Vlaams Bouwmeester, maar ook een kwaliteitskamer van een middelgrote stad of de regionale commissie monumentenzorg scheppen een discursieve ruimte waar in de veelheid aan belangen en criteria prioriteiten worden gelegd. Wanneer Vlaams Bouwmeesters vanuit hun mandaat, bijvoorbeeld in erfgoeddossiers advies moeten verlenen zal hun architectuuropvatting – kennis van het veld, professionele ervaring, persoonlijke visie op architectuur – ook hun oordeel kleuren. Bij het initiëren van ontwerpend onderzoek zoals de Pilootprojecten – een ander instrument van het team Vlaams Bouwmeester – werd een regelluw kader geschapen, waardoor bepaalde criteria die tellen bij de ontwikkeling van een omgeving tussen haakjes worden geplaatst, opdat andere eigenschappen een groter belang krijgen.

Onderhandeling tussen betrokkenen

Publieke instellingen zoals de Vlaams Bouwmeester creëren een democratische gespreksomgeving. In de onderhandeling wordt ruimte gemaakt voor het geschetste proces van verantwoording. Hiertoe verzamelt het overheidsorgaan, naast de directe betrokkenen bij het betreffende project zoals opdrachtvoerende architecten en opdrachtgevers, ook collega-architecten en externe deskundigen om over de 'kwaliteit' van de leefomgeving te waken. De betrokkenen vertegenwoordigen – en bewaken, zo men wil – de verschillende waardesystemen die bij het oordeel kunnen worden gemobiliseerd. Publieke opdrachtgevers en het bevoegde bestuur hebben in principe het maatschappelijke belang – of specifieke maatschappelijke belangen – voor ogen. Politici en lokale mandatarissen kunnen ook het prestige van hun stad of economische motieven behartigen. De gebruikers en bewoners zien toe op de bruikbaarheid, de identiteit en herkenbaarheid van hun leefomgeving in transformatie. Dit terwijl ambtenaren, academici of andere deskundigen vanuit de eigen achtergrond en discipline, en dus vanuit zeer specifieke bekommernissen over toekomstige architectuurprojecten debatteren: monumentenzorg, milieubeleid, circulair bouwen, bestuurszaken, sociale inclusie, welzijn en gezondheid, enzovoort. De exacte samenstelling van de groep representeert de belangen die tijdens de onderhandeling zullen spelen. Het democratische proces van onderhandeling is de tweede actie die we hier aan een analyse onderwerpen.
En daarin speelt ook de scenografie van de setting een rol. De vorm van het samenkomen van mensen en dingen is een belangrijk thema in het architectuurdebat, maar ook in de hedendaagse kunst.[9]

9 Anne Davidian en Laurent Jeanpierre (red.), *What Makes an Assembly? Stories, Experiments, and Inquiries* (Antwerpen/Londen: Evens Foundation & Sternberg Press, 2022); Markus Miessen (red.), *Agonistic Assemblies: On the Spatial Politics of Horizontality* (Berlijn: Sternberg Press, 2024); Bruno Latour en Peter Weibel (red.), *Making Things Public: Atmospheres of Democracy* (Cambridge, MA: MIT Press, 2005).

Meanwhile, civil servants, academics or other experts approach future architectural projects from the perspective of their respective backgrounds and disciplines, that is, from highly specific concerns such as monument preservation, environmental policy, circular building, governance, social inclusion, welfare, health and so on. The precise composition of this group reflects the interests that will shape the negotiation process. This democratic negotiation process forms the second phase of our analysis. The scenography of the setting also plays an important role in this: the way in which people and elements come together is a central theme in both architectural discourse and contemporary art.[9]

Kobe Matthys invited several stakeholders to the meeting, including artists, ecologists, lawyers and urban designers, but the photos of the event at Atelier Bouwmeester primarily show the carefully crafted scenography: a temporary setup with three rows of tiered seating arranged in a U-shape around a low stage displaying a concrete scale model of the community garden. The open end of the U faces the Atelier's glass display. A diverse audience sits on the stage, thoughtfully engaging with the theme issue at hand. The archive plays an important role in Agency's work: the same stages then contain labelled boxes containing the files of countless 'boundary things', pieces of evidence taken from the boxes in the context of the conversation. In various setups, Agency uses very different institutional formats, corresponding to architectural typologies through which specific meanings are made public: the salon, archive, parliament, exhibition and even showroom.

The ad hoc nature of Agency's setup resonates strongly with the minimalist design of Atelier Bouwmeester. This space also mixes programme elements in a deliberate departure from the conventional office environment. While Agency's scenography exudes a certain fragility, is in a sense a temporary presence in the Atelier, both the Atelier's setting and its design are more affirmative. In the scenography of Atelier NU, the occurrences at Atelier Bouwmeester unfold as a sequence of activities ranging from informal one-on-one meetings around a small kitchen table to a more theatrical setup at the opposite end of the gallery, where presentations and actions assume an audience, acquiring a more formal tone. In addition, the curved glass cabinetwork wall that opens onto a busy urban passage both literally and symbolically displays this transition from the informal to the formal.

Beyond the explicit reference to Latour's 'parliament of things', the theatrical arrangement also evokes late-eighteenth-century salon culture, echoing Jürgen Habermas's vision of this setting as embodying the utopian contours of a democratic project.[10] In salons and literary circles, citizens gathered to view paintings and listen to music and literature. Free from personal concerns and immediate material needs this audience, according to Habermas, could openly and freely discuss art, culture and social issues. Habermas's ideas on art criticism remain widely respected, and his perspectives on the public sphere continue to resonate as well. In the relaxed atmosphere of the salon, this thinker from the Frankfurt School saw the seeds of a revolutionary political project that would later have a wider social impact with the French Revolution. In some ways, the culture of the salons – their societies and circles – can provide a model for the debates on architectural quality that take place in aesthetics committees, urban ateliers or design review panels, as well as the pursuit of consensus on the desired quality of the living environment. However, such an idealised

9 Anne Davidian and Laurent Jeanpierre (eds.), *What Makes an Assembly? Stories, Experiments, and Inquiries* (Antwerp/London: Evens Foundation & Sternberg Press, 2022); Markus Miessen (ed.), *Agonistic Assemblies: On the Spatial Politics of Horizontality* (Berlin: Sternberg Press, 2024); Bruno Latour and Peter Weibel (eds.), *Making Things Public: Atmospheres of Democracy* (Cambridge, MA: MIT Press, 2005).

10 Bruno Latour. *Het parlement van de dingen: Over Gaia en de representatie van niet-mensen* (Amsterdam: Boom, 2021); Jürgen Habermas, *The Structural Transformation of the Public Sphere: An Inquiry into a Category of Bourgeois Society*, translated by Thomas Burger and Frederick Lawrence (Cambridge, MA: MIT Press, 1989).

Kobe Matthys nodigde verschillende betrokkenen uit voor de bijeenkomst, onder wie kunstenaars, ecologen, juristen en stedenbouwkundigen, maar op de foto's van het evenement in het Atelier Bouwmeester is vooral de welbewuste scenografie te zien. In de ruimte is een tijdelijke stellage gebouwd: drie tribunes zijn in een U-vorm opgesteld rond een laag podium waarop een betonnen schaalmodel van de gemeenschapstuin is geplaatst. De open zijde van de U richt zich naar de glazen vitrine van het atelier. Op de tribunes zit een divers publiek dat zich over de zaak in kwestie buigt. In het werk van Agentschap speelt het archief een sleutelrol: op dezelfde stellingen staan dan gelabelde kisten waarin de dossiers van talloze 'grensgevallen' worden bijgehouden, bewijsstukken die tijdens het gesprek uit de kisten worden gehaald. In verschillende ensceneringen put Agenschap uit zeer verschillende institutionele formats die corresponderen met architectuurtypologische vormen, waarbij een bepaalde betekenisinhoud publiek wordt gemaakt: de salon, het archief, het parlement, de tentoonstelling en zelfs de showroom.

Het ad-hoc karakter van Agentschap's opstelling resoneert nadrukkelijk met de minimalistische inrichting van het Atelier Bouwmeester, dat door NU architectenatelier werd ingericht. De hybride mengvorm van programmaonderdelen vinden we ook terug in het atelier dat zich op een bewuste manier distantieert van de reguliere kantooromgeving. Terwijl Agentschap's provisorische tribune een zekere fragiliteit bezit en in zekere zin in het atelier slechts tijdelijk te gast is, is zowel de locatie als de inrichting van het atelier meer bevestigend. In de scenografie van NU toont het gebeuren in het atelier zich als een sequens van activiteiten die variëren van zeer informele 1 op 1 ontmoetingen rondom een kleine keukentafel, naar een meer theatrale omgeving aan het uiteinde van de galerij waar presentaties en handelingen een publiek veronderstellen en aldus een meer formeel karakter krijgen. Door de gebogen, glazen schrijnwerkwand die uitziet op een druk gefrequenteerde stedelijke passage, wordt deze overgang van eerder informeel naar formeel letterlijk en figuurlijk in de etalage gezet.

Naast de expliciete verwijzing naar Latour's 'parlement der dingen' refereert de theatrale configuratie aan de laat-achttiende-eeuwse saloncultuur en de manier waarop Jürgen Habermas in deze setting de utopische contouren van een democratisch project ontwaarde.[10] In salons en literaire kringen kwamen burgers samen om te kijken naar schilderijen, te luisteren naar muziek en literatuur. Onbezwaard door private kwesties en directe materiële noden kon het publiek, volgens Habermas, in alle vrijheid en openheid discussiëren over kunst, cultuur en maatschappelijke uitdagingen. Er wordt vandaag nog vaak in Habermasiaanse termen over kunstkritiek gedacht, terwijl zijn opvattingen over de publieke sfeer eveneens doorwerken. In de ongedwongen sfeer van de salon zag de denker van de *Frankfürter Schüle* de aankondiging van het revolutionaire politieke project dat met de Franse Revolutie een bredere sociale uitwerking kreeg. De saloncultuur, de gezelschappen en kringen kunnen ergens model staan voor het debat omtrent architectuurkwaliteit in welstandscommissies, stadsateliers of *design-review* panels en de zoektocht naar consensus over een gewenste kwalitatieve leefomgeving – al miskent een dergelijk idealistisch idee van de vrije dialoog wel de politiek-bestuurlijke reikwijdte van de kwaliteitsbemiddeling.

Conceptueel-theoretisch spoort de positie van Agentschap eerder met latere politieke kritieken die op Habermas' theorieën zijn geformuleerd. Chantal Mouffe problematiseerde vanuit politicologisch perspectief het

10 Bruno Latour. *Het parlement van de dingen. Over Gaia en de representatie van niet-mensen* (Amsterdam: Boom, 2021), Jürgen Habermas, *The Structural Transformation of the Public Sphere: An Inquiry into a Category of Bourgeois Society*, vertaling Thomas Burger en Frederick Lawrence (Cambridge, MA: MIT Press, 1989).

notion of open dialogue may overlook the political and administrative dimensions inherent in the mediation of quality standards.

Conceptually and theoretically, Agency's position aligns more closely with later political critiques of Habermas's theories. From a political science perspective, Chantal Mouffe critically examined the notion of social consensus and the ideal of power-free dialogue, both of which are central to Habermas's thinking.[11] According to Mouffe, political action is inherently centred on disagreements and conflicts of interest, which are resolved through democratic negotiation. For Mouffe, all forms of decision-making involve choices, meaning the political process is inherently antagonistic. Every political debate, in her view, is a struggle for hegemony. Her thinking thus raises the question of which value systems are prioritised in quality mediation, given a specific issue, and why. From a feminist perspective, Nancy Fraser challenged the inclusivity of Habermas's idea of the public sphere. She argued that Habermas's model too easily assumes that stakeholders can detach themselves from everyday needs and personal concerns to engage disinterestedly in conversation. Nineteenth-century salon culture was accessible only to a select few - mostly men. The ideal of power-free dialogue overlooks the reality that not everyone is equally socialised or has the resources - such as education, financial independence and cultural literacy - to navigate such elite environments.[12]

Following these theoretical positions, two aspects challenge the idea of the Quality Setting, both related to the idea of 'representation.' To understand the status of negotiation, first, a distinction can be made between what Latour calls interest-driven and fact-driven representation. The distinction

11
Chantal Mouffe, *Agonistics: Thinking the World Politically* (London: Verso, 2013).

12
Nancy Fraser, 'Rethinking the Public Sphere', *Social Text* 25/26 (1990), 56-80.

Open Call presentation, Atelier Bouwmeester, Brussels, 2012/ Open Oproep presentatie, Atelier Bouwmeester, Brussel, 2012

idee van maatschappelijke consensus en het verlangen naar de machtsvrije dialoog die de hoeksteen van Habermas' denken vormen.[11] Het politiek handelen draait volgens Mouffe a priori om meningsverschillen en belangenconflicten die in democratische onderhandeling worden beslecht. Volgens de politieke denker vragen alle vormen van besluitvorming om keuzes en dus is het politieke proces inherent antagonistisch. Elk politiek debat laat zich als een hegemoniestrijd karakteriseren. Mouffe's denken werpt dan ook de vraag op welke waardesystemen in het licht van een specifieke kwestie bij kwaliteitsbemiddeling meer belang krijgen dan andere, en waarom? Nancy Fraser stelde vanuit een feministisch perspectief het inclusieve karakter van Habermas' idee van de publieke sfeer ter discussie: Habermas' model veronderstelt al te gemakkelijk dat betrokkenen zich kunnen losmaken uit dagelijkse noden en privé beslommeringen, om belangeloos aan het gesprek deel te nemen. De toegang tot de negentiende-eeuwse saloncultuur was voor een select gezelschap (van vooral mannen) voorbehouden. Het machtsvrije ideaal gaat voorbij aan het feit dat niet iedereen zodanig gesocialiseerd is en dus over alle middelen beschikt – vorming, financiële onafhankelijkheid, culturele geletterdheid – om zich in een elitaire omgeving staande te houden.[12]

In het verlengde van deze theoretische posities zijn er twee aspecten die het idee van de *Quality Setting* uitdagen en verband houden met het idee van 'vertegenwoordiging'. Voor het statuut van de onderhandeling kan in eerste instantie een onderscheid worden gemaakt tussen wat Latour een belangen- en feiten-gedreven vertegenwoordiging heeft genoemd. Er is een verschil of men als directe belanghebbende in het gesprek participeert, dan wel of men als deskundige feiten opvoert of spreekt en oordeelt met een zekere afstand tot de zaak. In een technocratie of bureaucratie worden deze twee typen vertegenwoordiging doorgaans resoluut van elkaar gescheiden: de belangen horen thuis in de politieke arena, de feiten in administraties en technische diensten. Als betrokkene handelt men bijvoorbeeld als eigenaar, bewoner of toekomstige gebruiker, en heeft men dus directe belangen in het bouwproject. Externe deskundigen hebben daarentegen een andere rol. Van hun inbreng wordt verwacht dat die vertrekt vanuit hun expertise: vanuit academisch-wetenschappelijke of kennistheoretische perspectieven, technische knowhow of professionele ervaring. De rol van een expert lijkt afstandelijker dan die van de direct betrokkenen, maar is, zo leren we van Latour, evenmin waardenneutraal. Experts zijn evengoed betrokken, maar in principe wordt hun mening gekleurd door de disciplinaire positie van waaruit wordt gesproken.

Een tweede aspect heeft hier direct betrekking op en handelt over het proces van in- en uitsluiting, een politieke dimensie die minder speelt in Latour's denken. De vertegenwoordigde groepen bepalen immers in belangrijke mate vanuit welk perspectief een waardeoordeel wordt uitgesproken. Dit roept talloze vragen op. Wie krijgt in de onderhandeling welke stem? Vanuit welk mandaat wordt gesproken? Met welke achtergrond en voorkennis ageren de betrokkenen? Wie heeft de vaardigheden en middelen om in de discussie te participeren en krijgt aldus toegang tot het gesprek, en wie niet? De vertegenwoordiging bepaalt wie inspraak krijgt, maar ook welke stemmen stil worden gehouden. De instelling bepaalt welke instanties, agenda's en bekommernissen bij de onderhandeling worden uitgesloten. De socio-politieke samenstelling van de groep en de mate waarin de actoren zijn gesocialiseerd, zijn integraal onderdeel van de institutionele setting. De assemblee van actoren schept de contouren

11 Chantal Mouffe, *Agonistics: Thinking the World Politically* (Londen: Verso, 2013).

12 Nancy Fraser, 'Rethinking the Public Sphere', *Social Text* 25/26 (1990), 56-80.

lies in whether one participates as a direct stakeholder or contributes facts as an expert, or whether one speaks and judges from a certain distance from the issue. In technocracies or bureaucracies, these two types of representation are typically kept separate: interests belong in the political arena, while facts are confined to administrations and technical departments. A stakeholder acts as an owner, occupant or future user – and therefore has a vested interest in the construction project. External experts, by contrast, have a different role. Their input is expected to be based on their expertise, which can be based on academic, scientific or epistemological perspectives, technical skills or professional experience. While the role of an expert appears more detached than that of those directly involved, as Latour reminds us, it is not value-neutral. Experts are similarly invested, although their opinions are inherently shaped by the disciplinary position from which they speak.

A second aspect closely related to this concerns the process of inclusion and exclusion – a political dimension that plays a lesser role in Latour's thinking. Indeed, the groups represented largely determine the perspective from which value judgments are made. This raises many questions: Who has a voice in the negotiations? What is their mandate? What background and prior knowledge do they bring to the table? Who has the skills and resources to participate and thus gain access to the conversation? And who does not? Representation not only determines who has a say, but also which voices are silenced. The institution decides which institutions, agendas, and concerns are excluded from the negotiation. The sociopolitical composition of the group, along with the extent to which actors are socialised, is integral to the institutional setting. The assembly of actors shapes the contours inside which the negotiation of architectural quality unfolds. Many aspects of architectural quality cannot be precisely measured and seem subjective. Rather than being a matter of 'personal taste' or 'private interest', architectural quality is better understood as 'essentially contested' – in the sense that the trade-offs between different quality claims in the light of specific projects have in fact yet to be made and are therefore subject to negotiation.[13]

In the Open Call – Team Flemish Government Architect's best-known selection and negotiation procedure – the external expert plays an important part in the assessment process.[14] However, their insights are weighed alongside the opinion of the client who, in principle, has the final say in the selection of the design team. The Open Call fully embodies the interplay between fact-based and interest-based perspectives. Similarly, in Labo Ruimte's thematic research-by-design projects, designers and experts collaborate with relevant administrations and local actors in workshops focused on complex spatial challenges.[15] The contributions of social actors and the knowledge of scientists are integrated into several futures studies, aimed at inspiring and shaping spatial policy.

In democratically conducted negotiation processes, it is crucial not only to balance the representation of local interests with external, more abstract value-based knowledge perspectives, but also to acknowledge the boundaries of the institutional configuration. Indeed, democratic decision-making relies heavily on making room for dissent: fundamental disagreements, unspoken voices, doubts about decisions, discursive recalibrations and revisions. When Agency questions controversies, the artist collective actually demonstrates that most legal conflicts are shaped by defined power relations and differing ideological views.

13
Latour, *Het parlement van de dingen*, op. cit. (note 10), 27-28.

14
Maarten Van Den Driessche, 'Het omcirkelen van een lege plaats: "bouwheer" worden, kwaliteit verwachten', in: Maarten Liefooghe and Maarten Van Den Driessche (eds.), *Meer dan een Wedstrijd: De Open Oproep in een veranderende bouwcultuur* (Antwerp/Brussels: Vlaams Architectuurinstituut/Team Vlaams Bouwmeester, 2022), 38-56.

15
Labo Ruimte is a collaboration of the Department of the Environment and Team Flemish Government Architect, which celebrated its tenth anniversary in 2023. Els Vervloesem et al. (eds.), *10 jaar Labo Ruimte: Ontwerpen aan de Toekomst* (Brussels: Departement Omgeving, 2023).

waarbinnen de onderhandeling over architectuurkwaliteit zich zal ontvouwen. Veel eigenschappen met betrekking tot architectuurkwaliteit kunnen niet exact worden gemeten en lijken subjectief. Eerder dan een zaak van 'persoonlijke smaak' of 'privébelang' kan architectuurkwaliteit beter als 'wezenlijk betwist' worden beschouwd, in de zin dat de afweging tussen verschillende kwaliteitsaanspraken in het licht van specifieke projecten *de facto* nog dient te gebeuren, en dus voorwerp is van onderhandeling.[13]

Bij de Open Oproep – de bekendste selectie- en onderhandelingsprocedure van Team Vlaams Bouwmeester – heeft de externe expert een belangrijke stem tijdens het beoordelingsproces.[14] Diens inzichten worden evenwel gebalanceerd met het oordeel van de opdrachtgever die bij de toewijzing van het ontwerpteam principieel het laatste woord krijgt. Het spel tussen een feiten- en belangengedreven vertegenwoordiging wordt in de Open Oproep met andere woorden ten volle gespeeld. Ook in de thematische ontwerpend-onderzoekstrajecten van Labo Ruimte worden ontwerpers en experts samen met betrokken bestuurlijke afdelingen en lokale actoren in workshops rond een uitdagende ruimtelijke opgave verzameld.[15] De inbreng van maatschappelijke actoren en de kennis van de wetenschappers wordt in een aantal toekomstverkenningen gebundeld, met als doel het ruimtelijk beleid te inspireren en aan te sturen.

In democratisch gevoerde onderhandelingsprocessen is het niet alleen van belang om het juiste evenwicht te vinden tussen de vertegenwoordiging van lokale belangen en externe, meer abstracte, waardengedreven kennisperspectieven; ook de limieten van de institutionele configuratie moeten worden onderkend. Voor de democratische besluitvorming blijft het immers van groot belang om ook ruimte te maken voor *dissensus*: fundamentele meningsverschillen, de stille stem, twijfel over de genomen beslissing, discursieve herijkingen en revisies. Wanneer Agentschap controverses ter discussie stelt, laat het collectief eigenlijk zien dat de meeste juridische geschillen door afgetekende machtsverhoudingen en divergente ideologische opvattingen worden getekend.

De rol van media en bemiddeling

In een recent boek heeft Sven Lütticken de aard van de bijeenkomsten van Agentschap geduid en daarbij ook de componenten van die bijeenkomsten aangewezen:

> De bijeenkomsten brengen een uiteenlopende reeks voorwerpen en onderwerpen (of dingen en mensen) samen. Meestal wordt een 'specimen' van een of meer dingen tentoongesteld als onderdeel van de bijeenkomst en is er een overleg waarbij experts en betrokkenen debatteren over de ins en outs van een bepaalde zaak. Agency's artefacten en hun gebruik, die aanleiding hebben gegeven tot rechtszaken, genereren uiteindelijk Agency's bijeenkomsten, waar advocaten, kunstenaars, theoretici en andere betrokkenen discussiëren over het ding in kwestie – of er deel van uitmaken.[16]

De voorwerpen op tafel zijn niet alleen onderwerp van gesprek, ze zetten aan tot debat.

In de architectuur wordt de term 'specimen' zelden in de mond genomen. De notie is afkomstig uit natuurwetenschappelijk onderzoek: staalafnamen – levende of afgestorven organismen, plantensoorten en mineralen – worden tijdens het veldwerk aan hun natuurlijke habitat onttrokken en daarna in een laboratorium nader onderzocht of in een museale context

13 Latour, *Het parlement van de dingen*, op. cit. (noot 10), 27-28.

14 Maarten Van Den Driessche, 'Het omcirkelen van een lege plaats: "bouwheer" worden, kwaliteit verwachten', in: Maarten Liefooghe en Maarten Van Den Driessche (red.), *Meer dan een Wedstrijd: De Open Oproep in een veranderende bouwcultuur* (Antwerpen/ Brussel: Vlaams Architectuurinstituut/Team Vlaams Bouwmeester, 2022), 38-56.

15 Labo Ruimte is het samenwerkingsverband tussen Departement Omgeving en Team Vlaams Bouwmeester dat in 2023 zijn 10-jarig bestaan mocht vieren. Els Vervloesem et al. (red.), *10 jaar Labo Ruimte: Ontwerpen aan de Toekomst* (Brussel: Departement Omgeving, 2023).

16 Sven Lütticken, *Objections, Vol. I: Forms of Abstraction* (Berlijn: Sternberg Press, 2022), 72.

The Role of Media and Mediation

In a recent book, Sven Lütticken has interpreted the nature of Agency meetings, also identifying the components of those meetings:

> The assemblies bring together a disparate array of objects and subjects (or things and people). Usually, a 'specimen' of one or more things is exhibited as part of the assembly, and there is a gathering during which experts and concerned parties debate the ins and outs of a particular case. Agency's artifacts and their uses, which have triggered legal actions, eventually generate Agency's assemblies, in which lawyers, artists, theorists, and other concerned parties discuss the thing in question – or become part of it.[16]

16 Sven Lütticken, *Objections, Vol. I: Forms of Abstraction* (Berlin: Sternberg Press, 2022), 72.

The objects on the table are more than just the subject of conversation; they actively provoke debate.

Architects rarely use the term 'specimen'. Originating in the natural sciences, the notion refers to the collection of samples – living or non-living organisms, plant species and minerals taken from their natural environment during fieldwork, then closely examined in a laboratory or displayed in a new context in a museum. Specimens are also the focus of the meeting organised by Agency at Atelier Bouwmeester. In this particular case, they take the form of historical evidence curated by the artist and presented as a paper file. This includes the full court decision in the Chico Mendez Mural Garden case, as well as Andreas Müller's pale orange concrete model. The comparison between the 'material sample' and the 'scale model' proves valuable here for a number of reasons.

Both the 'scale model' and the 'collected sample' serve as representations of and references to a reality beyond the institutional setting. Through the use of the concrete model, Agency's spatial installation bears a strong resemblance to the way in which architectural projects are discussed using drawings and models at Atelier Bouwmeester. Here, discussions are introduced and guided by texts, images or other media representations. These media – scale models, maps, architectural drawings, photographs, books and other media used in architectural design – establish a relationship to real-world settings, or project new realities that are represented by the media that are used. However, such media representations also change the nature and meaning of the objects themselves: a surveyed landscape becomes a map, a built environment becomes a scale model, and an ecological habitat is shown by placing representative 'species' in a museum. Processed by the media, the 'outside' reality is transported into a discursive 'inside' environment, where it can be studied and debated.

Clearly, media transubstantiation is also tied to vested interests. Whether through mapping, modelling, data entry via templates, calculation tables or scoring grids: formatting channels raw data and information into the institutional apparatus. The production of drawings and descriptions is linked to knowledge, control and power – in the Foucauldian sense of the word. As Lisa Gitelman has pointed out, this 'paperwork' has tangible power effects:

> Documents are integral to the ways people think, as well to the social order they inhabit. Knowing-Showing, in short, can never be disentangled from power – or more properly, control. . . . In the modern era documents have cultural weight mostly according to their institutional frames – the university, the corporation, and the state

Competition model, Atelier Bouwmeester, Brussels, 2012/ Prijsvraagmaquette, Atelier Bouwmeester, Brussel, 2012

ORBIS
OVER THE EDGES
AKERMAN
DAAN BIRNBAUM
vacant city

in een nieuw verband gepresenteerd. Ook tijdens de bijeenkomst die Agentschap in het Atelier Bouwmeester organiseerde, worden specimens centraal gezet. In dit specifieke geval is het de historische evidentie die door de kunstenaar werd verzameld en in een papieren dossier is samengevat. Het betreft de gerechtelijke uitspraak in de zaak van *Chico Mendez Mural Garden* die integraal kan worden geraadpleegd, maar ook de vaal-oranje betonnen maquette van de hand van architect Andreas Müller. De vergelijking tussen het 'materiaalstaal' en het 'schaalmodel' is hier om meerdere redenen bruikbaar.

Het 'schaalmodel' en het 'genomen staal' zijn allebei representaties van, en verwijzingen naar een werkelijkheid buiten de institutionele omgeving. Door het gebruik van het betonnen model, vertoont de ruimtelijke installatie een sterke verwantschap met de manier waarop architectuurprojecten via tekeningen en maquettes in het Atelier Bouwmeester ter discussie worden gesteld. Via teksten, beelden of andere mediale voorstellingen wordt het gesprek ingeleid en aangestuurd. Als echte media installeren maquettes maar ook kaarten, architectuurtekeningen, foto's, boeken en alle andere middelen die in het architectuurontwerp worden gebruikt, een verhouding tot de realiteit in het veld. Door de mediale voorstelling verandert echter ook de aard en betekenis van het voorwerp: het onderzochte gebied wordt een kaart, de gebouwde omgeving een schaalmodel, de ecologische habitat wordt getoond door middel van representatieve 'soorten' in een museale enscenering. Het is door deze mediale bewerkingen dat de werkelijkheid 'buiten' naar een discursieve omgeving 'binnen' wordt getransporteerd, en op deze manier voorwerp van studie en debat kan worden.

Het mag duidelijk zijn dat in de mediale transsubstantiatie ook belangen spelen. Of het nu het in kaart brengen of modelleren betreft, het invoeren van data door middel van sjablonen, rekentabellen of *score-grids*, door de formattering worden ruwe data en informatie in het institutioneel apparaat ingevoegd. Het maken van tekeningen en beschrijvingen is verbonden met kennis, controle en macht – in de Foucaultiaanse betekenis van het woord. Lisa Gittelman heeft erop gewezen dat dit papierwerk concrete machtseffecten heeft:

> Documenten zijn onlosmakelijk verbonden met de manier waarop mensen denken en met de sociale orde waarin ze zich bevinden. Weten-Zien, kortom, kan nooit los worden gezien van macht – of beter gezegd, controle. (...) In onze hedendaagse maatschappij hebben documenten een cultureel gewicht dat meestal verbonden is met de betrokken institutionele kaders – van de universiteit, het bedrijf en de overheid bijvoorbeeld – zelfs indien deze institutionele inbedding soms veraf lijkt.[17]

Door het gebruik van de media of de wijze van representeren worden de dingen ingelijfd in een gespecialiseerde professionele cultuur. De beeldtaal in prijsvraagbundels, de obligate nota's van ingenieurs die de constructieve haalbaarheid moeten bewijzen, de codes en conventies eigen aan de meeste architectuurtekeningen, vereisen een zekere geletterdheid van de participanten en beperken aldus ook de toegang tot het debat. Het is zelfs zo dat allerhande deskundigen via de gehanteerde media in belangrijke mate invloed op het beoordelingsproces uitoefenen: denk maar aan de manier waarop certificaten en allerlei indicatoren hun weg in het beoordelingsproces hebben gevonden.

17 Lisa Gitelman, *Paper knowledge: Toward a Media History of Documents* (Durham, NC: Duke University Press, 2014).

for instance – however remote the contextual framework can sometimes seem.[17]

Through the use of media or particular forms of representation, objects are absorbed into a specialised professional culture. The imagery in competition books, the engineering notes required to demonstrate structural feasibility, and the codes and conventions typical of most architectural drawings all require participants to have a certain level of literacy, effectively limiting access to the debate. Indeed, different experts significantly influence the evaluation process through the media they use: consider, for example, how certifications and various indicators have become embedded in the evaluation criteria.

However, reducing the role of media to the mere expression of hidden power dynamics is too simplistic, as Susan Leigh Star has shown. Media also function as communication tools that can unite different social worlds, bridging gaps between different fields and social domains. In a text exploring the concept of translation from *Science and Technology Studies*, Star reflects on the social significance of the 'specimen' in shaping the collection of the Museum of Vertebrate Zoology. Here, not only human actors but also objects – the specimens collected and displayed in the museum – give colour to the institutional setting. The media character thus encompasses both the descriptive tools created to make the outside world discussable and the reality that these specimens represent. In this seminal text, Star also describes boundary objects in terms that resonate strongly with Agency's discourse:

> Boundary objects are objects which are both plastic enough to adapt to local needs and constraints of the several parties employing them, yet robust enough to maintain a common identity across sites. They are weakly structured in common use, and become strongly structured in individual-site use.[18]

Susan Leigh Star sees each institutional setting as part of a wider ecosystem in which different social worlds intersect and interact. The media that circulate information in these settings provide a foothold and play a crucial role in this mediation process. As mediators, they both connect different social groups and facilitate exchanges between different spheres.

Given the nature of the discipline of architecture and the arsenal of representational tools available to designers – field notes and maps, sophisticated digital visualisations and scale models, as well as calculation tables and sets of plans – architects are well equipped to represent spatial challenges. This is especially true in competition formats, where visual materials must not only inform professionals, but also persuade and sometimes captivate clients. Just as carefully crafted rhetoric can influence discussions, well-designed images can guide the selection of a design proposal. The same can be said of the use of cartography in Labo Ruimte's research by design, where diagrams and maps make the collected findings imaginable.

The media used – what Gittelman refers to as 'the paperwork' – play a part very similar to that of the vocabularies that trigger processes of justification. However, unlike the generalising, linguistic criteria that frame quality ambitions, media representations also highlight the material object under discussion. The graphic file, the spreadsheet and the scale model provide a counterweight, a substance, to what is otherwise a purely

17 Lisa Gitelman, *Paper Knowledge: Toward a Media History of Documents* (Durham, NC: Duke University press, 2014).

18 Susan Leigh Star and James R. Griesemer, 'Institutional Ecology, "Translations", and Boundary Objects: Amateurs and Professionals in Berkeley's Museum of Vertebrate Zoology, 1907-1937', in: Geoffrey C. Bowker et al. (eds.), *Boundary Objects and Beyond: Working with Leigh Star* (Cambridge Mass.: MIT Press, 2016).

Het is echter te beperkend om de rol van de gehanteerde media te verengen tot deze versluierde machtseffecten, zoals Susan Leigh Star heeft laten zien. De media zijn even zo goed communicatiemiddelen die verschillende sociale werelden bij elkaar kunnen brengen, waardoor de afstand tussen verschillende velden en maatschappelijke domeinen wordt overbrugd. In een tekst die voortbouwt op het concept van translatie uit de *Science and Technology Studies*, heeft Susan Leigh Star nagedacht over de sociale betekenis van 'specimen' bij de totstandkoming van de collectie van het Museum for Verberate Zoology in Berkeley (Verenigde Staten). Niet alleen menselijke actoren maar ook de dingen – de specimens die in het museum verzameld en getoond worden – bepalen de institutionele setting. Het mediale karakter betreft dan zowel het beschrijvende instrumentarium dat werd ontwikkeld om het buiten bespreekbaar te maken, als de werkelijkheid waarnaar deze specimen verwijzen. In deze klassiek geworden tekst maakte ze ook een omschrijving van *boundary objects* (grensobjecten) in termen die overduidelijk een weerklank vinden in het vertoog van Agentschap:

> Grensobjecten zijn objecten die plastisch genoeg zijn om zich aan te passen aan de lokale behoeften en beperkingen van de verschillende partijen die ze gebruiken, maar toch robuust genoeg om een gemeenschappelijke identiteit te behouden op verschillende locaties. Ze zijn zwak gestructureerd in gemeenschappelijk gebruik en worden sterk gestructureerd in het gesitueerde individueel gebruik.[18]

18 Susan Leigh Star en James R. Griesemer, 'Institutional Ecology, "translations", and Boundary Objects: Amateurs and Professionals in Berkeley's Museum of Vertebrate Zoology, 1907-1937', in: Geoffrey C. Bowker et al. (red.) *Boundary Objects and Beyond: Working with Leigh Star* (Cambridge, MA: MIT Press, 2016).

Susan Leigh Star beschouwt elke institutionele setting als deel van een breder ecosysteem. Instellingen zijn plekken waar verschillende sociale werelden elkaar ontmoeten en met elkaar interageren. De media die informatie in circulatie brengen, bieden houvast en spelen een cruciale rol in dit bemiddelingsproces. Als intermediair houden ze zeer verschillende sociale groepen samen en bemiddelen ze tussen verschillende sferen.

Door de aard van de architectuurdiscipline en het arsenaal aan representatiemiddelen waarover ontwerpers beschikken – veldnotities en kaarten, vernuftige digitale visualisaties en schaalmodellen, maar ook rekentabellen en ontwerpen – zijn architecten goed geplaatst om ruimtelijke uitdagingen te verbeelden. Dit speelt bij uitstek bij prijsvragen, waar het beeldmateriaal niet enkel de specialisten moet informeren, maar opdrachtgevers moet overtuigen en soms ook verleiden. Net zoals retorisch woordgebruik het gesprek kan kleuren, zo kunnen goed gemaakte beelden de keuze voor een ontwerpvoorstel sturen. Hetzelfde kan worden gezegd over het gebruik van cartografie in het ontwerpend onderzoek van Labo Ruimte, waar diagrammen en kaartmateriaal de bijeengebrachte inzichten voorstelbaar maken.

De gehanteerde media – 'het papierwerk' waarover Gittelman spreekt – hebben aldus een zeer analoge rol als de *vocabulaires* die processen van verantwoording inleiden. In tegenstelling tot de generaliserende, talige criteria waarmee kwaliteitsambities worden vooropgesteld, trekken de mediale voorstellingen echter ook het materiële voorwerp waarover wordt gedebatteerd naar de voorgrond. Het grafische dossier, het rekenblad of het schaalmodel bieden tegenwicht en substantie aan een bij uitstek talig discours. De foto's verwijzen dan naar die specifieke gemeenschapstuin 'daar' in New York. De collage die de omheining van de Chico Mendez Garden als een replica rondom het Lapperfortbos plaatst, demonstreert een plausibele en betekenisvolle artistieke ingreep in de publieke ruimte

linguistic discourse. The photographs, for example, refer to a specific community garden 'over there' in New York. The collage, which places the fence of the Chico Mendez Garden as a replica around the Lapperfort forest, demonstrates a plausible and meaningful artistic intervention in public space 'here in Bruges'. The competition package represents an urban district that will be 'effectively developed' in the near future. Mathematical models predict, in an 'extremely realistic' way, the expected construction and operating costs of the project. And so on.

'Assembly (Going Public)' as a Critical Analogue

Agency's Assembly was part of the cultural programme at Atelier Bouwmeester, but in this text, it serves as a conceptual figure to characterise a Quality Setting.

Matthys's performance demonstrated that processes of quality mediation can be understood through the interplay of words, people and things. The setting is primarily a discursive space, in which different concepts are deliberately introduced to make qualitative distinctions as well as assessments. It is also a sociopolitical configuration, bringing together stakeholders and engaged experts around the case. Lastly, the setting is defined by the object on which agreement is sought – the things that are made present in the discussion through various media.

Clearly, the processes of justification, negotiation and mediation cannot be considered in isolation; they are inherently intertwined and unfold in a dynamic interplay. Finally, the artistic intervention by Agency serves as a reminder that in any process of quality mediation, power dynamics inevitably come into play – whether well-intentioned or unintentional. Doubts about the decision-making process are always justified, and the components of that process can always be critically examined.

Translation: InOtherWords, Maria van Tol

'hier in Brugge'. De prijsvraagbundel representeert een stadsdeel dat in de zeer nabije toekomst 'effectief' zal worden ontwikkeld. Rekenmodellen voorspellen op 'uiterst realistische' manier de verwachte bouw- en exploitatiekosten van het project. Enzovoort.

'Vergadering (Openbaarheid)' als kritisch analogon

De Vergadering van Agentschap was onderdeel van het culturele programma van het Atelier Bouwmeester, maar fungeerde in deze tekst als een denkfiguur om een *Quality Setting* te typeren. Matthys' performance liet zien dat processen van kwaliteitsbemiddeling kunnen worden begrepen in het samenspel van woorden, mensen en dingen. De setting is in eerste plaats een discursieve ruimte, waar doelbewust verschillende begrippen in stelling worden gebracht, om kwalitatief onderscheid te maken en te evalueren. De setting is eveneens een socio-politieke configuratie van belanghebbenden en betrokken experts die rondom de zaak worden samengebracht. De setting definieert zich op de derde plaats vanuit het voorwerp waarover overeenstemming wordt gezocht: de dingen die via allerhande media in de discussie aanwezig worden verondersteld.

Het mag duidelijk zijn dat de processen van Verantwoording, Onderhandeling en Bemiddeling niet onafhankelijk van elkaar kunnen worden bekeken, maar intrinsiek met elkaar zijn verweven en in een dynamisch samenspel voorkomen. De artistieke interventie van Agentschap herinnert er ons ten slotte aan dat er in elk proces van kwaliteitsbemiddeling ongewild, dan wel goedbedoeld of onbewust, machtseffecten optreden – dat twijfel over het beslissingsproces aldus ook steeds gerechtvaardigd is en de componenten van dit proces ook altijd kritisch voor het licht kunnen worden gehouden.

Thinking and Acting in a Design-Oriented Way: Interview with Chief Government Architect Francesco Veenstra

Kirsten Schipper

1 Wouter Veldhuis and Jannemarie de Jonge were members of the board from December 2020 to April 2025, and were succeeded by Thijs van Spaandonk and Noël van Dooren.

Who you gonna call? It's the summer of 2008 and during the farewell event for the first Board of Government Advisors in its current form – although a body with the same name briefly existed as early as 1874 – the next board makes its debut. Led by Chief Government Architect Liesbeth van der Pol, the new board introduces itself in a film by Jord den Hollander, set to the soundtrack of the 1984 hit film *Ghostbusters*. The message is clear: the board is ready to tackle the many challenges facing the Dutch government.

Van der Pol was succeeded as Chief Government Architect by Frits van Dongen and Floris Alkemade; Francesco Veenstra, who took over in September 2021, has since been shaping the statutory mandate of quality assurance. Together with urban designer Wouter Veldhuis and landscape architect Jannemarie de Jonge, he forms the current Board of Government Architect and Government Advisors (CRa).[1]

The CRa provides the Dutch government with both solicited and unsolicited advice on national spatial planning issues, addressing specific building projects as well as engaging in broad public debates. It also initiates various projects and methods to safeguard spatial quality. Through the NL2100 platform, whose motto is 'The 22nd Century Starts Now', the CRa promotes design-oriented thinking and organises various 'Future Ateliers'. It organises competitions on current spatial challenges, such as water security and sustainable energy transition. Notably, in 2022, these included initiatives for biobased and nature-inclusive building. Through its Young Innovators programme, the CRa invites talented young designers to contribute innovative ideas. From 2023, the CRa has also coordinated the Bouwmeesternetwerk, a network of local architects including the Regional Architect for the Groningen earthquake area, an appointment initiated by Veenstra. As part of his independent advisory role, the Chief Government Architect is involved in various projects of the Central Government Real Estate Agency (RVB), which manages the central government's buildings and land – including ministry buildings, prisons, palaces, museums, court buildings and natural and agricultural areas. The interview with Veenstra focuses on the latter role and highlights how design-oriented acting and thinking are applied in the Netherlands' largest real estate organisation.

Appreciated and Difficult

Despite the energetic soundtrack, 'ghost busting' may not be the best description of the CRa's work. Although according to Chief Government Architect Francesco Veenstra, making, having and maintaining contacts is necessary to carry out the function. This is necessary, 'especially to influence projects of the Central Government Real Estate Agency' where the Chief Government Architect is the main advisor to the Director-General of

Ontwerpend denken en handelen: Interview met Rijksbouwmeester Francesco Veenstra

Kirsten Schipper

Who you gonna call? Het is zomer 2008, en tijdens het afscheid van het eerste College van Rijksadviseurs (dat wil zeggen het eerste in deze samenstelling, want al in 1874 wordt voor een korte periode een gremium met dezelfde naam ingesteld), presenteert ook het volgende college zich. Onder aanvoering van Rijksbouwmeester Liesbeth van der Pol kondigt het nieuwe college zich aan in een film van Jord den Hollander op de soundtrack van de succesvolle film *Ghostbusters* uit 1984. De boodschap is duidelijk: het college staat paraat om aan de slag te gaan met de diverse opgaven waarvoor het Rijk aan zet is. Na Van der Pol, volgen Frits van Dongen en Floris Alkemade als Rijksbouwmeester. Sinds september 2021 heeft Francesco Veenstra de estafettestok in handen en geeft hij inhoud aan de wettelijke taak van kwaliteitsborging. Samen met stedenbouwkundige Wouter Veldhuis en landschapsarchitect Jannemarie de Jonge vormt hij het College van Rijksbouwmeester en Rijksadviseurs (CRa).[1]

1 Wouter Veldhuis en Jannemarie de Jonge waren lid van het college van december 2020 tot april 2025 en zijn opgevolgd door Thijs van Spaandonk en Noël van Dooren.

Het CRa adviseert de Nederlandse regering gevraagd en ongevraagd over nationale ruimtelijke inrichtingsvraagstukken omtrent concrete bouwprojecten en maatschappelijk bredere discussies, en initieert diverse projecten en instrumenten om de ruimtelijke kwaliteit te borgen. Via het platform NL2100 met als motto 'De 22e eeuw begint nú' stimuleert het college ontwerpend denken onder meer via breed samengestelde 'toekomstateliers'. Voor actuele ruimtelijke opgaven, te denken valt aan waterveiligheid en duurzame energietransitie, schrijft het college prijsvragen uit, zoals in 2022 voor *biobased* en natuurinclusief bouwen, en nodigt het, onder de noemer Young Innovators, jonge talentvolle ontwerpers uit vanwege hun vernieuwende inbreng. Sinds 2023 coördineert het CRa ook het Bouwmeesternetwerk, bestaande uit lokale bouwmeesters, onder wie de op initiatief van Veenstra aangestelde Regiobouwmeester voor het aardbevingsgebied in Groningen. Vanuit zijn onafhankelijke adviesrol is de Rijksbouwmeester betrokken bij diverse projecten van het Rijksvastgoedbedrijf, dat verantwoordelijk is voor het beheer van de gebouwen en de gronden van de rijksoverheid: ministeriegebouwen, gevangenissen, paleizen, musea, rechtbanken en natuur- en landbouwgronden. Het interview met Veenstra concentreert zich op laatstgenoemde rol, op de inzet van ontwerpend handelen en denken in het grootste vastgoedbedrijf van Nederland.

Gewaardeerd en lastig

Ondanks de daadkrachtige filmsound, is de bestrijding van spoken wellicht niet de beste omschrijving van de werkzaamheden van het CRa. Al is *call,* wanneer dit geïnterpreteerd wordt als het maken, hebben en onderhouden van contacten, noodzakelijk voor de uitvoering van de functie volgens Rijksbouwmeester Francesco Veenstra. Dit is nodig, 'vooral om invloed uit

the Central Government Real Estate Agency (RVB) on government housing policy.[2] The Central Government Real Estate Agency was formed in 2014 from four real estate organisations: the Rijksgebouwendienst (Government Buildings Agency), the Dienst Vastgoed Defensie (Defence Real Estate Agency), the Rijksvastgoed- en ontwikkelingsbedrijf (Government Real Estate and Development Agency) and the Directoraat Rijksvastgoed (Government Real Estate Agency).

The RVB, with its vast land and real estate portfolio, has a profound impact on our living environment. It is a huge organisation, employing some 2,900 people, including around 100 architects. Most of them work in The Hague in the Ministry of Finance building, which also houses the the Chief Architect's Studio. However, some work elsewhere in the Netherlands. Some people working at the RVB have us on their radar and involve us in various projects; others overlook us or do not involve us due to time constraints.' According to Veenstra, this is not specific to the culture of the RVB, but is a common dynamic in large organisations.

'Personal relationships are essential for me to fulfil my role as Chief Government Architect and to ensure quality. Our involvement depends on the people working on different projects and the relationships we have built up over decades. Of course, there is a legal mandate that might suggest I should be involved in everything, but in practice it doesn't work that way. The challenge is to make yourself as visible as possible and to do your work in such a way that you are invited to participate.' In addition to maintaining existing contacts and consulting regularly with the management, Chief Government Architect Veenstra is actively working on positioning his function in the organisation as a whole. Veenstra calls this 'internal acquisition'. 'To inspire the RVB staff to involve us, the Board of Government Architect and Government Advisors has produced a guideline that not only explains our role, but also provides a roadmap outlining the moments when we can best fulfil our role in collaboration with the RVB.'[3] Unlike the memorandum Chief Government Architect Tjeerd Dijkstra drew up on behalf of the Rijksgebouwendienst some 40 years ago, this guideline does not primarily contain evaluation criteria, but rather the working methods and vision of the Chief Government Architect and the Government Advisors for achieving quality.[4] 'To influence quality, you want to be involved as early as possible in the process. That way it will be clear whether one meeting is enough or whether you need to meet more often.'

Veenstra takes it as a compliment that the RVB seeks his advice. A coordinating architect recently asked for his advice on the renovation and sustainability of prisons and the new Directorate of Real Estate Investment and Development, which wants to focus not only on time and money but also on quality, asked for his opinion as well. But the Chief Government Architect also offers unsolicited advice. For example, the CRa has pointed out to the RVB the potential of their real estate as a lever for creating social value.[5] 'The RVB can set an example for other clients by giving substance to the concept of stewardship, taking a long-term view and investing counter-cyclically.'

It comes as no surprise to Veenstra that not everyone welcomes advice. 'If, as a partner at an architecture office, you provide last-minute input on a tender that needs to be submitted urgently, it's unlikely to please the architects, either. Once again, the earlier you are involved in a project, the greater the impact you can have.'

2
The Chief Government Architect is appointed by royal decree for a term of three to five years. The tasks and roles of the Chief Government Architect are formally defined in the (*Royal*) *Decree Rijksgebouwendienst 1999*. This decree states that the Chief Government Architect – both on request and unsolicited – advises the Director-General of the Central Government Real Estate Agency as well as all government ministers. The Chief Government Architect may also respond to advisory requests from other government entities. The independent advisory tasks of the Chief Government Architect are further elaborated in the 1999 *Positiedocument Rijksbouwmeester*.

3
Board of Government Advisors, *Leidraad College van Rijksadviseurs 2021-2024*, September 2022.

4
Dijkstra's memorandum (1985) was widely used by building standards, at first in stencilled form – the Rijksgebouwendienst distributed hundreds of them – and later, from 2001, slightly adapted, in book form (*Een notitie over architectuurbeleid*, Rotterdam 2001).

5
Board of Government Architect and Government Advisors, *Rijk als rentmeester #2*, 2024.

te oefenen bij projecten van het Rijksvastgoedbedrijf', waar de Rijksbouwmeester de eerste adviseur is van de directeur-generaal van het Rijksvastgoedbedrijf (RVB) voor het rijkshuisvestingsbeleid.[2] Het RVB is in 2014 ontstaan uit vier vastgoedorganisaties: de Rijksgebouwendienst, de Dienst Vastgoed Defensie, het Rijksvastgoed- en ontwikkelingsbedrijf en de directie Rijksvastgoed.

'Het RVB, dat met al zijn grond en vastgoed een enorme invloed heeft op onze leefomgeving, is een gigantisch bedrijf, met circa 2.900 medewerkers, onder wie ongeveer 100 architecten. De meesten werken in Den Haag, in het gebouw van het ministerie van Financiën, waar het Atelier Rijksbouwmeester ook onderdak heeft, maar een deel is verspreid over Nederland. Een aantal personen binnen het RVB heeft ons op het netvlies en betrekt ons bij de diverse projecten, bij anderen zijn we nog een blinde vlek of worden we door tijdsdruk niet gevraagd.' Dit is volgens Veenstra niet uniek voor de cultuur van het RVB, maar zie je terug in alle grotere organisaties.

'De persoonlijke contacten zijn evident om mijn taak als Rijksbouwmeester, als borger van de kwaliteit te kunnen uitoefenen. Onze betrokkenheid is afhankelijk van de mensen die aan de diverse projecten werken en de relaties die de afgelopen decennia zijn gevormd. Er is natuurlijk een wettelijke taak van waaruit je zou kunnen stellen dat je overal bij betrokken bent, maar in de praktijk werkt dat niet zo. De kunst is jezelf zo zichtbaar mogelijk te maken en zodanig je werk te doen dat je gevraagd wordt.'

2 De Rijksbouwmeester wordt per koninklijk besluit benoemd voor een periode van drie tot vijf jaar. De taken en rollen van de Rijksbouwmeester zijn met name formeel vastgelegd in het (Koninklijk) besluit Rijksgebouwendienst 1999. Hierin staat dat de Rijksbouwmeester – gevraagd en ongevraagd – adviseert aan de directeur-generaal van het Rijksvastgoedbedrijf én ook aan alle bewindspersonen. De Rijksbouwmeester mag ook ingaan op adviesvragen van andere overheden. In het 'Positiedocument Rijksbouwmeester' uit 1999 zijn de onafhankelijke adviestaken van de Rijksbouwmeester nader uitgewerkt.

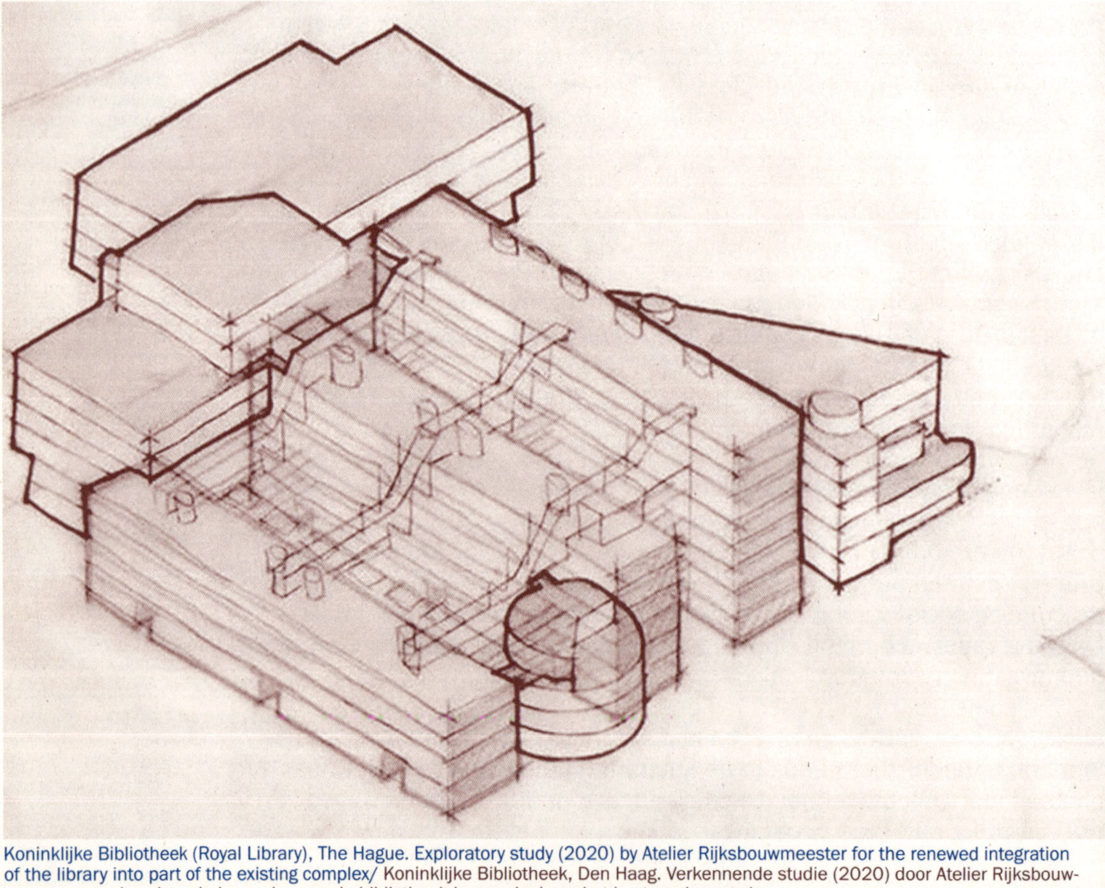

Koninklijke Bibliotheek (Royal Library), The Hague. Exploratory study (2020) by Atelier Rijksbouwmeester for the renewed integration of the library into part of the existing complex/ Koninklijke Bibliotheek, Den Haag. Verkennende studie (2020) door Atelier Rijksbouwmeester naar hernieuwde inpassing van de bibliotheek in een deel van het bestaande complex

'If, on one hand, you are appreciated and, on the other, seen as difficult – if both ends of the spectrum are experienced across the entire real estate portfolio – then you're doing a good job,' says Veenstra.

A Long-Standing Tradition

Traditionally, the Dutch government has entrusted quality assurance to experts. The Chief Government Architect safeguards and promotes the quality of government buildings, while various municipalities have their own (city) architects or spatial quality committees (the successors of the building standards committees).

The role of Chief Government Architect has a long-standing tradition. The first Chief Government Architect, Jean Thomas Thibault (1806), known as the King's Architect, was tasked with providing housing for the monarch and drawing up plans for the reconstruction of Leiden, which had been badly damaged by a gunpowder explosion. He also worked to establish a strong architecture education system and awarded scholarships for experience abroad. After Thibault, this critical advisory role was further expanded and strengthened. As well as ensuring quality, the Dutch government increasingly wanted to set a good example. Subsequently, in 1957, the role of the Chief Government Architect was adapted from that of lead architect and head of the Department of New Buildings to that of an independent advisor on architecture and related policy areas. The Chief Government Architect became responsible for the selection and supervision of architects and artists. To attract architects with significant professional experience, the position was made part-time, allowing them to maintain their own practices. From 1958, the Chief Government Architect stopped designing buildings directly and since 1972, the role has been purely advisory. The most important tool at their disposal is the selection of architects for government buildings. The redefinition of the Chief Government Architect's position – from the lead architect of the Rijksgebouwendienst to an advisor – was partly a response to criticism regarding the agency's insular nature in the early 1970s.

Since 2004, the institution of the Chief Government Architect has been extended to include Government Advisors in related disciplines.[6] Together, they form the Board of Government Architect and Government Advisors (CRa): a multidisciplinary body representing various spatial design disciplines. Compared with other countries, it is remarkable that the Dutch interpretation of the role of the Chief Government Architect is rooted in a centuries-old tradition.

You Cannot Do Everything

The Dutch national real estate portfolio is vast: some 900 km^2 of land and 12 million m^2 of buildings. The RVB is involved in hundreds of projects, ranging from the replacement of doors in a courthouse to the renovation and refurbishment of the Binnenhof in The Hague, the administrative centre of the Netherlands since the thirteenth century. This site comprises a number of buildings of considerable spatial complexity, including several national monuments.

According to Veenstra, the scope for influence is relatively limited. The Chief Architect's Studio, which supports the CRa and is part of the RVB organisation, employs some 40 people, three-quarters of whom work on RVB projects, with some focusing exclusively on buildings.[7] 'We are involved in dozens of projects. Some of them are dormant,' says Veenstra. In a

6
The 'first' Board of Government Advisors, officially active from 1 January 2005, consisted of Chief Government Architect Mels Crouwel, Government Advisor on Landscape Dirk Sijmons, Government Advisor on Infrastructure Jan Brouwer and Government Advisor on Cultural Heritage Fons Asselbergs. The latter position was discontinued in 2012 and from 2016, the two remaining advisors are both described as National Advisor for the Physical Living Environment. The CRa has been operating under the name Board of Government Architect and Government Advisors since 2024.

7
The Chief Architect's Studio consists of architects, urban designers, landscape architects, heritage experts, policy advisors and visual arts consultants, among others. The staff of the Studio are not tied to a specific term and thus provide continuous support for the Chief Government Architect and the Government Advisors.

Naast het onderhouden van de bestaande contacten en het reguliere overleg met de directie, is Rijksbouwmeester Veenstra daarom actief bezig met het positioneren van zijn functie in de gehele organisatie. Veenstra spreekt over 'acquisitie binnen de organisatie'. 'Om de medewerkers van het RVB geïnspireerd te krijgen om ons in te schakelen, heeft het College van Rijksbouwmeester en Rijksadviseurs een leidraad opgesteld met daarin niet alleen uitleg over onze rol, maar ook een routekaart die duidelijk maakt op welke momenten wij onze rol het beste kunnen vervullen in de samenwerking met het RVB.'[3] In tegenstelling tot de notitie die Rijksbouwmeester Tjeerd Dijkstra circa 40 jaar geleden opstelde in opdracht van de Rijksgebouwendienst, bevat de leidraad niet zozeer beoordelingscriteria, maar de werkwijze en visie van de Rijksbouwmeester en de Rijksadviseurs om tot kwaliteit te komen.[4] 'Om invloed te kunnen uitoefenen op de kwaliteit, wil je zo vroeg mogelijk in het proces betrokken worden. Dan is ook duidelijk of bijvoorbeeld één overleg voldoende is of dat ik vaker moet aanschuiven.'

Veenstra beschouwt het als een compliment dat het RVB hem om advies vraagt. Onlangs vroeg bijvoorbeeld een coördinerend architect advies over de vernieuwing en verduurzaming van gevangenissen, en vroeg de nieuwe directie Gebieds- en vastgoedontwikkeling die niet alleen wil sturen op tijd en geld maar ook op kwaliteit, zijn mening. Maar de Rijksbouwmeester geeft ook ongevraagde adviezen. Zo hebben het College van Rijksbouwmeester en Rijksadviseurs het RVB geattendeerd op de mogelijkheden van hun vastgoed als hefboom voor maatschappelijke waarde.[5] 'Het RVB kan een voorbeeld zijn voor andere opdrachtgevers door invulling te geven aan het begrip rentmeesterschap, een langetermijnvisie te hanteren en anticyclisch te investeren.'

Dat niet iedereen zit te wachten op advies, vindt Veenstra niet verwonderlijk. 'Als je als partner bij een architectenbureau op het laatste moment nog een reactie geeft op een aanbesteding die de deur uit moet, dan worden de architecten daar ook niet blij van. Ook hier geldt, hoe eerder je bij een project betrokken bent, hoe meer resultaat je kunt boeken.'

'Als je aan de ene kant wordt gewaardeerd en aan de andere kant als lastig wordt gezien – als die twee kanten van het spectrum in de gehele portefeuille van het vastgoed worden ervaren – dan doe je het goed,' aldus Veenstra.

Een lange traditie

Van oudsher laat de Nederlandse overheid de kwaliteitsborging over aan deskundigen. De Rijksbouwmeester bewaakt en bevordert de kwaliteit van de rijksgebouwen, diverse gemeenten hebben hun eigen (Stads) bouwmeester en/of commissies Ruimtelijke Kwaliteit (de opvolger van de welstandscommissies).

De functie van de Rijksbouwmeester heeft een lange traditie. De eerste Rijksbouwmeester, de 'architect des Konings' Jean Thomas Thibault (1806), wordt belast met de huisvesting van de vorst, maar ook bijvoorbeeld met het maken van wederopbouwplannen voor Leiden, die zwaar getroffen was door een buskruitramp. Daarnaast is hij betrokken bij de ontwikkeling van een goede architectuuropleiding en verstrekt hij studiebeurzen om in het buitenland ervaring op te doen. Na Thibault wordt deze cruciale adviesrol verder verbreed en versterkt. Behalve kwaliteitsbewaking krijgt de rijksoverheid steeds meer ambitie om zelf het goede voorbeeld te geven. De functie van de Rijksbouwmeester wordt om deze reden in 1957

3 College van Rijksadviseurs, *Leidraad College van Rijksadviseurs 2021-2024*, september 2022.

4 De notitie van Dijkstra (1985) werd veel gebruikt door welstandscommissies, eerst in gestencilde vorm (de Rijksgebouwendienst verspreidde er honderden) later, vanaf 2001, iets aangepast, in boekvorm (*Een notitie over architectuurbeleid*, Rotterdam 2001).

5 College van Rijksbouwmeester en Rijksadviseurs, *Rijk als rentmeester #2*, 2024.

number of cases, the Chief Government Architect plays an active part, such as with the Binnenhof, 'the most important project in the Netherlands at the moment, which is about to be realised.'

Veenstra says that, more than his predecessors, he works from his professional experience. As well as looking at quality criteria, he also looks at other aspects that affect the process in order to be able to assess quality. Is the brief clear, is the fee reasonable and is there enough time for proper preliminary research? Veenstra has regular face-to-face meetings with the various architecture offices selected for the Binnenhof – which not only accommodates the House of Representatives and the Senate, but also the Council of State and the Ministry of General Affairs. The RVB architects take part in these meetings as well. 'I mainly focus on the overall design, such as the placement of the new public entrance.' He is less involved in details such as the choice of materials. 'In my role as quality guardian, I mainly appeal to the professionalism and craftsmanship of the designers in discussions; that is where the responsibility ultimately lies,' says Veenstra. 'I can also act as the direct link between the work floor and the RVB management.'

'The trick is to be involved in projects that can serve as examples for the setting of frameworks in areas such as innovation or engaging young, talented designers, as we did with the Paleis van Justitie (Palice of Justice).'

Veenstra believes that as a Chief Government Architect, you are part of a relay team. 'This makes it a challenge to ensure quality over a longer period of time. When I started as Chief Government Architect, I had to attune to the projects that the Chief Architect's Studio, and thus my predecessor(s), had already been involved in: the renovation of the Algemene Rekenkamer (Dutch Court of Audit) in The Hague, the conversion of Rijkskantoor Mandemaat (Dutch Inland Revenue Office) in Assen and the area development around The Hague Central Station. All these projects are at different stages. You step into ongoing projects, which you often hand over again, and if you're involved in projects from the start, you will have to hand them over again before they are completed. National projects have a much longer timeline than the tenure of the Chief Government Architect. In general, however, the approach is the same, in the sense that the established requirements and their assessment remain the same, regardless of who is involved.'

The Right Moment

'Ensuring quality is first and foremost about finding the right moment,' says Veenstra. In this context, he refers to 'synchronising the various interests in time of the parties involved, which have to lead to the formulation of the design brief'. Take the Dutch Court of Audit, for example. The municipality has to adjust the zoning procedure, the user has to have his programme in order and the RVB has to have enough people available. The interests and time investments of each organisation are different and unless there is sufficient overlap of interests, you won't get the optimum result. It takes patience to get everyone on the same page, on the same wavelength, but as Chief Government Architect, you also have to exert influence. This approach may be different from that of previous Chief Government Architects. Often the emphasis is on building a quality team or awarding criteria, but my focus is on process.' Veenstra sees bringing

Binnenhof, Den Haag. Met de renovatie van het Binnenhof wordt de Hofgracht hersteld. Ontwerp: Merk X en Karres en Brands

Binnenhof, The Hague. With the renovation of the Binnenhof, the Hofgracht is being restored. Design: Merk X and Karres en Brands

aangepast. Van hoofdarchitect en chef van de afdeling Nieuwbouw wordt hij een zelfstandig adviseur op het gebied van de architectuur en aan verwante beleidsterreinen. De Rijksbouwmeester wordt verantwoordelijk voor de selectie en begeleiding van architecten en kunstenaars. Om architecten met een zekere staat van dienst aan te trekken voor de positie van Rijksbouwmeester, wordt het ambt omgezet in een deeltijdfunctie. Rijksbouwmeesters hoeven zo hun eigen architectenpraktijk niet op te geven. Vanaf 1958 ontwerpt de Rijksbouwmeester niet meer zelf en vanaf 1972 is hij of zij uitsluitend adviseur. Het belangrijkste instrument waarover hij of zij beschikt is de architectenkeuze voor rijksgebouwen. De herdefiniëring van de positie van de Rijksbouwmeester, als hoofdarchitect van de Rijksgebouwendienst naar adviseur, is onder meer het gevolg van het commentaar op het gesloten karakter van de Rijksgebouwendienst begin jaren 1970.

Sinds 2004 is het instituut van de Rijksbouwmeester verbreed met Rijksadviseurs voor de aangrenzende disciplines.[6] Samen vormen zij het College van Rijksbouwmeester en Rijksadviseurs, een multidisciplinair college waarbinnen de verschillende ruimtelijke ontwerpdisciplines vertegenwoordigd zijn. In vergelijking met andere landen is het uitzonderlijk te noemen dat de Nederlandse invulling van het Rijksbouwmeesterschap gebaseerd is op een traditie die al eeuwen standhoudt.

Je kunt niet alles doen

De rijksvastgoedportefeuille is enorm; circa 900 km^2 grond en 12 miljoen m^2 aan gebouwen. Het RVB werkt aan honderden projecten, van de vervanging van deuren in een rechtbank, tot de renovatie en verbouwing van het Binnenhof in Den Haag, sinds de dertiende eeuw hèt bestuurlijk centrum van Nederland en bestaande uit een reeks gebouwen met een grote ruimtelijke complexiteit, waaronder diverse rijksmonumenten.

Het deel waarop je invloed kunt uitoefenen is volgens Veenstra maar beperkt. Bij het Atelier Rijksbouwmeester, dat het CRa ondersteunt en deel uitmaakt van de organisatie van het RVB, werken circa 40 mensen, waarvan driekwart aan projecten van het RVB en daarvan een deel alleen aan de gebouwen.[7] 'Wij zijn bij vele tientallen projecten betrokken. Een deel hiervan is slapend,' aldus Veenstra. Bij een aantal heeft de Rijksbouwmeester een actieve functie, zoals bij het Binnenhof, 'de belangrijkste opgave in Nederland op dit moment, die aan de vooravond staat van uitvoering'.

Veenstra opereert, naar eigen zeggen in tegenstelling tot zijn voorgangers, meer vanuit de beroepspraktijk. Naast de aandacht voor de criteria voor kwaliteit, verdiept hij zich ook in andere aspecten die van invloed zijn op het proces, om zich uiteindelijk over de kwaliteit te kunnen uitspreken. Is de opdracht wel helder, is het honorarium toereikend, is er tijd gereserveerd om goed vooronderzoek te doen? Met de verschillende architectenbureaus die voor het Binnenhof zijn geselecteerd, waar naast de Eerste en Tweede Kamer, ook de Raad van State en het ministerie van Algemene Zaken zetelen, heeft Veenstra regelmatig een-op-een contact. Daarbij schuiven ook de architecten van het RVB aan. 'Ik let vooral op de hoofdopzet, zoals bijvoorbeeld de situering van de nieuwe publieksentree.' Met afwerkingen, zoals de materiaalkeuze bemoeit hij zich minder. 'In mijn rol als hoeder van de kwaliteit doe ik in de discussies vooral een beroep op de professionaliteit en het ambacht van de ontwerpers, daar ligt uiteindelijk de verantwoordelijkheid,' volgens Veenstra. 'Ook kan ik de directe schakel vormen tussen de werkvloer en de RVB-directie.'

6
Het 'eerste' College van Rijksadviseurs, dat vanaf 1 januari 2005 officieel actief is, bestaat uit: Rijksbouwmeester Mels Crouwel, Rijksadviseur voor het Landschap Dirk Sijmons, Rijksadviseur voor de Infrastructuur Jan Brouwer en Rijksadviseur voor het Cultureel Erfgoed Fons Asselbergs. De Rijksadviseur voor het Cultureel Erfgoed verdwijnt in 2012 en vanaf 2016 krijgen de twee overgebleven adviseurs de omschrijving: Rijksadviseur voor de Fysieke Leefomgeving. Sinds 2024 opereert het CRa onder de naam: College van Rijksbouwmeester en Rijksadviseurs.

7
Het Atelier bestaat onder andere uit architecten, stedenbouwkundigen, landschapsarchitecten, erfgoeddeskundigen, beleidsadviseurs en adviseurs beeldende kunst. De medewerkers van het Atelier zijn niet gebonden aan een termijn en zijn dus een continue factor van ondersteuning voor de Rijksbouwmeester en de Rijksadviseurs.

together different interests as a key role of the Chief Government Architect: 'Otherwise you won't achieve what you were hired for.'

The start of the commission for the conversion and renovation of the various buildings of the Royal Netherlands Meteorological Institute (KNMI) in De Bilt coincides almost exactly with Veenstra's appointment as Chief Government Architect. Meanwhile, work on formulating the brief has been going on for three years. According to Veenstra, the fact that not everyone is on the same wavelength also has to do with the approach taken by the client (RVB) and the user (KNMI). In his view, the Chief Government Architect has a part to play in this as well. 'The KNMI needs to assert itself in a new role, that of the client/user. It is really about the emancipation of the user. The RVB tends to take on the role of user, but the KNMI needs to position itself more as a client, perhaps by exploring possibilities with an architect before formulating the brief. What are the possibilities in terms of sustainability, appearance and the relationship between the buildings, land and the surrounding environment that will allow the KNMI to present itself more strongly as an authoritative climate institute?' Veenstra believes this also applies to other users, such as the Dutch Court of Audit. 'When clients and users better understand what is possible and what they want, selections also improve. Involving designers can help with this.'

A Proper Preparation

'I find it interesting to be part of a selection committee, but once the architects have been selected, the rest should run smoothly. In principle, they could all carry out the project if the criteria were well defined. They would produce different results, but these would all be quality results.' With this statement, Veenstra emphasises the importance of proper preparation. He cites the example of the conversion and extension of the Museum Catharijne Convent, a national museum of Christian art and heritage in Utrecht, where he had no official role but was asked to participate in the evaluation committee as the Chief Government Architect. The museum had already made preparations for a multiple negotiated tender but, in eenstra's view, had overlooked a number of fundamental aspects. Veenstra believes that a fixed fee should be determined so that the price does not influence the assessment, that a proper fee should be provided, that offices should be free to present their work as they see fit and that there should be room for dialogue (a conversation between the client/user and the architect). The museum adjusted the conditions for the commission to ensure Veenstra would take a seat on the committee. 'After that, my participation was no longer truly relevant, as the quality had already been ensured at the outset.'

'If the RVB, or any client for that matter, has a solid grasp of the project requirements at the outset, the process, including quality assurance, runs much more smoothly. When you involve design or designers early on, the likelihood of issues arising later is significantly reduced – that is my deepest conviction.' Veenstra observes this step – using the design expertise of landscape architects, urban designers and architects in the early stages of the process to clarify and refine the scope of the project – also being taken at the RVB and organisations like Rijkswaterstaat.

Involving designers early in the process, through feasibility studies, design research or other means, is the most important tool for defining and ensuring quality criteria, according to Veenstra. The lack of design expertise at this stage is a risk to the quality of the project,' says Veenstra.

'De kunst is om bij projecten betrokken te zijn, die een voorbeeld kunnen zijn om kaders te stellen op het gebied van innovatie of het inschakelen van jonge talentvolle ontwerpers, zoals bij het Paleis van Justitie.'

Als Rijksbouwmeester ben je in de ogen van Veenstra onderdeel van een estafetteploeg. 'Dat maakt het bewaken van kwaliteit over een langere periode een opgave. Toen ik startte als Rijksbouwmeester moest ik mij opnieuw verhouden tot de projecten waar het Atelier Rijksbouwmeester en daarmee mijn voorganger(s) al betrokken waren: zoals de verbouwing van de Algemene Rekenkamer in Den Haag, de renovatie van rijkskantoor Mandemaat in Assen en de gebiedsontwikkeling van Den Haag Centraal Station. Al deze projecten bevinden zich in andere fasen. Je stapt in lopende projecten die je vaak weer overdraagt, en mocht je er vanaf het begin bij zijn betrokken, dan moet je ze vaak al voor de oplevering weer overdragen. De rijksprojecten hebben een hele andere tijdspanne dan de aanstelling van de Rijksbouwmeester. Over het algemeen hanteer je wel eenzelfde aanpak, in de zin dat de gestelde eisen en toetsing daarvan, ongeacht de persoon, hetzelfde blijven.'

Het juiste moment

'In de eerste plaats gaat het bij de borging van kwaliteit om het vinden van het juiste moment.' Veenstra heeft het in dit verband over het 'synchroniseren van de verschillende belangen in tijd van de betrokken partijen die tot de formulering van de ontwerpopgave moeten leiden'. 'Neem bijvoorbeeld de Algemene Rekenkamer. De gemeente moet de bestemmingsplanprocedure aanpassen, de gebruiker moet zijn programma op orde hebben en het RVB moet voldoende mensen beschikbaar hebben. De belangen en de inzet in tijd is bij iedere organisatie anders en zolang er onvoldoende overlap in belangen ontstaat, bereik je niet het optimale resultaat. Om iedereen op één lijn, op dezelfde golflengte te krijgen is geduld nodig, maar moet je als Rijksbouwmeester ook invloed uitoefenen. Deze benadering is wellicht anders dan die van de vorige Rijksbouwmeesters. Vaak ligt de nadruk in het opstellen van een kwaliteitsteam en/of gunningscriteria, maar ik richt mij vooral op het proces.' Het samenbrengen van verschillende belangen ziet Veenstra als een belangrijke taak van de Rijksbouwmeester, 'anders krijg je niet voor elkaar waarvoor je bent aangenomen'.

De start van de opdracht voor de verbouwing en renovatie van de diverse gebouwen van het Koninklijk Nederlands Meteorologisch Instituut (KNMI) in De Bilt valt bijna gelijk met het aantreden van Veenstra als Rijksbouwmeester in het najaar van 2021. Ondertussen wordt al drie jaar gewerkt aan het formuleren van de opgave. Dat nog niet iedereen op dezelfde golflengte zit heeft volgens Veenstra ook te maken met de taakopvatting van de opdrachtgever (RVB) en gebruiker (KNMI). Ook hier is naar zijn mening een taak voor de Rijksbouwmeester weggelegd. 'Het KNMI moet zich gaan manifesteren in een nieuwe rol, die van opdrachtgever/gebruiker. Eigenlijk gaat het hier om de emancipatie van de gebruiker. De RVB heeft de neiging om de gebruikersrol op zich te nemen, maar het KNMI moet zich sterker als opdrachtgever profileren, wellicht door samen met een architect de mogelijkheden te verkennen alvorens de opgave te formuleren. Wat zijn de kansen op het gebied van duurzaamheid, uitstraling en de samenhang tussen gebouwen, landgoed en omgeving, die ervoor moeten zorgen dat het KNMI zich sterker kan tonen als gezaghebbend klimaatinstituut?' Dit geldt volgens Veenstra ook voor andere gebruikers, zoals de Rekenkamer. 'Wanneer opdrachtgevers en gebruikers beter weten

'The approach chosen depends on the brief and the ambition. The research is carried out by the Chief Architect's Studio, possibly with the support of external designers or offices.'

According to Veenstra, the biggest opportunities for the design sector will continue to lie in the early stages of the construction process. 'Our profession is undergoing huge changes throughout the production side, partly due to AI.' The advantage of involving designers early on, he says, is that 'you get a more robust programme that better meets the user's needs, which leads to a smoother process and better control of costs. In short, more manageable projects, faster realisation and better architecture.'

Royal Netherlands Meteorological Institute (KNMI), De Bilt. Model of the site and buildings to explore spatial scenarios for the future/ Koninklijk Nederlands Meteorologisch Instituut (KNMI), De Bilt. Maquette van terrein en bebouwing om ruimtelijke scenario's voor de toekomst te verkennen

wat mogelijk is en wat ze willen, worden selecties ook beter. Het betrekken van ontwerpers kan hierbij helpen.'

Een goede voorbereiding

'Ik vind het interessant om in een gunningscommissie te zitten, maar als er eenmaal architecten zijn geselecteerd, dan moet het goed komen. In principe zouden ze allen de opdracht kunnen uitvoeren als de criteria goed zijn. Je krijgt een ander resultaat, maar allemaal van kwaliteit.' Met deze stelling onderstreept Veenstra het belang van een goede voorbereiding. Als voorbeeld noemt de Rijksbouwmeester de verbouwing en uitbreiding van Museum Catharijneconvent, een rijksmuseum voor christelijke kunst en erfgoed in Utrecht, waar hij geen officiële rol had, maar als Rijksbouwmeester werd gevraagd deel te nemen in de beoordelingscommissie. Het museum had reeds voorbereidingen voor een meervoudige onderhandse aanbesteding getroffen, maar had met een aantal, voor Veenstra, fundamentele zaken geen rekening gehouden. Zo is Veenstra onder meer van mening dat een vast honorarium moet worden bepaald, zodat de prijs geen invloed heeft op de beoordeling; dat er een behoorlijke vergoeding moet zijn; dat bureaus de vrijheid moeten hebben hoe zij hun werk presenteren en dat er ruimte is voor een dialooggesprek (een gesprek tussen opdrachtgever/ gebruiker en architect). Het museum heeft vervolgens de voorwaarden voor de opdracht aangepast, zodat Veenstra zitting zou nemen in de commissie. 'Deelname was voor mij vervolgens niet meer echt relevant, de kwaliteit was nu immers aan de voorkant al gewaarborgd.'

'Als het RVB, of welke opdrachtgever ook, aan het begin de opgave goed in de vingers heeft, dan verloopt het proces, waaronder de kwaliteitsborging, veel soepeler. Op het moment dat je aan de voorkant gebruik maakt van het ontwerp of ontwerpers, is de kans kleiner dat er later iets misgaat, dat is mijn diepste overtuiging.' Veenstra ziet deze beweging – het inschakelen van ontwerpkracht van landschapsarchitecten, stedenbouwkundigen en architecten in de voorfase van het proces om de opgave scherp te stellen en in de vingers te krijgen – ook bij het RVB en organisaties als Rijkswaterstaat.

Het betrekken van ontwerpers in het voortraject, bijvoorbeeld aan de hand van haalbaarheidsstudies of ontwerpend onderzoek, is volgens Veenstra het belangrijkste instrument om de criteria voor kwaliteit scherp te stellen en te borgen. 'Het gebrek aan ontwerpdeskundigheid in deze fase is een risico voor de kwaliteit van de opgave,' stelt Veenstra. 'Welke manier je kiest is afhankelijk van de opgave en de ambitie. Onderzoek wordt uitgevoerd door het Atelier Rijksbouwmeester, eventueel met ondersteuning door externe ontwerpers/bureaus.'

Aan de voorkant van het bouwproces liggen volgens Veenstra in de toekomst ook de meeste kansen voor de ontwerpsector. 'Ons vak ondergaat een enorme verandering aan de gehele productiekant, onder meer door AI.' Het voordeel van het vroegtijdig betrekken van ontwerpers is in zijn ogen dat je 'een steviger programma krijgt, dat beter aansluit bij de eisen van de gebruiker, waardoor het proces beter verloopt en je beter greep hebt op de kosten. Kortom: beter beheersbare projecten, sneller gerealiseerd en betere architectuur.'

Critici van deze manier van werken zeggen wellicht dat de manier van Veenstra de eigenlijke ontwerpopgave ondermijnt. Veenstra zelf ziet dit anders. 'Je laat in deze voorfase geen gebouw maken, maar de uitgangspunten om te kunnen starten met het daadwerkelijk ontwerpen. Als

Critics of this approach might argue that Veenstra's method undermines the actual design brief. But Veenstra sees it differently. 'In this preliminary stage, you are not creating a building, but laying the groundwork for the actual design work to begin. As a designer, you get a role in the process much earlier, and thus influence the conditions.'

Opportunities for Experimentation and Young Talent

'Using design in the preliminary stage also creates opportunities for experimentation, and experimentation helps people to think differently about challenges.' Veenstra believes it is important to 'broaden the pool of architects who win tenders'. 'Experimentation is not necessary everywhere, but there are plenty of opportunities where emerging designers and smaller firms should be given a chance to realise a public building.' He also sees this as a responsibility of the larger offices. They should involve young architects, 'give them a leg up'. Veenstra believes that the Chief Government Architect also has a role to play in this respect, which is why he started organising debates on tendering in 2023.

A recent debate focused on the Open Call, the tool introduced in 2000 shortly after the appointment of the first Flemish Government Architect, aimed at strengthening architecture culture.[8] The Flemish Government Architect, whose organisation is largely structured around this approach, primarily advises public clients and enables them to contact designers. One of the few criteria is that designers must be able to present three reference projects designed under their own name. The results are made publicly available so that others can learn from them. Chief Government Architect Veenstra recently introduced a similar method for private tenders in the Netherlands: the Architects' Index, a procedure for investigating which designers are interested and eligible for commissions from the RVB.

Since the formation of the new Dutch cabinet in July 2024, a coordinating minister tasked with overseeing spatial planning, public housing, the Central Government Real Estate Agency and spatial quality has once again been appointed, after more than ten years. A fundamental question is how policy will develop in the coming years. The role of the Chief Government Architect has remained fairly consistent for over two centuries, despite various political changes and differing viewpoints. Numerous Chief Government Architects have come and gone, and while their approaches, choice of tools and methods of addressing challenges differ, quality assurance has always been a top priority. Central to this are promoting good commissioning practices and strengthening the role of design, or as Veenstra puts it: design-oriented acting and thinking.

Translation: InOtherWords, Maria van Tol

8 This call is comparable to the procedure once used by Chief Government Architect Wytze Patijn for selecting architects for (smaller) government projects – the 'restricted European tender procedure' designed with the aim of selecting young designers. After his term ended in 2000, the method was discontinued, partly due to resistance from the legal experts at the Rijksgebouwendienst.

ontwerper krijg je veel eerder een rol in het proces en daarmee invloed op de condities.'

Kansen voor experiment en jong talent

'Het inzetten van het ontwerp in de voorfase biedt ook kansen voor experimenten, en experimenten helpen om anders te denken over opgaven.' Het is volgens Veenstra noodzakelijk de 'vijver van architecten die de aanbestedingen winnen' te vergroten. 'Niet overal is het nodig om te experimenteren, maar er zijn genoeg mogelijkheden waar beginnende ontwerpers en kleinere bureaus een kans zouden moeten krijgen om een publiek gebouw te realiseren.' Hij ziet hier ook een verantwoordelijkheid voor de grotere bureaus. Deze zouden jonge architecten moeten betrekken, 'een lift moeten bieden'. Hier heeft volgens Veenstra ook de Rijksbouwmeester een taak. Dit is ook de reden dat hij in 2023 is gestart met het organiseren van discussies over aanbesteden.

Onlangs werd gedebatteerd over de Open Oproep, het instrument dat in 2000, vlak na de aanstelling van de eerste Vlaams Bouwmeester, is ingevoerd om de architectuurcultuur te versterken.[8] De Vlaams Bouwmeester, die een groot deel van zijn organisatie hierop heeft ingericht, biedt begeleiding aan voornamelijk publieke opdrachtgevers en stelt ze in de gelegenheid in gesprek te gaan met ontwerpers. Een van de weinige criteria is het kunnen aanleveren van drie referentieprojecten die onder eigen naam zijn ontworpen. De resultaten worden openbaar bekend gemaakt, zodat er ook van geleerd kan worden. Rijksbouwmeester Veenstra introduceerde onlangs in Nederland een vergelijkbare methode voor onderhandse aanbestedingen: de Architectenindex, een procedure om te onderzoeken welke ontwerpers geïnteresseerd zijn en in aanmerking komen voor opdrachten van het RVB.

Sinds de start van het nieuwe Kabinet in juli 2024 is na ruim tien jaar weer een coördinerend minister benoemd, die de regie krijgt over de ruimtelijke ordening, de volkshuisvesting, het Rijksvastgoedbedrijf en de ruimtelijke kwaliteit, benoemd. Fundamentele vraag is hoe het beleid zich de komende jaren gaat ontwikkelen. De rol van de Rijksbouwmeester is al ruim twee eeuwen redelijk standvastig, ondanks diverse politieke wisselingen en opvattingen. Inmiddels passeerden al veel Rijksbouwmeesters de revue. Kwaliteitsborging staat telkens hoog in het vaandel, al verschilt hun aanpak, de keuze van instrumenten en de wijze waarop ze de opgaven tegemoet treden. Hierbij speelt het stimuleren van goed opdrachtgeverschap en de versterking van het nut van ontwerp een prominente rol, of zoals Veenstra het benoemt: 'ontwerpend handelen en denken'.

8 Deze oproep is vergelijkbaar met de procedure die Rijksbouwmeester Wytze Patijn ooit gebruikte voor architectenselecties bij (kleinere) overheidsopdrachten – de 'niet openbare Europese aanbestedingsprocedure', met het idee om jonge ontwerpers te selecteren. Na zijn aftreden in 2000 wordt de methode afgeschaft, onder andere door weerstand bij de juristen van de Rijksgebouwendienst.

We Need to Talk about Quality: The Urban Workshop in Ostend and the Zilverlaan

Stefan Devoldere

In the southern outskirts of the Belgian seaside city of Ostend lies the historical village of Stene. The village, probably dating from the time of Charlemagne, developed around a fortified castle built to protect the coastal inhabitants from Viking invasions. Over time, it merged with the twentieth-century suburban developments encircling the heart of Ostend, marking the boundary between the city and the surrounding polders. While the protected village landscape is now dominated by hospitality businesses, Ostend is working on a short supply chain initiative involving local food production and innovative water management in its backyard. Agricultural park De Tuinen van Stene is part of the elongated green area known as the Groen Lint that connects various green spaces around the city like pearls on a string. Along the 37-km-long route, wooden platforms, resting places, waterfronts and avenues punctuate the landscape, all linked by cycling paths.

De Tuinen van Stene, a highlight along the cycling route, is proving to be a successful link in realising the ambitions of the Groen Lint as a new urban framework. The park not only provides a strong identity to the undefined city fringe, but also brings a range of experiences and meanings to the otherwise generic suburban residential landscape. Recently, the residential fabric around De Tuinen has also begun to transform, driven by Urban Workshop Ostend, an expert group that supports the city's ambition to develop innovative housing projects for young families.[1] Several of the housing projects supervised by Urban Workshop Ostend are rethinking the traditional suburbanisation model and the associated real estate logic, while establishing a network of slow traffic routes and shared green spaces throughout the residential district.

Housing Quality as a Joint Project

The first housing project in line is located at the intersection of the Groen Lint and a major access road to the village of Stene, Zilverlaan. Three adjacent plots are the property of a nonprofit care organisation (Duinhelm), a social housing company (WoonWel) and a private developer (Condor Red). Together, they form a green residential environment that deliberately blurs the boundaries between private plots and the collective landscape, between public and private space, between individual and communal housing preferences, and between a traditional profit model and the value generated by communal added value. A shared development vision transcends both plot boundaries and the traditional division in housing sectors, creating benefits for both residents and the neighbourhood. By sharing space, everyone gains more than what would be possible within the confines of their individual plot.

At the heart of the housing project on Zilverlaan lies a 60-m-wide and 140-m-deep landscaped area: a publicly accessible park, half of it on private land and the other half on land owned by a housing association. On the private side of the green space, 32 apartments and 37 terraced houses are arranged around an enclosed communal outdoor area. All

1 For a detailed description of the operation of the Urban Workshop Ostend, on which this article is partly based, see: Stefan Devoldere, 'Constructing a Common Vision: The Stadsatelier Oostende as a Proactive Tool for Quality in Urban Development', in: Aglaée Degros et al. (eds.), *Territorial Urbanism Now! Call for a Social and Ecological Urban Planning and Design* (Berlin: Jovis Verlag, 2024), 175-188.

We moeten het over kwaliteit hebben: Het Stadsatelier in Oostende en de Zilverlaan

Stefan Devoldere

In de zuidelijke periferie van de Belgische badplaats Oostende ligt de historische dorpskern van Stene. Het dorp ontstond – wellicht onder Karel de Grote – rondom een versterkte burcht die de kustbewoners moest beschermen tegen de invasie van de Noormannen. Intussen is het vergroeid met de twintigste-eeuwse verkavelingswijken die het centrum van Oostende omgorden, en markeert het de grens tussen de stad en de omliggende polders. Het beschermde dorpsgezicht wordt vandaag ingepalmd door horecazaken, maar in de achtertuin werkt de stad aan een korte keten van lokale voedselproductie en innovatief waterbeheer. Het landbouwpark De Tuinen van Stene is onderdeel van een langgerekt Groen Lint dat als een kralensnoer de verschillende groengebieden rondom de stad met elkaar verbindt. Langs het 37 km lange traject leggen houten platformen, rustplekken, waterboorden en dreven accenten in het landschap, onderling verbonden met fietspaden.

De Tuinen van Stene functioneert als een verbijzondering van het fietstraject en blijkt een succesvolle schakel in de ambities van het Groen Lint als nieuwe stedelijke drager. Het park geeft niet alleen een sterke identiteit aan de onbenoemde stadsrand, het zorgt ook voor beleving en betekenis in het generiek verkavelde woonlandschap. Dat woonweefsel is intussen ook rondom de Tuinen bezig te transformeren, aangevuurd door Stadsatelier Oostende, een groep experts die de stad ondersteunt in haar ambitie om innovatieve woningprojecten te ontwikkelen voor jonge gezinnen.[1] Verschillende van die projecten die door het Stadsatelier worden begeleid, sleutelen aan het traditionele verkavelingsmodel en de bijhorende vastgoedlogica, en bouwen door de wijk heen een netwerk uit van langzaam verkeer en collectief groen.

Woonkwaliteit als gedeeld project

Het eerste woonproject dat aan de beurt was, ligt aan de kruising van het Groen Lint en een belangrijke toegangsweg naar Stene Dorp, de Zilverlaan. Drie naast elkaar gelegen percelen zijn in handen van een vereniging zonder winstoogmerk (vzw) uit de zorgsector (Duinhelm), een sociale woningbouwvereniging (WoonWel) en een private ontwikkelaar (Condor Red). Deze percelen vormen samen een groene woonomgeving die bewust met de grenzen speelt tussen de eigen kavel en het collectieve landschap, tussen publieke en private ruimte, tussen individuele en gemeenschappelijke woonwensen, tussen een traditioneel verdienmodel en het rendement van collectieve meerwaarde. Een gezamenlijke ontwikkelingsvisie overschrijdt zowel de perceelsgrenzen als de klassieke opdeling in huisvestingssectoren, en levert zo winst op voor de bewoners én de buurt. Door ruimte te delen, krijgt iedereen meer dan wat binnen de grenzen van het eigen perceel mogelijk is.

Centraal in het terrein van de Zilverlaan ligt een landschapskamer van 60 m breed en 140 m diep: een publiek toegankelijk park waarvan de ene helft op private grond ligt en de andere helft op grond van de

1 Voor een uitgebreide beschrijving van de werking van het Stadsatelier Oostende, waarop dit artikel deels is gebaseerd, zie: Stefan Devoldere, 'Constructing a Common Vision: The Stadsatelier Oostende as a Proactive Tool for Quality in Urban Development', in: Aglaée Degros et al. (red.), *Territorial Urbanism Now! Call for a Social and Ecological Urban Planning and Design* (Berlijn: Jovis Verlag, 2024), 175-188.

front doors, the lifts of two apartment blocks, the bicycle storages and a multipurpose space with a kitchen open onto this car-free courtyard. On the other side, a residential area will be built with 57 social housing units, 11 of which will be sold without land ownership (using the Community Land Trust model). Behind this area, nonprofit care organisation Duinhelm is constructing two curved residential buildings, each designed for two groups

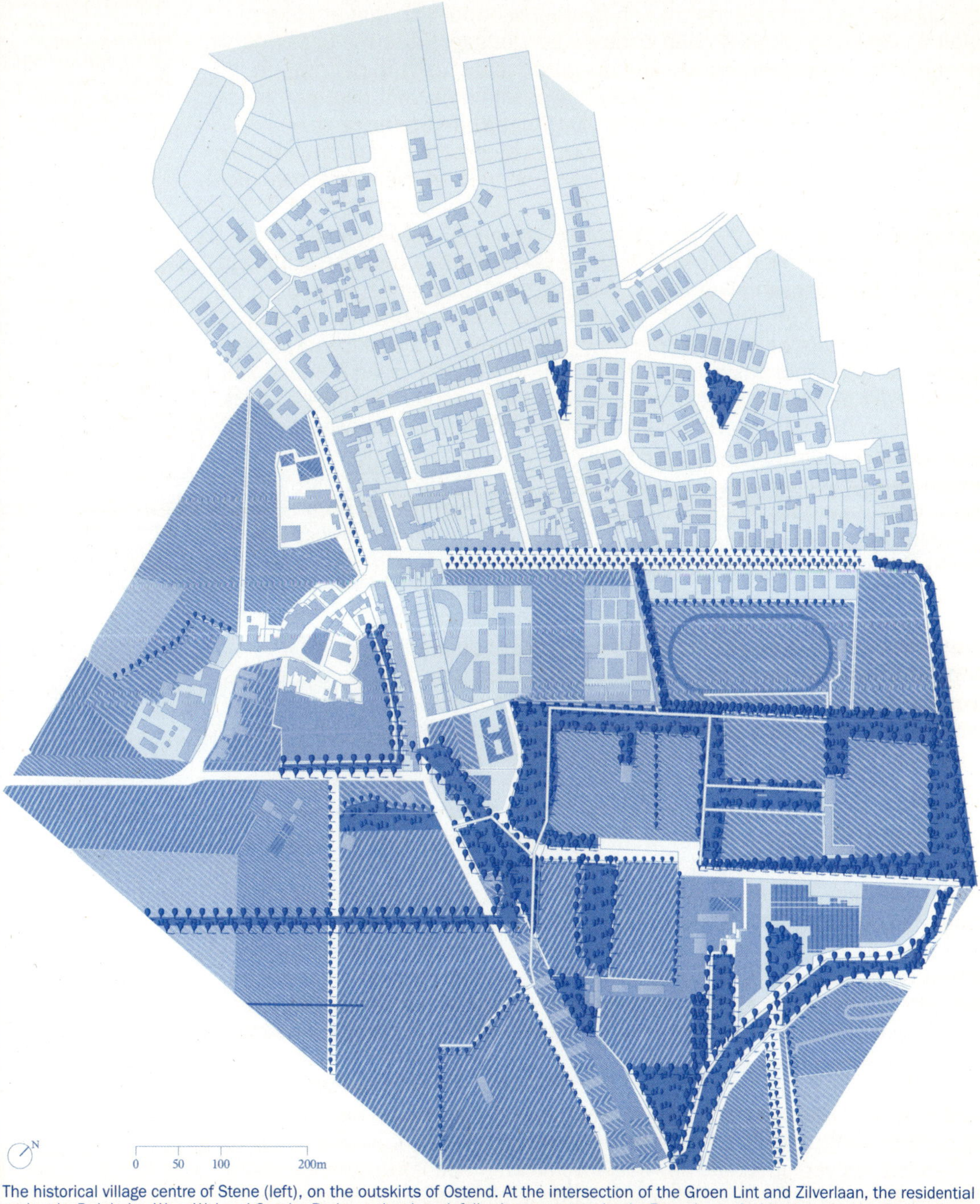

The historical village centre of Stene (left), on the outskirts of Ostend. At the intersection of the Groen Lint and Zilverlaan, the residential project by Duinhelm, WoonWel and Condor Red was developed, following a master plan by Bovenbouw Architectuur and landscape firm CLUSTER/ De historische dorpskern van Stene (links) aan de rand van Oostende. Op de kruising van het Groen Lint en de Zilverlaan kwam het woonproject van Duinhelm, WoonWel en Condor Red tot stand, volgens een masterplan van Bovenbouw Architectuur en landschapsbureau CLUSTER

corporatie. Aan de private zijde van het groen zijn 32 appartementen en 37 grondgebonden rijtjeshuizen rond een omsloten, collectieve buitenruimte geschikt. Alle voordeuren, de liften van twee appartementenblokjes, de fietsbergingen en een activiteitenruimte met keuken komen uit op dit autovrije binnenplein. Aan de andere kant komt een woonerf met 57 sociale woningen, waarvan 11 zullen worden verkocht met de grond in erfpacht. Daarachter bouwt de vzw Duinhelm twee gekrulde woonvolumes voor telkens twee leefgroepen van tien bewoners met een verstandelijke beperking. Elk volume schermt een gemeenschappelijke tuin af die aansluit op de woonruimte via een patio en een langgerekt terras onder de schuin aflopende dakrand. De kamers zitten in de nok van het dak en kijken uit over de omgeving. Tussen de twee volumes door leidt een fiets- en wandelpad naar het Groen Lint en De Tuinen van Stene.

Parallel aan de Zilverlaan komt een brede dreef die als een gezamenlijke vestibule toegang geeft tot de drie woonprojecten. Hier komen collectieve voorzieningen, maar ook het parkeren wordt er opgevangen. Eén garagepoort leidt naar een parkeergarage die onder de private woonontwikkeling is geschoven. Elk van de drie grondeigenaars heeft zo zijn eigen bouwplannen ingeschreven in een groter geheel. De compacte voetafdruk zorgt ervoor dat één derde van elk perceel onbebouwd blijft en gereserveerd is voor een 'polderpark' dat de woningen een fantastisch uitzicht garandeert en mooi past in het landschap van Groen Lint en polders. Het park maakt de verbinding tussen de woonwijk en de achtergelegen sportterreinen, maar zorgt ook voor de waterbuffering van de nieuwe woningen. Het park zal onderhouden worden door de stad, maar de grond blijft eigendom van de bewoners. Elke toekomstige aanpassing van het polderpark wordt daardoor uitgesloten, zonder het akkoord van de buren. Een gezamenlijke visie levert een bijzondere kwaliteit op voor de individuele bewoner en een park van 1,5 ha groot voor de buurt.

Stadsatelier als gespreksruimte

Het project in de Zilverlaan telt vele kwaliteiten: de landschappelijke inplanting van de woningen, de link met sport en recreatie, de vlotte fietsverbinding naar de stad, de meerwaarde van collectieve voorzieningen, de mix van private en gedeelde buitenruimte, de uitzonderlijke architecturale uitwerking, enzovoort. Dat is in de eerste plaats een verdienste van het Stadsatelier Oostende dat de ontwikkeling vanaf het begin intensief begeleidt. De kwaliteitskamer functioneert daarbij niet louter als een adviesraad, maar vooral als een plek waar wederzijds vertrouwen kan worden opgebouwd. Een 'veilige plek' voor open gesprekken waar coalities worden gesmeed, eigen agenda's kunnen worden uitgesproken en vervolgens bijgesteld ten voordele van een grotere, gedeelde ambitie. Het Stadsatelier overstijgt daarbij de rol van de traditionele kwaliteitskamer of welstandscommissie, door een specifieke positie ten opzichte van ambtenarij en bestuur (onafhankelijk, maar ook ingebed) en met een effect dat het resultaat is van visievormend ontwerpend onderzoek tot en met de uitwerking en begeleiding van selectieprocedures en bouwprojecten.[2]

Vanaf de oprichting in 2015 beslaat het werkterrein van het Stadsatelier twee complementaire niveaus: het maken van een strategische ontwikkelingsvisie voor de stad op de lange termijn, en het opstarten en aansturen van concrete voorbeeldprojecten op de korte termijn.[3] Het Stadsatelier opereert dus op verschillende snelheden, maar tracht een voortdurende terugkoppeling te voorzien tussen die snelheden. Het bestaat

2 Een heldere analyse van het Stadsatelier Oostende, vergeleken met de welstandscommissie en kwaliteitskamers van Antwerpen, Gent en Mechelen, is te vinden in: Stéphanie De Somer, 'De rol van kwaliteitskamers in het recht van de ruimtelijke ordening: over smaken en kleuren moet je soms kunnen twisten', *Tijdschrift voor ruimtelijke ordening, omgeving en stedenbouw* 92 (2018), 279-306.

3 Het Stadsatelier Oostende werd op 28 augustus 2015 door de gemeenteraad opgericht naar aanleiding van het hernieuwde Woonplan van de stad, met de ambitie om innovatieve woonprojecten voor jonge gezinnen te helpen realiseren. De verantwoordelijke schepen en de burgemeester behoorden tot de twee belangrijkste politieke partijen binnen de coalitie, wat het Stadsatelier vanaf de start een potentieel sterk politiek mandaat gaf, dat evenwel in de eerste jaren nog moest worden hard gemaakt.

of ten residents with intellectual disabilities. Each building embraces a communal garden connected to the living space via a patio and an elongated terrace beneath the sloping roofline. The rooms are located in the attic and offer views of the surroundings. The cycling and walking path running between the two buildings connects to the Groen Lint and De Tuinen van Stene.

Parallel to Zilverlaan, a wide avenue will serve as a common forecourt providing access to the three housing projects. This space will accommodate communal facilities and parking needs. A single garage entrance will lead to an underground parking garage beneath the private development. Each of the three landowners has integrated their individual development plans into the ensemble. The compact footprint of the development ensures that one third of each plot remains undeveloped, reserved for a 'polder park' that offers stunning views from the dwellings and connects seamlessly with the Groen Lint and the surrounding polders. The park will not only link the residential district with the nearby sports fields, but also provide a water buffer for the new dwellings. While the park is maintained by the city, ownership of the land will remain with the residents, ensuring that any future changes to the polder park will require their collective approval. This shared vision provides an exceptional housing quality for individual residents while creating a 1.5-ha park for the wider neighbourhood.

The Urban Workshop as a Room for Dialogue

The Zilverlaan project has many qualities: the embedding of the dwellings into the landscape, the connection to sport and recreation facilities, the seamless cycling connection to the city, the added value of the communal facilities, the mix of private and communal outdoor spaces, and the exceptional architectural design. This success is largely due to the Urban Workshop Ostend, which has been closely involved in its development from the outset. The quality panel functions not only as an advisory body, but especially as a place where mutual trust can develop – a safe space for open discussion, where coalitions are formed and individual agendas are expressed and then adjusted to fit a broader, shared ambition. The Urban Workshop goes beyond the traditional role of quality panels or building standards committees by maintaining a unique position relative to city administration and governance – independent yet embedded. Its scope ranges from vision-forming research by design, to the development and monitoring of selection processes and construction projects.[2]

Since its inception in 2015, the Urban Workshop has operated on two complementary levels, developing a long-term strategic vision for the city's development and initiating and managing concrete pilot projects in the short term.[3] The Urban Workshop operates at different speeds, but seeking to ensure continuous feedback between these speeds is a key part of its approach. This is why it is made up of both independent experts and members of the local administration, combining an external perspective and expertise with local knowledge and insight.[4] The long-term vision takes shape through stakeholder workshops, external sub-studies and inhouse research by design. At the same time, housing projects are set up and realised that translate this vision into specific contexts and bring it to life, as in the case of Zilverlaan.

The aim of Urban Workshop Ostend is not only to combine the traditional quality control of building projects with vision forming, but also to assess the implementation of these visions on the ground. This is done

2
A clear analysis of the Urban Workshop Ostend, compared with the building standards committees and quality panels of Antwerp, Ghent and Mechelen, can be found in: Stéphanie De Somer, 'De rol van kwaliteitskamers in het recht van de ruimtelijke ordening: over smaken en kleuren moet je soms kunnen twisten', *Tijdschrift voor ruimtelijke ordening, omgeving en stedenbouw* 92 (2018), 279-306.

3
The Urban Workshop Ostend was established by the city council on 28 August 2015 in response to the city's renewed Housing Plan, with the ambition to help realise innovative housing projects for young families. The responsible councillor and the mayor were members of the two main political parties in the coalition, which gave the Urban Workshop a potentially strong political mandate from the start, but one that had yet to be substantiated in the first years of operation.

4
The composition of the Urban Workshop has varied over the years, but it usually consists of about six external architects or urban designers from professional practice or academia, including the chair, supplemented by a lawyer, the project director of the Autonoom Gemeentebedrijf Stadsvernieuwing Oostende (Autonomous Municipal Company for Urban Renewal Ostend) and Ostend's municipal environmental officer.

daarom uit zowel onafhankelijke experts als leden van de lokale administratie, en combineert dus een externe blik en expertise met lokale knowhow en terreinkennis.[4] De langetermijnvisie krijgt vorm in ateliersessies met stakeholders, extern uitgevoerde deelstudies en eigen ontwerpend onderzoek. Op hetzelfde moment worden woonprojecten opgetuigd en gerealiseerd die die visie naar een specifieke context vertalen en in de praktijk brengen, zoals bijvoorbeeld in de Zilverlaan.

Het Stadsatelier Oostende wil niet alleen de klassieke kwaliteitsbewaking van bouwprojecten koppelen aan visievorming, het wil ook

4 Het Stadsatelier kent een wisselende bezetting door de jaren heen, maar bestaat doorgaans uit zes externe architecten of stedenbouwkundigen uit de beroepspraktijk of het academische veld, onder wie de voorzitter, aangevuld met een jurist en de projectdirecteur van het Autonoom Gemeentebedrijf Stadsvernieuwing Oostende en de gemeentelijke mgevingsambtenaar.

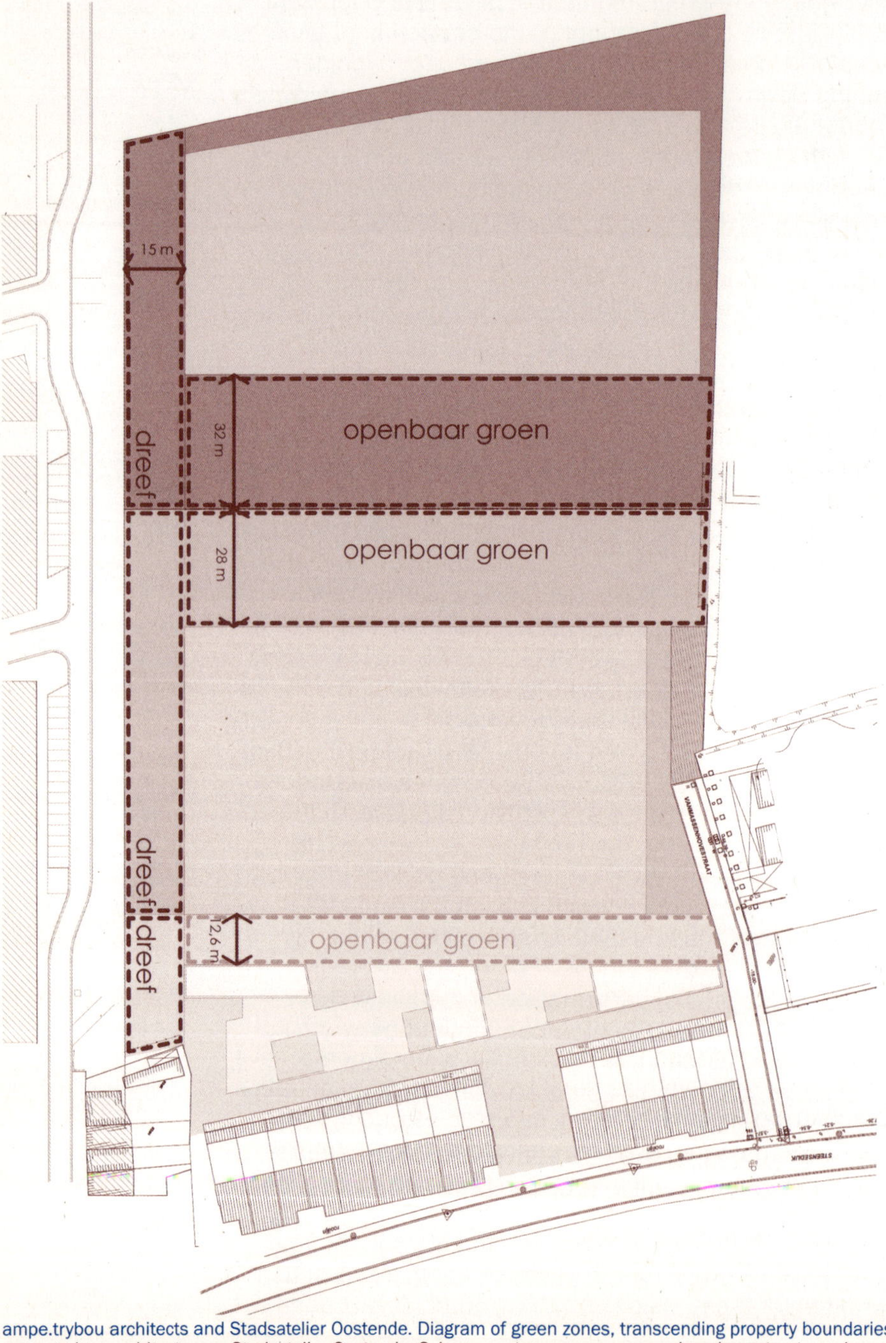

ampe.trybou architects and Stadsatelier Oostende. Diagram of green zones, transcending property boundaries/
ampe.trybou architecten en Stadsatelier Oostende. Schema met groenzones, over eigendomsstructuren heen

not only by monitoring projects, but also by actively initiating and framing them, by bringing together the necessary actors and by searching for flexible tools for urban development. As chair of the Urban Workshop until the end of 2020, I have contributed to this quest for methodological innovation. The Zilverlaan project was the first exemplary case in this search. Several vision documents were produced during the preparation stage and throughout the process. Procedures were introduced and memoranda of understanding were drawn up. In this article, I will look at the mechanisms and tools that were used to bring the project – and the quality it embodies – to life. Which tools were used at which stages, what guarantees for quality did they ultimately provide and how did they influence each other along the way?

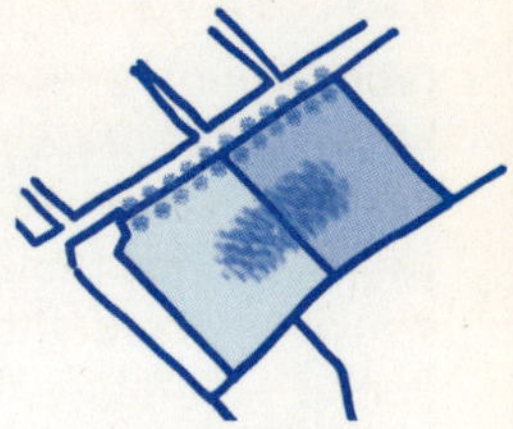

Stadsatelier Oostende. Sketch of the design framework for the Zilverlaan residential project/ Stadsatelier Oostende. Schets ontwerpkader voor woonproject Zilverlaan

Faites vos jeux

When the Autonoom Gemeentebedrijf Grond- en Bouwbeleid (Autonomous Municipal Department for Land and Building Policy, AGGB) of the city of Ostend puts a plot of land on Zilverlaan up for sale in the summer of 2016, 6,000 m^2 of available land has already been sold to Duinhelm, a nonprofit organisation that provides supported living for people with intellectual disabilities. Duinhelm had been looking for land for a new sheltered housing project for some time and when the *kerkfabriek* (the public institution that manages the material resources of the local church community) put a plot of land up for sale, the mayor of Ostend sees an opportunity to combine this need with the ambitions of the newly established Urban Workshop. The remaining 1.5 ha are put on the market at a fixed price (the purchase price plus administrative costs), but with a clear demand for high quality. This must be ensured, not only via the assessment of the application for planning permission, but also by skilfully managing the development process itself.

Private developers are invited to make an offer with a high-quality design proposal, taking into account a guiding design framework established by the Urban Workshop. This design framework links the plot to the neighbouring plots of Duinhelm and housing association WoonWel, both of which share the ambition of creating a cohesive residential neighbourhood. The call is for a cross-plot vision for a shared landscape including a parking avenue along Zilverlaan serving as the entrance to the three housing projects, a significant green space on the site itself, and a public passage to the adjacent sports park. In addition, the project must focus on the communal use of infrastructure and space: underground parking (that is, not directly in front of the houses), compact and clustered living, communal service spaces and utility systems, and usable shared green spaces for the residents.

Six developers attend the official presentation of the design framework on 19 August 2016. By the end of September, three of them accept the invitation to an interim consultation with the Urban Workshop to discuss potential designing trajectories. Two proposals are finally submitted and presented to a jury on 10 November 2016. The jury, made up of members of the Urban Workshop and representatives from WoonWel, Duinhelm and the city's Autonoom Gemeentebedrijf (Autonomous Municipal Department), unanimously decide to award the site to developer Condor. Its design, drawn up by Bovenbouw Architectuur and landscape architects Cluster, proposes a compact development around a communal

bemiddelen bij de uitvoering van die visie op het terrein. Niet louter door projecten op te volgen, maar ook door ze actief op te starten en te omkaderen, en er de nodige actoren voor samen te brengen, op zoek naar een flexibel instrumentarium om aan stadsontwikkeling te doen. Als voorzitter van het Stadsatelier tot eind 2020 zette ik mede de schouders onder dat streven naar methodische vernieuwing. Het traject in de Zilverlaan was een eerste exemplarische casus in die zoektocht. Meerdere visiedocumenten werden in de voorbereiding, maar ook in de loop van het traject gemaakt. Procedures werden uitgerold en afsprakennota's opgesteld. In deze tekst wil ik ingaan op de mechanismen en middelen om het project, en de kwaliteit die het belichaamt, waar te kunnen maken. Welke instrumenten zijn op welk moment gebruikt, welke garanties hebben ze uiteindelijk geboden op kwaliteit, en hoe hebben ze elkaar *en cours de route* beïnvloed?

Faites vos jeux

Als het Autonoom Gemeentebedrijf Grond- en Bouwbeleid (AGGB) van de stad Oostende in de zomer van 2016 een perceel in de Zilverlaan te koop aanbiedt, is 6.000 m² van de beschikbare grond al doorverkocht aan Duinhelm, een vzw die begeleid wonen aanbiedt voor mensen met een mentale beperking. Duinhelm is al een tijdje op zoek naar grond voor een nieuw zorg-woonproject, en als een terrein van de kerkfabriek (de openbare instelling die de materiële middelen van de lokale kerkgemeenschap beheert) te koop staat, ziet de burgemeester van Oostende zijn kans om die wens te koppelen aan de ambities van het zopas opgerichte Stadsatelier. De resterende 1,5 ha wordt in de markt gezet tegen een vaste prijs (het aankoopbedrag plus administratieve kosten), maar met een uitgesproken ambitie voor kwaliteit. Die moet worden waargemaakt, door niet enkel bij de vergunningsaanvraag te bemiddelen, maar ook het ontwikkelingsproces zelf slim aan te sturen.

Private ontwikkelaars wordt gevraagd een bod te doen met een hoogwaardig ontwerpvoorstel dat rekening houdt met een richtinggevend ontwerpkader dat door het Stadsatelier is opgesteld. Dat ontwerpkader maakt de koppeling met de buurpercelen van Duinhelm en de sociale corporatie WoonWel, die allebei meestappen in de ambitie om samen één woonbuurt te maken. Er wordt een perceel-overschrijdende visie gevraagd voor een gedeeld landschap, met een parkeerdreef langs de Zilverlaan die toegang biedt tot de drie woonprojecten, een belangrijke groenzone op het terrein zelf en een publieke doorsteek naar het achtergelegen sportpark. Daarnaast moet het project inzetten op het collectief gebruik van infrastructuur en ruimte: parkeren ondergronds en dus niet voor de deur, compact en geclusterd wonen, gemeenschappelijke dienstruimten en nutssystemen, en bruikbaar gedeeld groen voor de bewoners.

Zes ontwikkelaars zijn op 19 augustus 2016 aanwezig bij de officiële presentatie van het ontwerpkader. Drie daarvan gaan eind september in op de uitnodiging voor een tussentijds overleg met het Stadsatelier over hun inzendingen voor het ontwerp. Twee daarvan worden uiteindelijk ingediend en gepresenteerd op 10 november 2016 aan een jury. De jury is samengesteld uit leden van het Stadsatelier en vertegenwoordigers van WoonWel, Duinhelm en het Autonoom Gemeentebedrijf van de stad. Ze beslist unaniem om de grond toe te wijzen aan ontwikkelaar Condor, met als ontwerpers Bovenbouw Architectuur en landschapsbureau Cluster. De inzending adviseert om compact rondom een collectieve hof te bouwen

courtyard garden, with a third of the total area reserved for publicly accessible green space.

Split Costs and Shared Benefits

WoonWel and Duinhelm decide to adopt the landscape vision of the private developer, which they have jointly selected. Duinhelm exchanges the land it has bought for part of the land owned by WoonWel, so that the sheltered accommodation can move to the far corner of the site and the space needed for the centrally located, undeveloped polder park becomes available. A diagram of the redefined plots is attached to the collaboration agreement that formalises the ambitions for the joint master plan and sets out agreements for the further monitoring of the construction projects.[5] The agreement stipulates that the three partners will uniformly develop the area along Zilverlaan as a parking avenue and that each partner will make 28 per cent of their land available for a public park running across the different plots. They ask Cluster to develop an overarching landscape design.

As far as possible, the work and studies required to prepare the construction projects are combined and carried out for the entire area of the three plots. The associated costs are shared according to the percentage of the total area that each plot represents. The partners agree that Duinhelm will select a designer through an Open Call by the Flemish Government Architect, under the supervision of the chairman of the Urban Workshop.[6] In order to monitor and coordinate the further development of the projects – each of which has very specific conditions in terms of allocation and funding – a timetable is drawn up that includes feedback sessions with the Urban Workshop. In addition, the chair meets regularly with the partners and various city departments. What begins as a joint commitment to create an innovative housing project continues to be supervised and monitored through the work of the Urban Workshop, ensuring that all partners continue to meet regularly and that any obstacles are addressed together.

The first major obstacle is quickly revealed to lie beneath the surface. Preliminary archaeological research shows that archaeological finds can be expected on each of the three plots. Especially on the exchanged Duinhelm plot – which borders on the historical village of Stene – excavations for a medieval dwelling are likely to cause considerable additional costs. Shared ambitions and interpersonal relationships are immediately put under pressure and the Urban Workshop, in consultation with the Flanders Heritage Agency, diligently seeks creative solutions to cover the unexpected costs. In the end, the mayor, through the Autonoom Gemeentebedrijf, allocates additional funds to cover the extra archaeological costs Duinhelm faces. The project is back on track and in 2019 both Duinhelm and Condor submit their applications for planning permission for their plots. In 2021, Duinhelm starts construction and by the end of 2023, the first 20 residents are welcomed into their new dwellings. After a procedural dispute with a lady living in an adjacent villa, Condor begins construction on the first stage of 32 apartments and 20 houses in the autumn of 2022. WoonWel receives planning permission in 2022 and, following a major merger with regional housing association Woonsprong, resumes construction in 2024.

5
The collaboration agreement was ceremonially signed by the partners on 31 March 2017 in the meeting rooms of the Urban Workshop Ostend.

6
On 28 March 2018, Raamwerk was selected as the designer for the Duinhelm residential project. A detailed analysis of the Flemish Government Architect's selection process can be found in: Maarten Liefooghe and Maarten Van Den Driessche (eds.), *Meer dan een wedstrijd: De Open Oproep in een veranderende bouwcultuur* (Antwerp/Brussels: Vlaams Architectuurinstituut, Team Vlaams Bouwmeester, 2021).

en een derde van het volledige terrein te reserveren voor publiek toegankelijk groen.

Gedeelde kosten en baten

WoonWel en Duinhelm beslissen om de landschapsvisie van de private ontwikkelaar (die ze mede hebben gekozen) over te nemen. Duinhelm wisselt zijn aangekochte perceel met een deel van de grond van WoonWel, waardoor de zorgwoningen naar de uiterste hoek van het terrein verhuizen en de nodige ruimte vrijkomt voor het centraal gelegen, onbebouwd te laten polderpark. Een schema met de opnieuw ingetekende percelen wordt toegevoegd aan een samenwerkingsovereenkomst waarin de ambities voor het gezamenlijk masterplan worden vastgelegd en afspraken gemaakt voor de verdere opvolging van de bouwprojecten.[5] In de overeenkomst staat dat de zone aan de Zilverlaan door de drie partners uniform zal worden ingericht als parkeerdreef en dat elke partner 28 procent van het eigen terrein ter beschikking stelt voor een publiek park dat over de verschillende eigendommen heen loopt. Aan Cluster wordt gevraagd om hiervoor een overkoepelend landschapsontwerp uit te werken.

Het werk en onderzoek dat nodig is om de bouwprojecten voor te bereiden, wordt zoveel mogelijk gekoppeld en uitgevoerd voor het totaal van de drie percelen. De hieraan verbonden kosten worden verdeeld volgens het percentage dat elk perceel vertegenwoordigt in het geheel. Er wordt afgesproken dat Duinhelm een ontwerper zoekt via de Open Oproep van de Vlaams Bouwmeester, onder begeleiding van de voorzitter van het Stadsatelier.[6] Om de verdere uitwerking van de projecten – elk met zeer specifieke randvoorwaarden naar toewijzing en financiering – op te volgen en op elkaar af te stemmen, wordt een kalender opgesteld met terugkoppelmomenten met het Stadsatelier. Daarnaast vergadert de voorzitter geregeld mee met de partners en de verschillende stadsdiensten. Wat begon als een gezamenlijk engagement rond een innovatief woonproject, wordt verder begeleid en bewaakt binnen het Stadsatelier, zodat alle partners elkaar op regelmatige basis blijven ontmoeten en eventuele obstakels samen worden aangepakt.

Een eerste, stevige hindernis blijkt al snel verscholen te zitten in de ondergrond. Archeologisch vooronderzoek toont aan dat op elk van de drie percelen archeologische vondsten te verwachten zijn. Vooral op het omgeruilde perceel van Duinhelm, dat tegen de historische dorpskern van Stene ligt, zullen opgravingen naar een middeleeuws huis voor een aanzienlijke meerprijs zorgen. Gedeelde ambities en interpersoonlijke relaties komen meteen onder druk te staan, en het Stadsatelier zoekt in overleg met de dienst Onroerend Erfgoed van de Vlaamse Overheid, ijverig naar creatieve oplossingen voor de onverwachte kosten. Uiteindelijk maakt de burgemeester via het autonoom gemeentebedrijf budget vrij om de extra kosten van het archeologisch onderzoek voor Duinhelm op te vangen. Het project staat terug op de rails en in 2019 dient zowel Duinhelm als Condor een bouwaanvraag in voor zijn perceel. Duinhelm start in 2021 met de bouw en eind 2023 worden de eerste 20 bewoners ontvangen in hun nieuwe thuis. Na een procedureslag met de buurvrouw van de naastgelegen villa begint Condor in het najaar van 2022 te bouwen aan een eerste fase met 32 appartementen en 20 woningen. WoonWel krijgt in 2022 een bouwvergunning en pakt in 2024, na een ingrijpende fusie met de regionale corporatie Woonsprong, de draad weer op.

5 De samenwerkingsovereenkomst wordt plechtig ondertekend door de partners op 31 maart 2017 in de vergaderlokalen van het Stadsatelier Oostende.

6 Op 28 maart 2018 wordt Raamwerk geselecteerd als ontwerper voor het woonproject van Duinhelm. Een uitgebreide analyse van de selectieprocedure van de Vlaams Bouwmeester is te vinden in: Maarten Liefooghe en Maarten Van Den Driessche (red.), *Meer dan een wedstrijd: De Open Oproep in een veranderende bouwcultuur* (Antwerpen/Brussel: Vlaams Architectuurinstituut en Team Vlaams Bouwmeester, 2021).

Drawing (on) the Bigger Picture

The Zilverlaan approach sets the tone for several housing projects that are developed in the area in collaboration with the Urban Workshop. Other plots are put up for sale, with the invitation to submit not only a financial bid, but also a high-quality design proposal that focuses on communal added value. For each project, the Urban Workshop establishes a reference framework, provides interim feedback, assesses the quality of the final proposal submitted and, once the land has been allocated, continues to guide the buyer through the process of applying for planning permission. In some cases the design framework simply calls for a public cycling path and clustered parking along the road, while in others the Urban Workshop drafts a full development scenario, weighing factors such as how much residential development is required to generate the necessary return to create a high-quality neighbourhood park, thus determining what hard conditions can be attached to the sale.

The focus of the Urban Workshop shifts to a long-term vision that anticipates future developments and places ongoing projects in a broader context, aiming at new forms of collective housing, shared green spaces and sustainable mobility. The ambitions tested in the design framework for Zilverlaan thus form the blueprint for a strategy at the district level. Through research by design, the Urban Workshop develops three trajectories for the gradual transformation of Stene. The development of a network of cycling paths removes the district from its isolation and provides a smooth connection to the city centre and the Groen Lint. This network for slow traffic becomes the basis for a sustainable and car-free public space that makes the homogeneous residential fabric more legible and enriches it with new functions and residential densification. Private housing projects are an integrated part of the vision, ensuring its gradual implementation. They provide public passageways, cycling paths and communal green spaces as a mandatory condition, contributing to the systematic upgrading of the entire neighbourhood.

The vision for Stene combines an analysis of the social and spatial challenges of the district with the quality control of individual building projects, aiming to reconcile different scales and speeds. The design of projects and processes is used both as a basis for policy and as a litmus test on the ground. In 2017, the vision forms the basis of a grant application to the Vlaams Stadsvernieuwingsfonds (Flemish Urban Renewal Fund) which yields 2 million euros for investments in the public space and the cycling infrastructure. Under the title *Stapstenen voor Stene*, a digital booklet is published, documenting analysis, vision and examples in around 30 pages. The Urban Workshop starts to prepare similar vision booklets for other urban districts. These so-called ‘cahiers’ are intended to inspire and influence policy at various levels, without carrying the weight of officially ratified policy documents. They contain maps, design sketches and diagrams in an attractive and recognisable style, but also show how the vision is translated into concrete construction projects. On 10 May 2019, booklets for Stene, Raversijde and Westerkwartier are presented to the mayor and councillors, after which they are made available for internal use. They are easy to understand and thought-provoking and can easily be taken up by politicians, spatial designers and social workers.

The Zilverlaan as one of six strategic project sites within 'Stepping Stones for Stene'. This map (by Ellen Verbiest) also appeared on the cover of the eponymous publication/ De Zilverlaan als een van zes strategische projectsites binnen 'Stapstenen voor Stene'. Deze kaart van (gemaakt door Ellen Verbiest) kwam ook op de cover van het gelijknamige cahier

Research by Design

The strength of *Stapstenen voor Stene* lies in the visualisation and naming of spatial quality through the project, both at the district level and at the plot scale. The design frameworks established by the Urban Workshop provide an initial translation of a district-wide vision around sustainable mobility and communal housing into a high-quality and feasible project, taking into account the qualities of the site, what is spatially achievable and financially feasible, and the constellation of partners that need to be brought together. The booklets and design frameworks aim to clarify what is difficult to describe or measure. They provide the vocabulary for conversations that are to lead to strong design proposals. They are the starting point of a trajectory inspired in part by the Flemish Government Architect's Open Call, with the aim of bringing its procedural lightness and practical designer perspective to the typically legally rigorous context of Design & Build. This is not a heavy-handed procedure, but a sale under conditions, where the checklist is replaced by a good design and the time and space necessary for discussion.

But when architectural quality takes the lead, average property developers lose all sense of direction. And when this quality is not explicitly described, they lose their way altogether. When the plots in Zilverlaan were sold, most private developers struggled to understand exactly what was expected of their design proposals. The design framework provided was deliberately schematic and the overarching vision of *Stapstenen voor Stene* was developed step by step throughout the process. During the initial presentation of the project, the participants gratefully made use of another tool of the Flemish Government Architect to which the Zilverlaan project is indebted. In 2012 Flemish Government Architect Peter Swinnen launched the Pilootprojecten Collectief Wonen (Pilot Projects for Collective Housing) to bridge the gap between urgent policy challenges, research by design and the realisation of innovative projects on the ground. The Pilootprojecten Collectief Wonen encourage researchers and designers to investigate how meeting the projected need for 330,000 additional homes in Flanders can result in a better and more sustainable living environment. The research by design, carried out by Bovenbouw Architectuur in collaboration with Ghent University, starts from the observation that more housing leads to less landscape, and seeks to restore this lost landscape by using new housing projects to create green corridors and free up space in Flemish suburbs. 'By changing the rules slightly, the existing dynamic can help to create a new alliance between housing and landscape. Compact housing and communal living thus contribute to a high-quality, collective landscape.'[7]

The previous quote could have been the starting point for Zilverlaan. The design exercises in which the new rules are tested are a valuable reference for the start of the land sale. Condor, the developer that eventually won the project, was well aware of this when it asked Bovenbouw to prepare a proposal for its bid. A second project that appears in the PowerPoint presentation intended to clarify the intentions of the Urban Workshop is the Groen Lint. Designed by Tractebel and Georges Descombes, it shows how the fringes of Ostend can be revitalised by creating a link between greenery and communal value in the suburban residential area of Stene.[8] With its shared avenue and green space, the housing project in Zilverlaan can serve as a new link to the Groen Lint, located between food park De Tuinen van Stene and the sports fields of De

7
Joachim Declerck, Stefan Devoldere and Michael Ryckewaert, *Pilootprojecten Wonen: Nieuwe vormen van collectiviteit* (Brussels: Team Vlaams Bouwmeester, 2013), 31.

8
In 2010 Ostend, together with the Rother District in the south of England, carried out an Interreg Europe study on '21st Century Parks'. This project led to the concept for the Groen Lint, for which Tractebel and Georges Descombes were appointed designers in 2012 following an Open Call by the Flemish Government Architect.

Het grotere plaatje

De aanpak van de Zilverlaan zet de toon voor meerdere woonprojecten die in de buurt samen met het Stadsatelier worden ontwikkeld. Andere gronden worden te koop aangeboden met de vraag niet alleen een financieel bod te doen, maar ook een kwalitatief ontwerpvoorstel in te dienen dat inzet op collectieve meerwaarde. Het Stadsatelier stelt daarvoor telkens een referentiekader op, koppelt tussentijds terug, beoordeelt de kwaliteit van het uiteindelijk ingediende voorstel, en begeleidt na toewijzing van de grond, de koper verder richting bouwaanvraag. Het ontwerpkader beperkt zich in het ene geval tot een vraag naar een publieke fietsdoorsteek en geclusterd parkeren aan de straat, in het andere geval werkt het Stadsatelier een uitgebreid ontwikkelingsscenario uit, waarin onder meer wordt afgewogen hoeveel woonontwikkeling het nodige rendement oplevert voor een hoogwaardig buurtpark, en dus welke harde voorwaarden aan de verkoop kunnen worden verbonden.

De focus van het Stadsatelier verschuift daarbij naar een visie op lange termijn die anticipeert op toekomstige ontwikkelingen en de lopende projecten in een breder perspectief plaatst, gericht op nieuwe vormen van collectief wonen, gedeeld groen en duurzame mobiliteit. De ambities die in het ontwerpkader voor de Zilverlaan werden getest, vormen zo de blauwdruk voor een strategie op de schaal van de wijk. Via ontwerpend onderzoek binnen het Stadsatelier worden drie voorstellen uitgewerkt voor de geleidelijke transformatie van Stene. Het uitwerpen van een netwerk aan fietspaden haalt de wijk uit zijn isolement en maakt een vlotte verbinding mogelijk met het stadscentrum en het Groen Lint. Dat netwerk voor langzaam verkeer wordt de drager voor een duurzaam en autovrij publiek domein, dat het homogene woonweefsel leesbaarder maakt en wordt geïntensifieerd met nieuwe functies en een grotere dichtheid, waaronder initiatieven voor private woningbouw, die stapsgewijs worden uitgevoerd. Ze realiseren publieke doorsteken, fietspaden en collectief groen als opgelegde randvoorwaarde en bouwen zo aan een systematische opwaardering van de buurt als geheel.

De visie op Stene verbindt een analyse van de sociale en ruimtelijke uitdagingen van de wijk aan de kwaliteitsbewaking van individuele bouwprojecten, en tracht zo verschillende schaalniveaus en snelheden op elkaar af te stemmen. Zowel projecten als processen worden ingezet om het beleid te onderbouwen en als lakmoesproef op het terrein te functioneren. In 2017 wordt voor de visie een subsidie aangevraagd bij het Vlaamse Stadsvernieuwingsfonds die wordt gehonoreerd met 2 miljoen euro voor investeringen in publieke ruimte en fietspaden. Onder de titel 'Stapstenen voor Stene' wordt een digitaal boekje gemaakt, waarin analyse, visie en voorbeeldcasussen in een 30-tal pagina's zijn gedocumenteerd. Ook voor andere stadswijken begint het Stadsatelier dergelijke visiebundels samen te stellen. Deze 'cahiers' moeten het beleid op verschillende niveaus inspireren en beïnvloeden, zonder het gewicht van een officieel bekrachtigd beleidsdocument. Ze bevatten kaarten, ontwerpschetsen en diagrammen in een aantrekkelijke en herkenbare stijl, maar ze tonen ook hoe de visie vertaald kan worden in concrete bouwprojecten. Op 10 mei 2019 worden de cahiers voor Stene, Raversijde en Westerkwartier gepresenteerd aan het College van Burgemeester en Schepenen, waarna ze beschikbaar zijn voor intern gebruik. Ze zijn eenvoudig te begrijpen, stemmen tot nadenken en worden gemakkelijk ter hand genomen door zowel politicus, ruimtelijk ambtenaar als straathoekwerker.

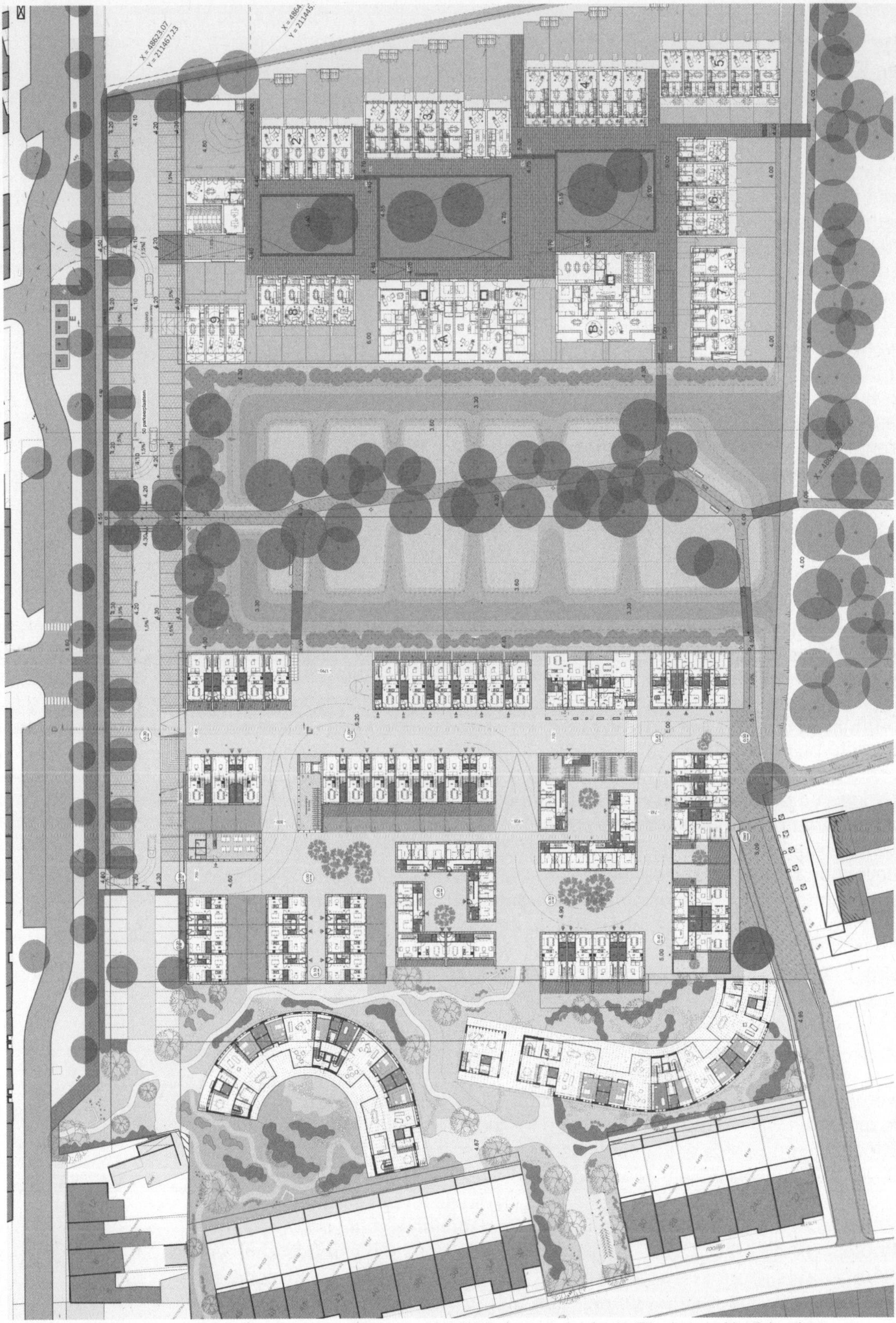

Raamwerk, ampe.trybou architects, Bovenbouw Architectuur and CLUSTER. General plan for the Zilverlaan residential project, with the landscape room at its centre/ Raamwerk, ampe.trybou architecten, Bovenbouw Architectuur en CLUSTER. Overzichtsplan voor woonproject Zilverlaan, met centraal de landschapskamer

Ontwerpend onderzoek

De kracht van het cahier 'Stapstenen voor Stene' ligt in het verbeelden en benoemen van ruimtelijke kwaliteit via het project, zowel op de schaal van de wijk als op die van de kavel. De ontwerpkaders die het Stadsatelier opstelt, maken een eerste vertaalslag van een wijkbrede visie rond duurzame mobiliteit en collectief wonen naar een hoogwaardig en uitvoerbaar project, rekening houdend met de eigenschappen van de plek, met wat ruimtelijk haalbaar en financieel rendabel is, en met de constellatie van partners die in stelling moet worden gebracht. Cahier en ontwerpkaders trachten datgene te verduidelijken, wat moeilijk te beschrijven of te meten valt. Ze reiken het vocabularium aan voor de gesprekken die tot een sterk ontwerpvoorstel moeten leiden. Ze zijn het vertrekpunt voor een traject dat deels inspiratie vond in de Open Oproep van de Vlaams Bouwmeester, waarvan ze de procedurele lichtheid en praktische ontwerpersblik tracht te introduceren in de doorgaans juridisch dichtgetimmerde context van Design & Build. Geen zwaar overladen procedure, maar een verkoop onder voorwaarden, waarbij de afvinklijst wordt vervangen door een goed ontwerp, en de nodige tijd en ruimte om daarover in gesprek te gaan.

Als architecturale kwaliteit de maat bepaalt, verdwijnt echter voor de doorsnee bouwpromotor alle houvast. En als die kwaliteit bovendien niet letterlijk benoemd wordt, is het noorden helemaal zoek. Bij de verkoop van de grond in de Zilverlaan hebben de meeste private ontwikkelaars de grootste moeite om te begrijpen wat precies van hun ontwerpbieding wordt verlangd. Het meegeleverde ontwerpkader is bewust schetsmatig, en de overkoepelende visie van het cahier wordt pas tijdens het traject al doende ontwikkeld. Bij de startpresentatie wordt dan ook dankbaar geput uit een ander instrument van de Vlaams Bouwmeester waaraan het Zilverlaan-project schatplichtig is. In 2012 lanceerde Vlaams Bouwmeester Peter Swinnen de zogenaamde 'Pilootprojecten' om een brug te slaan tussen urgente beleidsopgaven, ontwerpend onderzoek en de realisatie van vernieuwende projecten. De Pilootprojecten Collectief Wonen zetten onderzoekers en ontwerpers aan het werk om na te gaan hoe een voorspelde behoefte aan 330.000 extra woningen in Vlaanderen een betere en duurzamere woonomgeving kan opleveren. Het ontwerpend onderzoek dat Bovenbouw Architectuur samen met de Universiteit Gent voerde, stelde om te beginnen vast dat meer woningbouw tot steeds minder landschap leidt, en probeerde dat verloren landschap te herstellen door via nieuwe woonprojecten groene verbindingen te leggen en ruimte vrij te maken in de Vlaamse verkavelingen. 'Door de spelregels nét iets te wijzigen, kan de bestaande dynamiek meebouwen aan een nieuwe alliantie tussen wonen en landschap. Compact en collectief wonen bouwt zo mee aan een kwalitatief, collectief landschap.'[7]

Het voorgaande citaat lijkt wel de basislijn voor de Zilverlaan. De ontwerpoefeningen waarbij de nieuwe spelregels worden getest, zijn een dankbare referentie voor het startschot van de verkoop. Dit is goed begrepen door Condor, de ontwikkelaar die het project uiteindelijk binnenhaalt, wanneer hij Bovenbouw engageert om een voorstel uit te tekenen voor zijn bod. Een tweede project dat opduikt in de PowerPoint die de intenties van het Stadsatelier moet verduidelijken, is het Groen Lint. Plannen van het ontwerp van Tractebel en Georges Descombes tonen hoe de rafelrand van Oostende een nieuw elan krijgt en een aanknopingspunt levert voor groen en collectieve waarden in de suburbane woonwijk van Stene.[8] Met zijn gedeelde dreef en groene ruimte kan het woonproject in de Zilverlaan een nieuwe schakel

7 Joachim Declerck, Stefan Devoldere en Michael Ryckewaert, *Pilootprojecten Wonen: Nieuwe vormen van collectiviteit* (Brussel: Team Vlaams Bouwmeester, 2013), 31.

8 In 2010 voerde Oostende samen met het Rother District in Zuid-Engeland een Interreg Europe onderzoek naar '21st Century Parks'. Hieruit groeide het idee voor het Groen Lint, waarvoor Tractebel en Georges Descombes in 2012 als ontwerpers werden geselecteerd via de Open Oproep van de Vlaams Bouwmeester.

Schorre. The seed for the Groen Lint was planted much earlier, however, as part of a European study programme that linked the need for sustainable urban parks with urban agriculture, climate change and sustainable mobility. Next, the food park is developed by MAAT-Ontwerpers as a strategic component of the Pilootproject Productief Landschap (Pilot Project Productive Landscape).[9] The innovative housing project proves to be the direct heir to a cascade of designs and quality tools that follow and reinforce each other: a family tree of research by design that ultimately leads to Zilverlaan.

Commitments and Vision Documents

The Zilverlaan project is characterised by a clever combination of different tools, complemented by the collective commitment of several actors: a knowledgeable and enthusiastic quality panel that sets high-enough standards, a convinced politician who is bold and dependable, and a partnership of project partners that is solid enough to overcome political pressure, personal mistrust and unforeseen costs. Quality comes from shared ambition and endures through shared ownership. They are patiently being built over the long process of Zilverlaan. The sales process explicitly allows space for the discussion of ambition and design. Previous studies and projects provide points of connection and persuasion. However, the real driving force of the project is the focus on personal interaction that is maintained throughout the process. At the heart of this is the Urban Workshop, which gives a clear place and meaning to the quality of the project. With the chair as the unwavering motivator, the Urban Workshop sessions regularly manage and 'nurture' complex relationships as the foundation for sustainable, high-quality spatial development.[10]

Quality is determined by an approach, rather than a clear-cut definition. Therefore, the design of the process is as important as the design drawing that is on the meeting table. The methodology of the Urban Workshop

9 The Pilootprojecten Productief Landschap were launched in 2014 by the Flemish Government Architect and the Instituut voor Landbouw- en Visserijonderzoek (Institute for Agricultural and Fisheries Research, ILVO). The programme offered resources for project direction and design to realise interesting interactions between agriculture, recreation, nature management, society and policy.

10 Alice Haddad, 'De kaart ontrafelen, werken met het grondgebied', in: Liefooghe and Van Den Driessche, *Meer dan een wedstrijd*, op. cit. (note 6), 100.

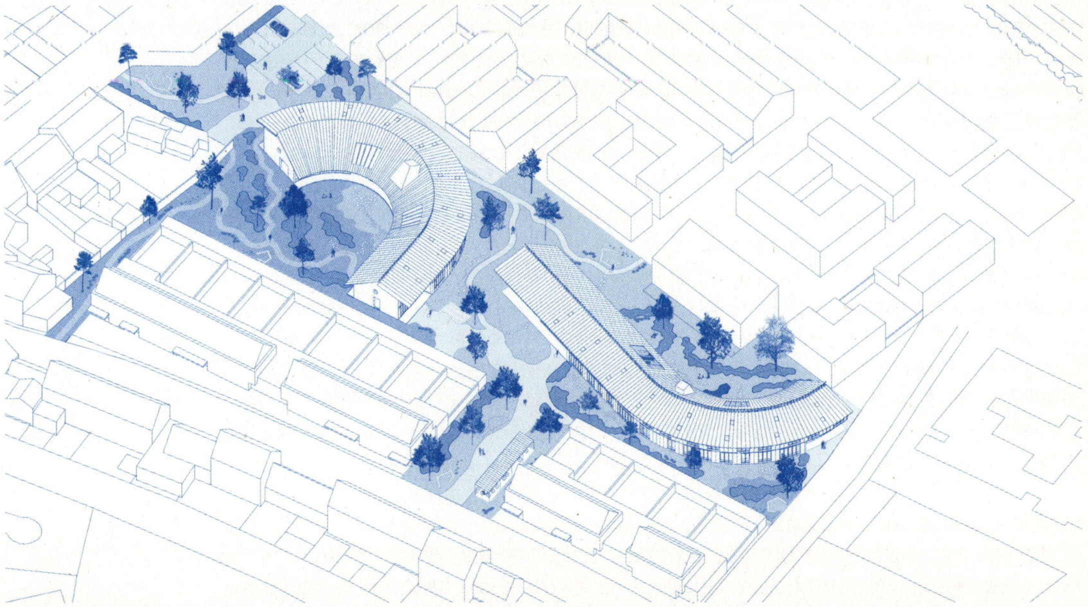

Raamwerk, housing facility for Duinhelm, Stene. Two curved residential volumes around a garden provide sheltered living for people with intellectual disabilities. A cycling and walking path runs between them toward the Groen Lint/ Raamwerk, woonproject voor Duinhelm te Stene. Twee gekrulde volumes rondom een tuin zorgen voor beschermd wonen voor bewoners met een verstandelijke beperking. Er tussenin loopt een fiets- en wandelpad naar het Groen Lint

vormen op het Lint, tussen het voedselpark De Tuinen van Stene en de sportvelden van De Schorre in. De kiem van het Groen Lint wordt echter al veel eerder gelegd binnen een Europees studietraject dat de vraag naar toekomstbestendige stadsparken koppelt aan stadslandbouw, klimaatverandering en duurzame mobiliteit. Het voedselpark wordt vervolgens als strategisch onderdeel verder uitgewerkt door Maat-Ontwerpers in het kader van het Pilootproject Productief Landschap.[9] Het vernieuwende woonproject blijkt zo de rechtstreekse erfgenaam van een cascade aan ontwerpen en kwaliteitsinstrumenten die elkaar opvolgen en versterken: een stamboom van ontwerpend onderzoek die uiteindelijk leidt naar de Zilverlaan.

Engagementen en visiedocumenten

Het traject van de Zilverlaan wordt gekenmerkt door een slimme combinatie van verschillende instrumenten, aangevuld met het gezamenlijk engagement van verschillende actoren: een kwaliteitskamer die met kennis en enthousiasme de lat hoog genoeg legt, een overtuigde politicus die durft en betrouwbaar is, een entente van projectpartners die solide genoeg is om politieke druk, persoonlijk wantrouwen en onvoorziene kosten te overbruggen. Kwaliteit ontstaat door een gedeelde ambitie en houdt stand door een gedeeld eigenaarschap. Daar wordt voor en tijdens het lange proces van de Zilverlaan geduldig aan gebouwd. De verkoopprocedure voorziet expliciet ruimte voor discussie over ambities en ontwerp. Eerdere studies en projecten zorgen voor aanknopingspunten en overtuigingskracht. De ware motor van het project is echter de focus op persoonlijke interactie die gedurende het gehele traject wordt aangehouden. Het brandpunt daarvan ligt in het Stadsatelier dat de kwaliteit van het project een duidelijke plaats en betekenis geeft. Met de voorzitter als niet aflatende aanjager, zorgen de workshopsessies op regelmatige basis voor het managen en 'het voeden van complexe relaties' als basis voor een duurzame ruimtelijke ontwikkeling.[10]

Kwaliteit wordt bepaald door een aanpak, eerder dan een welomlijnde definitie. Het ontwerp van het gevoerde proces is daarom even cruciaal als de ontwerptekening die op de vergadertafel ligt. De methodiek van het Stadsatelier draait om het opzetten van gesprekken, niet om het uitschrijven en toepassen van richtlijnen. Kwaliteit blijft een moeilijk te vatten begrip, dat pas echt invulling krijgt tijdens een goed gesprek rond de keukentafel, zoals de oorspronkelijke Vlaams Bouwmeester bOb Van Reeth het zelf graag verwoordt.[11] Elk kwalitatief project heeft een plek nodig voor die keukentafel. In Oostende staat de keukentafel in het Stadsatelier, waar ze verschillende overheidsdiensten rondom zich verzamelt en met één stem laat spreken bij de begeleiding van grootschalige initiatieven, maar ze houdt ook een ingewikkeld project als de Zilverlaan op koers door misverstanden tijdig te neutraliseren en de gedeelde ambitie warm te houden. Een doorlopende dialoog zorgt bovendien voor wendbaarheid. Een goed plan laat steeds voldoende ruimte om ervan af te wijken, om zich aan te passen aan nieuwe randvoorwaarden tijdens de lange duur van een bouwtraject. Die flexibiliteit legt de lat niet lager, ze helpt vooral om de ambitie hoog te houden en op elk moment van het proces onderscheid te maken tussen essentie en bijzaak.

Een gedegen pilootproject is niets waard als herhaling uitblijft. Een zorgvuldige documentatie van de afgelegde route en een breed gedragen beleidsvisie waarin het pilootinitiatief een duidelijke plaats krijgt, moeten ervoor zorgen dat de Zilverlaan geen unicum is. De overkoepelende

9 De Pilootprojecten Productief Landschap werden in 2014 gelanceerd door de Vlaams Bouwmeester en het Instituut voor Landbouw- en Visserijonderzoek (ILVO). Ze boden middelen voor projectregie en ontwerp om een interessante wisselwerking te realiseren tussen landbouw, recreatie, natuurbeheer, maatschappij en beleid.

10 Alice Haddad, 'De kaart ontrafelen, werken met het grondgebied', in: Liefooghe en Van Den Driessche, *Meer dan een wedstrijd*, op. cit. (noot 6), 100.

11 bOb Van Reeth, interview 'Afscheid van Vlaams Bouwmeester bOb Van Reeth', in: Jan de Zutter (red.), *Een Bouwmeester bouwt niet: 1999-2005* (Brussel: Vlaams Bouwmeester, 2005), 35.

revolves around initiating conversations, not around writing and applying guidelines. Quality remains a difficult concept to grasp that only really takes shape during a good conversation around the kitchen table, as the original Flemish Government Architect bOb Van Reeth himself liked to put it.[11] Every high-quality project needs room for such a kitchen table. In Ostend, the kitchen table is at the Urban Workshop. It brings together various government departments and enables them to speak with one voice as they guide major projects, while keeping a complex project like Zilverlaan on track by neutralising misunderstandings in time and fostering a common ambition. Ongoing dialogue also ensures flexibility. A good plan always leaves enough room for deviation, to adapt to new conditions during the long duration of a construction project. This flexibility does not lower the bar; it helps to keep ambitions high and to distinguish the essential from the peripheral at any point in the process.

A high-quality pilot project is worthless if it is not followed by replication. Careful documentation of the route taken, and a broadly supported political vision in which the pilot project has a clear place, must ensure that Zilverlaan is not a one-off. The overarching *Stapstenen voor Stene* is as important as the realisation of the housing project itself, just like the research by design that preceded it, which served as a thought process and source of inspiration, always anticipating the next step in a productive chain of framing and designing. Such documents form a collective memory and protect the fragile ecosystem of an exemplary project in the face of political change of power or a loss of momentum. Architectural quality is not an objective fact, but an inspiring story that convinces and enthuses. Sometimes this story is more important than the plans drawn up. After all, told well, it can create the momentum to transform an entire district. Design is therefore an essential tool in the arsenal of administrators and politicians. It brings together the imaginations of different users and stakeholders, makes visible shared values and expectations, and helps people to understand and challenge each other. It is applicable at every stage of every spatial development process, and provides the necessary arguments and conditions for a high-quality living environment.

Translation: InOtherWords, Maria van Tol

11 bOb Van Reeth, interview 'Afscheid van Vlaams Bouwmeester bOb Van Reeth', in: Jan de Zutter (ed.), *Een Bouwmeester bouwt niet: 1999-2005* (Brussels: Vlaams Bouwmeester, 2005), 35.

visie 'Stapstenen voor Stene' is daarbij even essentieel als de bouw van de woningen zelf, net zoals het voorafgaande ontwerpend onderzoek dat dienstdeed als denkmethode en inspiratiebron, steeds anticiperend op een volgende stap in een productieve ketting van omkadering en ontwerp. Dergelijke documenten zorgen voor een collectief geheugen en beschermen de kwetsbare biotoop van een voorbeeldproject bij een politieke machtswissel of een dip in het momentum. Architectuurkwaliteit is geen objectief feit, maar een wervend verhaal dat overtuigt en enthousiasmeert. Soms blijkt dat verhaal belangrijker dan de uitgetekende plannen. Als het goed wordt verteld, creëert het immers een momentum om een hele wijk te transformeren. Ontwerp mag daarom als instrument niet ontbreken in het arsenaal van bestuur en beleid. Het bundelt de verbeelding van verschillende gebruikers en stakeholders, maakt gedeelde waarden en verwachtingspatronen zichtbaar, en helpt elkaar te begrijpen en uit te dagen. Het is bij elke ruimtelijk ontwikkeling op elk moment bruikbaar, en levert ons de nodige argumenten en omstandigheden voor een hoogwaardige leefomgeving.

The Return of Confidence? On the Quality Assurance of Prospective Planning: The Example of Luxembourg in Transition

Florian Hertweck

Compelled by the immense need for transformation that we are facing in the context of climate change and resource scarcity, many in our spatial disciplines are wondering how concepts, strategies and instruments of socioecological transformation can be scaled up to have the broadest possible effect. There are very different approaches in this regard, from legislative initiatives such as HouseEurope, which aims to prohibit demolition and reduce VAT on renovation at the European level, to the New European Bauhaus policy initiative, which supports pilot projects on various scales and expects them to actualise the European Green Deal.[1]

Upscaling is now also the ultimate goal of so-called prospective planning of cities and regions. However, its focus and methods have changed significantly over the last three decades. Whereas in the 1990s and early 2000s the primary aim was to generate regional growth; since the ground-breaking Consultation du Grand Paris pursued a paradigm for the city following the Kyoto Protocol, the focus has been on ecological transformation. Since then, many cities and regions in Europe have attempted to build on this consultation model and explore the question of how they need to change in order to become climate-neutral and resilient by 2050 – a key date established by the Paris Agreement (COP21) – in view of the effects of climate change and resource depletion that they face.

Of these prospective planning programmes, the international consultation Luxembourg in Transition stands out in terms of the innovation of its programme and methodology.[2] The aim of this research and planning programme was to develop planning strategies for 2050 at different scales and in different sectors, with two main objectives. On the one hand, it investigated how the functional area of Luxembourg, which currently has the highest carbon footprint per capita in Europe and the earliest Earth Overshoot Day in the year, can become climate-neutral and more careful in its use of resources. On the other hand, it explored how this region, which is locked into dependencies in terms of capital, goods, food and labour from the immediate hinterland to the global level, can become resilient over time.[3]

Buckminster Fuller's maxim that the best way to predict the future is to design it raises, in the context of prospective planning, the question of how the quality of this 'shaping of the future' can be effectively agreed, assured and monitored. With regard to Luxembourg in Transition, this mindset motivated a unique quality assurance agenda. A range of measures and instruments were employed to integrate the quantification of decarbonisation and resilience as evaluation criteria at various stages in the planning and design processes, both during the consultation itself and for the future implementation of the various approaches. After

1
See: houseeurope.eu and new-european-bauhaus.europa.eu.

2
The full title of the international consultation was Luxembourg in Transition: Spatial Visions for the Zero-Carbon and Resilient Future of the Luxembourg Functional Region, initiated by the Luxembourg Ministry of Energy and Land Planning from 2020 to 2022. See: luxembourgintransition.lu.

3
Markus Hesse and Catherine Mei Ling Wong, 'Cities Seen through a Relational Lens', *Geographische Zeitschrift* 108/2 (2020), 74-98.

De terugkeer van vertrouwen? Over kwaliteitsborging in langetermijnplanning: Het voorbeeld van Luxembourg in Transition

Florian Hertweck

Onder invloed van de immense behoefte aan transformatie, door de uitdagingen rond klimaatverandering en grondstoffenschaarste, vragen velen in de ruimtelijke disciplines zich af hoe socio-ecologische concepten, strategieën en instrumenten zo kunnen worden opgeschaald dat ze een zo groot mogelijk effect op de transformatie hebben. Er worden heel verschillende initiatieven ontplooid: van wetgevende zoals HouseEurope, dat sloop wil verbieden en de BTW op renovatie op Europees niveau wil verlagen, tot beleidsmatige als New European Bauhaus, dat proefprojecten op verschillende schaalniveaus ondersteunt en daarmee de Europese Green Deal wil concretiseren.[1]

Opschalen is tegenwoordig ook het ultieme doel van de zogenaamde toekomstverkenning van steden en regio's. De focus en methoden zijn de afgelopen 30 jaar echter aanzienlijk veranderd. In de jaren 1990 en de vroege jaren 2000 lag de nadruk vooral op het stimuleren van regionale groei, maar sinds het baanbrekende Consultation du Grand Paris een paradigma voor de stad volgens het Kyoto Protocol voorstelde, ligt de focus op ecologische transformatie. Sindsdien hebben veel Europese steden en regio's geprobeerd om voort te bouwen op dit raadplegingsmodel, op zoek naar manieren om zo te transformeren dat ze tegen 2050 – een belangrijk jaartal dat is vastgelegd in het Akkoord van Parijs (COP21) – klimaatneutraal en veerkrachtig zijn, dit met het oog op de gevolgen van klimaatverandering en de uitputting van hulpbronnen.

Onder deze programma's voor de lange termijn onderscheidt de internationale raadpleging Luxembourg in Transition zich door het vernieuwende programma en de methodologie.[2] Het idee erachter was om op verschillende schaalniveaus en binnen diverse sectoren, planningsstrategieën voor 2050 te ontwikkelen, met twee hoofdambities. Niet alleen werd onderzocht hoe Luxemburg als functioneel gebied, dat momenteel de hoogste koolstofvoetafdruk per hoofd van de bevolking in Europa heeft en als eerste de *Earth Overshoot Day* bereikt, klimaatneutraal kan worden en zorgvuldiger met hulpbronnen kan omgaan. Verder werd bekeken hoe deze regio, die voor wat betreft kapitaal, goederen, voedsel en arbeid sterk afhankelijk is van andere – van het directe achterland tot de rest van de wereld – mettertijd veerkrachtiger kan worden.[3]

De uitspraak van Buckminster Fuller dat de beste manier om de toekomst te voorspellen is om deze te ontwerpen, roept bij langetermijnplanning de vraag op hoe de kwaliteit van deze 'vormgeving van de toekomst' effectief kan worden overeengekomen, gewaarborgd en gecontroleerd. In het geval van Luxembourg in Transition resulteerde deze denkwijze in een unieke agenda voor kwaliteitsborging. Een reeks maatregelen en instrumenten werd ingezet om decarbonisering en veerkracht te kwantificeren

1 Zie: houseeurope.eu en new-european-bauhaus.europa.eu.

2 De volledige naam van het internationale overleg was: Luxembourg in Transition: Spatial Visions for the Zero-Carbon and Resilient Future of the Luxembourg Functional Region. Het overleg werd tussen 2020 en 2022 geïnitieerd door het Luxemburgse ministerie van Energie en Ruimtelijke Ordening. Zie: luxembourg-intransition.lu.

3 Markus Hesse en Catherine Mei Ling Wong, 'Cities Seen through a Relational Lens', *Geographische Zeitschrift* 108/2 (2020), 74-98.

contextualising the Luxembourg consultation, this article highlights its potentials and obstacles, in order to draw conclusions for further prospective planning. Because the gap between decarbonisation and the circular economy ambitions on the one hand, and the real ecological footprint and creeping Overshoot Day on the other is constantly widening, we urgently need scalable and monitorable strategies to deal with the effects of these ecological challenges, be they species and forest extinction, flooding, heat waves and heat islands, depleted soils and water, or material and resource shortages. This is also an opportunity for our spatial design disciplines. The more we develop narratives that convincingly link a qualitative understanding of what the socioecological transition means for our experience of the built environment, with the hard calculations that evidence corresponding improvements in environmental quality, and do not retreat into disciplinary autonomy, the more we can deliver scalable strategies for decarbonisation and resilience with confidence. This will increase our influence on the socioecological transition, which otherwise risks further domination by techno-solutionism in politics, business and science.

From Paris via Geneva to Luxembourg

After the oil crises and recessions of the 1970s put an end to the 'brief dream of perpetual prosperity', as sociologist Burkart Lutz aptly described the unique growth phase of the post-war period, an 'end to confidence' and an increasingly retrospective mentality also prevailed in the field of urban planning.[4] From the 1980s to the 1990s, the prevailing view in Europe was to promote the so-called 'reconstruction of the European city', which was moderate in terms of the morphology of the city, and deliberately conservative – especially in Germany, Eastern Europe and to some extent in the Netherlands – with regard to the cityscape and the façades of the buildings, and which led in some cases to an uncritical reconstruction of historical urban ensembles.[5]

In the 1990s, many cities saw a paradigm shift in their planning culture: fearing that they would be left behind in the international competition for globally active companies and skilled labour, cities increasingly turned to prospective planning, which was primarily concerned with strengthening their own branding. From Berlin 2000 to Rotterdam 2020, Chicago 2020, Melbourne 2030 and Abu Dhabi 2030: the visionary plans of this period were intended to signal that the respective city had a prosperous future that was worth investing in. Although the ecological dimension was suggested, it was not inscribed in any serious methodology. In other words, the neoliberalism that accompanied the triumph of postmodernism in the late 1970s and early 1980s triggered a renaissance of prospective planning, which was primarily intended to generate growth, but often only produced a cultural or creative flagship.

The Consultation internationale du Grand Paris was intended to change this, at least in terms of ambition. On the occasion of the inauguration of the Cité de l'architecture et du patrimoine, where the results would later be exhibited, President Nicolas Sarkozy announced the launch of an international consultation for the greater Paris area in September 2007. According to Sarkozy in his remarkable speech, it was once again time to think not only about the urban development of the 'next six months, but of the coming century'.[6] Architects should therefore work together to develop a 'prospective, urban and landscape diagnosis of the greater Paris area in

4
See, for example: Burkart Lutz, *Der kurze Traum immerwährender Prosperität* (Frankfurt am Main/New York: Campus Verlag, 1984); Wolfgang Pehnt, *Das Ende der Zuversicht: Architektur in diesem Jahrhundert: Ideen – Bauten – Dokumente* (Berlin: Siedler Verlag, 1983).

5
See also: Florian Hertweck, *Der Berliner Architekturstreit* (Berlin: Gebr. Mann Verlag, 2010); Florian Hertweck, 'De la réparation urbaine à la grande réparation', *Le Visiteur* 29 (2024), 75-86; Stephan Trüby (guest editor), 'Rechte Räume: Bericht einer Europareise', *ARCH+* 235 (2019).

6
'Déclararation de M. Nicolas Sarkozy, Président de la République, sur l'architecture et la politique du patrimopine, à Paris le 17 septembre 2007', elysee.fr/nicolas-sarkozy/2007/09/17/declaration-de-m-nicolas-sarkozy-president-de-la-republique-sur-larchitecture-et-la-politique-du-patrimoine-a-paris-le-17-septembre-2007 (accessed 2 July 2024).

en ze als evaluatiecriteria te integreren in de verschillende stadia van planning en ontwerp, zowel tijdens het overleg als bij uitvoering. In dit artikel wordt Luxembourg in Transition eerst in zijn context gesitueerd; vervolgens worden de mogelijkheden (en belemmeringen) van het overleg belicht en conclusies getrokken voor verdere langetermijnplanning. Er is immers dringend behoefte aan opschaalbare en controleerbare

2001-51N4E-LOLA / Philippe Nathan & Arya Arabshahi & VIVID. Sublime Suburbias: Helfent op de grens van Luxemburg-Stad in 2050. Hoogbouw speelt een sleutelrol in de vrijwaring van akkerland en bos. Plinten voorzien in economische, maatschappelijke en vrijetijdsvoorzieningen en diensten

the horizon of twenty, thirty or even forty years'.[7] The ten selected teams, whose expertise had to cover both practice and research, were supported by a scientific advisory board including Manuel Castells, Saskia Sassen and Thomas Sieverts – the latter had driven a discursive shift in urban planning discourse that foregrounded the globally networked metropolis, and the decentralisation of the compact self-contained European city to

7 Ibid.

2001-51N4E-LOLA / Philippe Nathan & Arya Arabshahi & VIVID. Sublime Suburbias: Helfent, on the fringe of Luxemburg-city in 2050. High-rises play a key role in preserving arable land and forests. Their plinths accommodate economic, civic and leisure facilities and services

strategieën, aangezien er een nog steeds groeiende kloof gaapt tussen enerzijds de ambities op het gebied van circulaire economie en het terugdringen van koolstof, en anderzijds de werkelijke ecologische voetafdruk of de steeds eerder plaatsvindende *Earth Overshoot Day*. De uitdaging is om de ecologische achteruitgang – of het nu gaat om het uitsterven van soorten en bossen, overstromingen, hittegolven en hitte-eilanden, uitgeputte bodems en water of materiaal- en grondstoffentekorten – het hoofd te bieden, en hier liggen meteen ook kansen voor de ruimtelijke ontwerpdisciplines. Hoe meer verhalen we creëren die op overtuigende wijze een verband leggen tussen een kwalitatief begrip van wat de sociaal-ecologische transitie betekent voor onze ervaring van de gebouwde omgeving met de harde data die verbeteringen in milieukwaliteit aantonen, hoe minder we ons terugtrekken in de autonomie van de architectuurdiscipline, des te beter zullen we in staat zijn met vertrouwen opschalingsstrategieën voor decarbonisering en veerkracht aan te reiken. Dit zal onze invloed op de sociaal-ecologische transitie vergroten, die anders verder gedomineerd zal blijven door het vertrouwen van de politiek, het bedrijfsleven en de wetenschap in puur technologische oplossingen.

Van Parijs via Genève naar Luxemburg

Nadat de oliecrisis en recessie van de jaren 1970 een einde maakten aan de 'kortstondige droom van eeuwigdurende welvaart', zoals de socioloog Burkart Lutz de unieke groeifase van de naoorlogse periode treffend omschreef, was er ook in de stedenbouw sprake van 'een einde aan het vertrouwen' en meer en meer een terugblikkende mentaliteit.[4] Van 1980 tot 1990 overheerste in Europa het idee dat de zogenoemde 'reconstructie van de Europese stad' moest worden aangemoedigd. Deze opvatting bleef gematigd waar het ging om de stedelijke morfologie en was bewust conservatief – vooral in Duitsland, Oost-Europa en tot op zekere hoogte in Nederland – waar het om het stadsbeeld en de gevels ging. In sommige gevallen resulteerde dit in een onkritische reconstructie van historische stedelijke ensembles.[5]

In de jaren 1990 vond in veel steden een paradigmaverschuiving plaats in de plancultuur. Uit angst om achter te blijven in de internationale concurrentiestrijd om wereldwijd actieve bedrijven en geschoolde arbeidskrachten, richtten steden zich steeds meer op langetermijnplanning, die primair was gericht op versterking van eigen merk en naamsbekendheid. Van Berlijn 2000 tot Rotterdam 2020, Chicago 2020, Melbourne 2030 en Abu Dhabi 2030: de visionaire plannen uit deze periode dienden vooral om aan te geven dat de betreffende stad een welvarende toekomst had, die het waard was om in te investeren. Hoewel deze plannen soms een ecologische dimensie suggereerden, werd deze zelden in een serieuze methodologie opgenomen. Met andere woorden: het neoliberalisme, dat gepaard ging met de triomf van het postmodernisme aan het eind van de jaren 1970 en het begin van de jaren 1980, leidde tot een heropleving van de toekomstverkenning. Deze was echter voornamelijk gericht op het genereren van groei en resulteerde vaak alleen maar in een cultureel of creatief prestigeproject.

De Consultation internationale du Grand Paris moest hierin verandering brengen, althans qua ambitie. Tijdens de opening van de Cité de l'architecture et du patrimoine, waar de resultaten later zouden worden tentoongesteld, lanceerde president Nicolas Sarkozy in september 2007 het idee voor een internationale ideeënconsultatie over de regio Groot-

4 Zie bijvoorbeeld: Burkart Lutz, *Der kurze Traum immerwährender Prosperität* (Frankfurt am Main/New York: Campus Verlag, 1984); Wolfgang Pehnt, *Das Ende der Zuversicht: Architektur in diesem Jahrhundert: Ideen – Bauten – Dokumente* (Berlijn: Siedler Verlag, 1983).

5 Zie ook: Florian Hertweck, *Der Berliner Architekturstreit* (Berlijn: Gebr. Mann Verlag, 2010); Florian Hertweck, 'De la réparation urbaine à la grande réparation', *Le Visiteur* 29 (2024), 75-86; Stephan Trüby (gastredacteur), 'Rechte Räume: Bericht einer Europareise', *ARCH+* 235 (2019).

what he called the *Zwischenstadt*. According to him, the state of the dense and mixed European city has become marginal compared to the dominant in-between areas, which are neither purely rural nor purely urban, but incorporate elements of both.

The consultation centred on the question of how the Paris agglomeration should be designed in the context of the Kyoto Protocol. While this initial question manifests a perspective of the city beyond the classic view of Paris within the Périphérique, the focus on climate change was also challenging for the spatial planning disciplines to assimilate, and translated most explicitly into a concern with counteracting any extensification of the agglomeration with strategies for intensification. The Protocol, which came into force in 2005, committed the European Union, among others, to reducing its greenhouse gas emissions by 8 per cent by 2012 compared with 1990 levels, which translated across all teams into strategies for fossil-free mobility, continuous green networks, reduced land consumption and a functional mix. With its high ambition, the Consultation du Grand Paris thus expressed a return of confidence that the transformation of urban agglomerations, which are responsible for the largest share of the ecological footprint, could overcome the ecological crisis.

As a result of the consultation, the Atelier International du Grand Paris (AIGP) was founded with the aim of having architects, urban planners and landscape planners work together with the Atelier Parisien d'Urbanisme (Apur) and the Institut Paris Région on the modelling of Greater Paris. This urban alteration project could 'not simply be a matter of bureaucracy', as the French president put it at the time.[8] The follow-through of the prospective planning process was therefore secured by means of a new institution, in which the respective teams acted as scientific advisory boards.

A decade later, architect and urbanist Panos Mantziaras, who was involved in preparing the tender text for the Paris Consultation, launched the Consultation du Grand Genève in his role as Director of the Fondation Braillard in Geneva.[9] Mantziaras wrote his doctoral thesis on Rudolf Schwarz's concept of *Stadtlandschaft*, and gave the Genève consultation the subtitle 'Visions prospectives pour le Grand Genève: Habiter la ville-paysage du 21e siècle'.[10] The consultation's call for proposals emphasised the ecological urgency, and the crucial role of urbanised land, declaring it to be 'the cornerstone of ecological transition . . . whose drastic reduction in CO2 emissions and its ecological footprint must be considered with rigour and imagination'.[11]

The demand for both rigour (scientific-rational thinking) and imagination (creative-visionary thinking) reflects a general tension of prospective planning. At the same time, the Genève call underlines the intention of this iteration of prospective planning to subject the approaches of the respective architects to scientific evaluation. This was to be achieved first through more precise requirements for the teams to combine experts in spatial planning, urban planning, architecture and landscape architecture with experts in the humanities, environmental technology and mobility 'in order to renew the instruments, tools and methods [of spatial production]',[12] and then through the provision of qualified feedback from various science disciplines to the seven selected teams at various instances during the consultation. The highlight of the research and planning programme was a workshop involving all teams as well as experts from the region, which resulted in a considerable transfer of knowledge. However, the final event also marked the end of the quality assurance processes that had fostered

8 'Déclaration de M. Nicolas Sarkozy, Président de la République, sur le projet du Grand Paris, à Paris le 29 avril 2009', francearchives.gouv.fr/fr/authorityrecord/FRAN_NP_051820 (accessed 2 July 2024).

9 Mantziaras, well acquainted with German planning history and in particular the Greater Berlin Competition of 1909-1910, is also said to have provided the impetus for the Consultation du Grand Paris as an employee of the architectural and urban planning research department of the French Ministry of Culture (Bureau de la Recherche Architecturale, Urbaine et Paysagère, BRAUP). As director of BRAUP, he subsequently launched and coordinated the long-term research programme 'Ignis Mutat Res: Penser l'architecture, la ville et les paysages au prisme de l'énergie' (2011-2015).

10 See: braillard.ch/consultation-grand-geneve.

11 See: braillard.ch/consultation-grand-geneve/objet-de-la-consultation (accessed 1 July 2024).

12 Ibid.

Parijs. In een opmerkelijke toespraak stelde Sarkozy dat het tijd was om niet alleen te denken aan de stedelijke ontwikkeling voor de komende zes maanden, maar aan die van de komende eeuw.[6] Architecten zouden daarom moeten samenwerken om een 'vooruitblik en diagnose van de stedelijke en landschappelijke ontwikkeling van de regio Groot-Parijs over twintig, dertig of zelfs veertig jaar' te formuleren.[7] De tien geselecteerde teams, die zowel praktijkervaring als onderzoeksexpertise hadden, werden bijgestaan door een wetenschappelijke adviesraad. Tot deze raad behoorden onder andere Manuel Castells, Saskia Sassen en Thomas Sieverts, welke laatste een verschuiving in het stedenbouwkundig discours had teweeggebracht, waardoor de nadruk kwam te liggen op de wereldwijd vernetwerkte metropool en de decentralisatie van de compacte, zelfvoorzienende Europese stad naar wat hij de *Zwischenstadt* noemde. Volgens

6 'Déclarararion de M. Nicolas Sarkozy, Président de la République, sur l'architecture et la politique du patrimopine, à Paris le 17 septembre 2007', elysee.fr/nicolas-sarkozy/2007/09/17/declaration-de-m-nicolas-sarkozy-president-de-la-republique-sur-larchitecture-et-la-politique-du-patrimoine-a-paris-le-17-septembre-2007 (geraadpleegd 2 juli 2024).

7 Ibid.

2001-51N4E-LOLA / Philippe Nathan & Arya Arabshahi & VIVID. Sublime Suburbias: Helfent in 2050 is een genereuze vallei geworden met herstelde natuur en met een levendige wijk met nieuwe hoogbouw in een combinatie van wonen en werken

the integration of scientific rigour and visionary thinking. The teams were not involved in any further planning steps.

Luxembourg in Transition: Planning and Metrics

Building on the Consultation du Grand Genève, the Luxembourg Ministry of Energy and National Planning, under the leadership of Claude Turmes, launched the consultation Luxembourg in Transition immediately after the Geneva 2020 programme. Turmes, who was previously a Member of the European Parliament and involved in many reports and initiatives on European energy policy, recruited Panos Mantziaras as scientific director, who in turn brought along the former director of the AIGP Bertrand Lemoine and the Geneva climate scientist Dominique Bourg, among others, as scientific advisors for the new programme.[13]

13 The UN Special Rapporteur Olivier de Schutter and the renowned sustainability researcher François Gemenne were also on board as scientific advisors.

2001-51N4E-LOLA / Philippe Nathan & Arya Arabshahi & VIVID. Sublime Suburbias: Helfent in 2050 has become a generous re-naturalised valley and a lively neighbourhood of new typologies of living and working in mixed-use high-rises

Sieverts was de traditionele, dichte en gemengde Europese stad steeds marginaler geworden in vergelijking met de dominante tussengebieden, die noch puur landelijk noch puur stedelijk zijn, maar elementen van beide combineren.

Het Parijse overleg concentreerde zich op de vraag hoe de Parijse agglomeratie kon worden ontworpen volgens de richtlijnen van het Kyotoprotocol. Hoewel uit deze initiële vraag een visie op de stad blijkt, die het klassieke idee van Parijs binnen de *périférique* (ringweg) overstijgt, was de focus op klimaatverandering voor de ruimtelijke planningsdisciplines wel een uitdaging. Dat vertaalde zich in het tegengaan van verdere uitbreiding van de agglomeratie door er verdichting en intensivering tegenover te stellen. Het protocol, dat in 2005 van kracht werd, verplichtte de Europese Unie onder andere om haar uitstoot van broeikasgassen tegen 2012 met 8 procent te hebben verminderd ten opzichte van 1990. Bij alle teams werd dit vertaald in strategieën voor fossielvrije mobiliteit, doorlopende groene netwerken, minder landgebruik en functiemenging. Via deze ambities sprak de Consultation du Grand Paris dus opnieuw het vertrouwen uit dat de transformatie van de stedelijke agglomeraties die verantwoordelijk waren voor een groot deel van de ecologische voetafdruk, zou bijdragen aan het overwinnen van de ecologische crisis.

In het verlengde van het Parijse overleg werd het Atelier International du Grand Paris (AIGP) opgericht, om architecten, stedenbouwkundigen en landschapsarchitecten samen met het Atelier Parisien d'Urbanisme (Apur) en het Institut Paris Région te laten samenwerken aan het ontwerp van Groot-Parijs. Deze stadsverbouwing mocht 'niet alleen een kwestie van bureaucratie' zijn, zoals de Franse president het destijds uitdrukte.[8] Voor de planning voor de lange termijn werd daarom een nieuwe instelling opgericht, waarin de verschillende teams als wetenschappelijke adviesraden fungeerden.

Architect en stedenbouwkundige Panos Mantziaras, die betrokken was geweest bij de aanbestedingstekst voor de Consultation du Grand Paris, lanceerde tien jaar later, toen hij directeur was van de Geneefse Fondation Braillard, de Consultation du Grand Genève.[9] Mantziaras, die een proefschrift over Rudolf Schwarz' concept *Stadtlandschaft* had geschreven, gaf dit Geneefse overleg de ondertitel Visions prospectives pour le Grand Genève: Habiter la ville-paysage du 21ᵉ siècle.[10] In de oproep om voorstellen in te dienen werd de ecologische urgentie benadrukt en de cruciale rol van het verstedelijkte gebied, dat als 'de hoeksteen van de ecologische transitie' bestempeld werd, en 'waarvan de drastische reductie van CO2-uitstoot en de verkleining van de ecologische voetafdruk stipt en met verbeeldingskracht moeten worden benaderd'.[11]

De vraag naar zowel accuratesse (wetenschappelijk-rationeel denken) als verbeelding (creatief-visionair denken) weerspiegelde een algemene spanning in de toekomstgerichte planning. Tegelijkertijd onderstreepte de Geneefse oproep de intentie om in dit specifieke proces van toekomstverkenning de voorstellen van de betrokken architecten wetenschappelijk te toetsen. Dit moest allereerst bereikt worden door uitgebreidere eisen aan de teams te stellen: deskundigen op het gebied van ruimtelijke ordening, stedenbouw, architectuur en landschapsarchitectuur moesten samenwerken met specialisten uit de geesteswetenschappen, milieutechniek en mobiliteit, om 'de instrumenten, gereedschappen en methoden [van de ruimtelijke productie] te vernieuwen'.[12] Daarnaast werd tijdens de raadpleging op verschillende momenten en vanuit diverse wetenschappelijke

8 'Déclaration de M. Nicolas Sarkozy, Président de la République, sur le projet du Grand Paris, à Paris le 29 avril 2009', francearchives.gouv.fr/fr/authorityrecord/FRAN_NP_051820 (geraadpleegd 2 juli 2024).

9 Mantziaras was goed bekend met de Duitse planningsgeschiedenis, vooral met de prijsvraag voor Groot-Berlijn van 1909-1910. Naar verluid heeft hij als medewerker van de onderzoeksafdeling voor architectuur en stedenbouw van het Franse ministerie van Cultuur (Bureau de la Recherche Architecturale, Urbaine et Paysagère, BRAUP) ook de aanzet gegeven tot de Consultation du Grand Paris. Als directeur van het BRAUP lanceerde en coördineerde hij vervolgens het langlopende onderzoeksprogramma 'Ignis Mutat Res: Penser l'architecture, la ville et les paysages au prisme de l'énergie' (2011-2015).

10 Zie: braillard.ch/consultation-grand-geneve.

11 Zie: braillard.ch/consultation-grand-geneve/objet-de-la-consultation (geraadpleegd 1 juli 2024).

12 Ibid.

When it came to the conception of this new programme, it immediately became clear that the actors involved in the preparation of the tender wanted to build on their previous experience and guarantee efficacy of the prospective planning process through various quality assurance instruments. As Mantziaras put it in retrospect: 'Despite their considerable conceptual depth, [the prospective plans for the Grand Paris and the Grand Genève] remained too descriptive, declarative and qualitative.'[14] First of all, the various teams, which had to be made up of a representative from the spatial planning disciplines (spatial planning, urban planning, architecture and landscape architecture), the environmental sciences (ecology, soil science, climatology, agroecology and others) and the human and social sciences, were no longer able to work relatively freely for a year with only an interim presentation, but were put into a three-phase competitive process. The programme therefore took on the character of a competition rather than a consultation, at least in the first two phases.

In an initial three-month phase, for which ten teams were selected in line with the Paris programme, the methodology and, above all, the evaluation metrics of the socioecological transition were to be defined.[15] This meant using either the categories defined in the tender document of soil, greenhouse gases, energy, waste, food, drinking water, biodiversity and climate; or the widely accepted sectors for carbon accounting (including mobility, construction, agriculture and industry) and measuring resilience (through air quality, water quality, soil quality, forest health, food security and energy supply) to inform a methodology for how to define and evaluate a transition pathway for Luxembourg towards decarbonisation and increased resilience. Basically, climatologists, economists and engineers used Excel tables and diagrams to demonstrate, via subcategories and numerous

14
Panos Mantzarias, 'Urban Strategic Foresight in European Territories: Lessons from Geneva and Luxembourg', *AGATHON* 15 (2024), 44.

15
Département de l'aménagement du territoire, Luxembourg in Transition: Consultation internationale urbano-architecturale et paysagère, Cahier des charges (version 15 June 2020), Luxembourg. The teams were AREP, MVRDV, University of Luxembourg, 2001, KCAP, TVK, Raum 404, AWP, Interland and Studio Paola Viganò. Only the lead institutions/offices are listed here. For the complete teams see: luxembourgintransition.lu/fr/la-consultation-internationale/, Ministère de l'Energie et de l'Aménagement du Territoire.

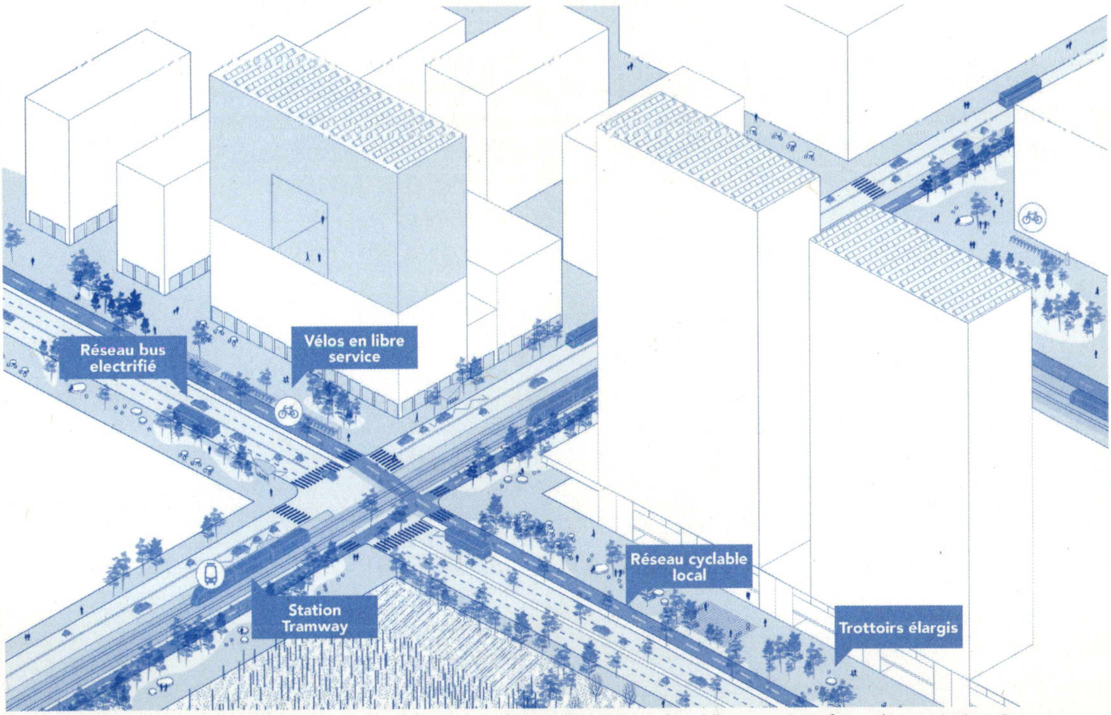

AREP, Taktyk, Quattrolibri, SU-ITE, Mobil'homme. Reducing car dependency through public space transformation: a strategy to convert car-centric streets into multimodal avenues in the Cloche d'Or district of Luxembourg City / AREP, Taktyk, Quattrolibri, SU-ITE, Mobil'homme. Afhankelijkheid van autoverkeer verminderen door de publieke ruimte te transformeren: een strategie om autogerichte straten te veranderen in multimodale lanen in de Cloche d'Or-wijk van Luxemburg-Stad

disciplines gekwalificeerde feedback gegeven aan de zeven geselecteerde teams. Hoogtepunt van het programma was een workshop, waaraan zowel de teams als regionale deskundigen deelnamen, wat resulteerde in een aanzienlijke kennisoverdracht. Het slotevenement markeerde echter ook het einde van de ambitieuze kwaliteitsborging die de integratie van wetenschappelijke nauwkeurigheid en visionair denken had ondersteund. De teams werden ook niet betrokken bij verdere planningsstappen in Genève.

Luxembourg in Transition: Planning en statistiek

In navolging van de Consultation du Grand Genève lanceerde het Luxemburgse ministerie van Energie en Nationale Planning, onder leiding van Claude Turmes, onmiddellijk na het Geneefse programma van 2020 het overleg Luxembourg in Transition. Turmes, voormalig lid van het Europees Parlement en betrokken bij talrijke rapporten en initiatieven rond het Europese energiebeleid, stelde Panos Mantziaras aan als wetenschappelijk directeur. Mantziaras bracht op zijn beurt onder andere de voormalige directeur van het AIGP, Bertrand Lemoine, en de Geneefse klimaatwetenschapper Dominique Bourg in als wetenschappelijke adviseurs voor het nieuwe programma.[13]

Het werd snel duidelijk dat Turmes, Mantziaras, Lemoine en Bourg bij de aanbesteding van het nieuwe programma wilden voortbouwen op hun eerdere ervaringen en de doeltreffendheid van de langetermijnplanning wilden garanderen via het opnemen van verschillende kwaliteitsborgingsinstrumenten. Want 'ondanks hun aanzienlijke conceptuele diepgang bleven [de toekomstverkenningen voor Grand Paris en Grand Genève] te beschrijvend, verklarend en kwalitatief', zoals Mantziaras achteraf vaststelde.[14] Ten eerste konden de verschillende teams – die moesten bestaan uit vertegenwoordigers van de ruimtelijke ordeningsdisciplines (ruimtelijke ordening, stedenbouw, architectuur en landschapsarchitectuur), de milieuwetenschappen (ecologie, bodemkunde, klimaatwetenschap, agro-ecologie en wat dies meer zij) en de mens- en maatschappijwetenschappen

13 Ook speciaal rapporteur bij de VN Olivier de Schutter en gerenommeerd duurzaamheidsonderzoeker François Gemenne werkten mee als wetenschappelijke adviseurs.

14 Panos Mantziaras, 'Urban Strategic Foresight in European Territories: Lessons from Geneva and Luxembourg', *AGATHON* 15 (2024), 44.

University of Luxembourg / Florian Hertweck & Céline Zimmer. Tien procent van alle gebouwen in Luxemburg kan worden opgetopt. Dat kan woonruimte bieden aan een kwart van de nieuwe inwoners tot 2050. Een dergelijke ontwikkeling kan betaalbare woonruimte opleveren, maar ook gemeenschappelijke en gedeelde voorzieningen, vooral door de garages op maaiveld een andere functie te geven

individual items, how net zero could be reached and resilience measures improved over a period of almost 30 years.

By focusing the first phase on defining appropriate ecological and decarbonisation metrics, the aim was to prevent the prospective plans from focusing 'primarily on the result and insufficiently on the process required to achieve it'.[16] This is because the Consultations du Grand Paris and du Grand Genève, according to Mantziaras, ultimately offered 'too few key indicators for managing the transformation process and insufficient criteria for holding those involved to account'.[17] This sharp formulation once again makes clear the intention to go beyond the affirmation of architectural and urban development visions to ensure their verifiability and capacity to be monitored against agreed metrics of decarbonisation and ecological resilience.

This first phase was particularly challenging for urban planners and architects, as they were deliberately held back in their conventional endeavours to develop spatial strategies. At the same time, however, they recognised the extent to which spatial planning concepts were able to trigger effects in different areas. In the area of agriculture, for example, the metrics showed that a relatively high impact can be achieved with relatively simple measures – in particular by changing diets or avoiding food waste. At the same time, it became clear that the mobility sector accounts for half of the ecological footprint in Luxembourg and that the strategy must therefore not only be based on a change in mobility patterns and infrastructure, but also on a reduction in mobility through urban planning strategies aiming at shorter travel distances for the most essential human activities. Reducing mobility in turn opened up the opportunity for planners to tap into a considerable reservoir of already sealed land, which in a small country like Luxembourg is all the more valuable for the desired intensification. No team was able to achieve a climate-neutral outcome against the metrics, without including the sequestration of CO_2 by natural soils. As a result, unsealed areas – or rather their renaturalisation – became an important component for all approaches.

16
Mantziaras, 'Urban Strategic Foresight', op. cit. (note 13), 44.
17
Ibid.

University of Luxembourg / Florian Hertweck & Céline Zimmer. Ten per cent of all buildings in Luxembourg could be topped up. This could provide housing for a quarter of the new residents by 2050. Such a development could not only create affordable housing, but also communal and shared amenities – especially by repurposing ground-level garages

– niet langer een jaar lang relatief vrij werken, waarbij ze alleen een tussentijdse presentatie hoefden te geven, maar moesten ze een competitief proces in drie fasen doorlopen. Hierdoor kreeg het programma meer het karakter van een competitie dan een raadpleging, althans in de eerste twee fasen.

Tijdens de eerste fase, die drie maanden duurde en waarin, net als bij het Parijse programma, tien teams werden geselecteerd, lag de focus op het vaststellen van de methodologie en vooral de evaluatiecriteria.[15] Dit hield in dat er hetzij gebruik werd gemaakt van de in het aanbestedingsdocument gedefinieerde categorieën bodem, broeikasgassen, energie, afval, voedsel, drinkwater, biodiversiteit en klimaat, hetzij van algemeen bekende sectoren voor koolstofboekhouding (zoals mobiliteit, bouw, landbouw en industrie) en het meten van veerkracht (via luchtkwaliteit, waterkwaliteit, bodemkwaliteit, gezondheid van bossen, voedselzekerheid en energievoorziening). Dit alles diende als basis voor de ontwikkeling van een methodiek om voor Luxemburg een overgang naar minder carbonisering en meer veerkracht te ontwikkelen en te evalueren. Klimaatwetenschappers, economen en ingenieurs maakten in feite gebruik van Excel-tabellen en diagrammen om via subcategorieën en talloze individuele items inzichtelijk te maken hoe klimaatneutraliteit bereikt kon worden en hoe de veerkracht over een periode van bijna 30 jaar vergroot kon worden.

Door in de eerste fase ecologische criteria en normen voor het terugdringen van koolstof vast te stellen, wilde men voorkomen dat langetermijnplannen 'voornamelijk op het resultaat [gericht zouden zijn] en onvoldoende op het proces om dat resultaat te bereiken'.[16] Volgens Mantziaras hadden de consultaties voor Groot-Parijs en Groot-Genève uiteindelijk 'te weinig sleutelindicatoren voor het beheer van het transformatieproces en onvoldoende criteria om de betrokkenen ter verantwoording te roepen' opgeleverd.[17] Deze scherpe formulering maakt opnieuw duidelijk dat het de bedoeling was om niet alleen verder te komen dan de conventionele architectonische en stedenbouwkundige visies, maar ze ook te kunnen verifiëren en opvolgen met rekenmodellen voor vermindering van koolstof en ecologische veerkracht.

Deze eerste fase was vooral uitdagend voor stedenbouwkundigen en architecten, omdat ze opzettelijk werden afgehouden van hun gebruikelijke werkwijze om ruimtelijke strategieën te ontwikkelen. Tegelijkertijd moesten ze erkennen dat ruimtelijke planningsconcepten op verschillende gebieden bepaalde effecten kunnen veroorzaken. Op het gebied van de landbouw, bijvoorbeeld, toonden de berekeningen aan dat er relatief grote effecten behaald konden worden met relatief eenvoudige maatregelen – vooral door eetgewoonten te veranderen of voedselverspilling te vermijden. Tegelijkertijd werd duidelijk dat de mobiliteitssector verantwoordelijk was voor de helft van Luxemburgs ecologische voetafdruk en dat een strategie daarom niet alleen gebaseerd moest zijn op een verandering van de mobiliteit en infrastructuur, maar ook op een vermindering van de mobiliteit door middel van stedenbouwkundige ingrepen met betrekking tot kortere reisafstanden voor de meest essentiële activiteiten. Met minder mobiliteit zouden planners vervolgens een aanzienlijke hoeveelheid reeds verhard land ter beschikking krijgen, grond die in een klein land als Luxemburg zeer waardevol is met het oog op de gewenste intensivering. Geen enkel team was in staat om met die statistieken een klimaatneutraal resultaat te bereiken, zonder de binding van CO2 door natuurlijke

15 Département de l'aménagement du territoire, Luxembourg in Transition: Consultation internationale urbano-architecturale et paysagère, Cahier des charges (versie 15 juni 2020), Luxemburg. De betrokken teams waren: AREP, MVRDV, Universiteit Luxemburg, 2001, KCAP, TVK, Raum 404, AWP, Interland en Studio Paola Viganò. De voornaamste instellingen en bureaus zijn hier opgesomd; zie voor een volledig overzicht: https://luxembourgintransition.lu/fr/la-consultation-internationale/, Ministère de l'Energie et de l'Aménagement du Territoire.

16 Mantziaras, 'Urban Strategic Foresight', op. cit. (noot 13), 44.

17 Ibid.

In this first phase, the teams had to establish clear priorities, even though everyone was aware that the different sectors and their decarbonisation objectives were interwoven in complex ways. This presented a methodological dilemma: should the individual competing prospective plans each deal comprehensively with all the fields in order to show how the overall footprint can be reduced in accordance with the Paris Agreement, namely by 90 per cent in the Luxembourg context? Or should they deal in a targeted way with individual sectors or topics, to demonstrate more in-depth approaches that could ultimately lead to complete decarbonisation when combined together, but which would, however, go against the intent of holistic prospective planning? Given the complexity of the task, it is no surprise that none of the teams' approaches, and neither the sectoral nor the holistic ones, were able to be developed consistently. In the end, certain focal points were visible, but the desire for a synthesis ultimately prevailed, even if, by its very nature, it could not easily be realised.

In the second phase, for which six teams qualified, the aim was to demonstrate how the 'principles, methods, tools and metrics for ecological transformation through a spatial project' developed in the first phase could be applied in practice.[18] Basically, the metrics were now to be spatialised, and the Excel tables and diagrams translated into spatial and planning strategies. The first challenge – in line with the concept of transition – was to describe the decarbonised and resilient state in 2050 and the strategies over time to get there. In contrast to conventional regional and urban planning or the classic prospective planning of the 1970s, the aim here was to use backcasting methods to plan 'back into the future' in order to set the right immediate course. Here too, metrics had to be considered at every step, but this was only feasible with specific strategies and certain scales.

18 See: tender text of 15 June 2020, op. cit. (note 14), 54.

University of Luxembourg / Florian Hertweck & Aristaviva, Foetz case study. The careful development of the perimeter areas of these parking lots and the renaturation of the spaces in between turns this commercial zone into an urban neighbourhood for more than 10,000 residents/ University of Luxembourg / Florian Hertweck & Aristaviva, Foetz-casus. De zorgvuldige ontwikkeling van de randen van deze parkeerterreinen en de verwildering van de ruimten ertussen maakt deze handelszone tot een stedelijke wijk voor meer dan 10.000 bewoners

bodems mee te tellen. Het gevolg was dat onverharde gebieden – of liever gezegd het natuurherstel aldaar – een belangrijke component van alle benaderingen vormden.

In deze eerste fase moesten de teams duidelijk prioriteiten stellen, ook al was men zich ervan bewust dat de verschillende sectoren en hun pogingen om de decarbonisering op te lossen, op een ingewikkelde manier met elkaar verweven waren. Dit veroorzaakte een methodologisch dilemma: moesten de concurrerende langetermijnplannen elk ingaan op alle domeinen om te laten zien hoe de totale voetafdruk kon worden verminderd in overeenstemming met het Akkoord van Parijs, namelijk met 90 procent in de Luxemburgse context? Of moesten ze zich specifiek richten op afzonderlijke sectoren of thema's om meer de diepte in te gaan, zodat de combinatie van die beter ontwikkelde voorstellen uiteindelijk tot volledige terugdringing van koolstof zou leiden, wat wel zou ingaan tegen de intentie van holistische toekomstverkenning? Gezien de complexiteit van de taak is het niet verrassend dat geen van de teams, noch de sectorgerichte, noch de holistisch werkende, hun voorstellen consequent konden uitwerken. Uiteindelijk kwamen er wel bepaalde aandachtspunten naar voren, maar het verlangen naar een synthese overheerste, ook al bleek die uiteraard moeilijk te realiseren.

De tweede fase, waarvoor zich zes teams kwalificeerden, was bedoeld om te laten zien hoe de in de eerste fase ontwikkelde 'principes, methoden, instrumenten en berekeningen voor ecologische transformatie via een ruimtelijk project' in de praktijk konden worden toegepast.[18] Met andere woorden, de data moesten ruimtelijk worden vertaald, en de Excel-tabellen en diagrammen omgezet in ruimtelijke en planningsstrategieën. De eerste uitdaging, aansluitend bij het concept van transitie, was de beschrijving van de gedecarboniseerde en veerkrachtige toestand van 2050 en de methoden die in de loop der tijd zouden moeten worden toegepast om die te realiseren. In tegenstelling tot conventionele regionale en stedelijke planning of de klassieke langetermijnplanning uit de jaren 1970 lag de focus hier op achterwaarts redeneren om 'terug te plannen vanuit de toekomst' en zo een directe en effectieve koers uit te stippelen. Ook hier moest bij elke stap rekening worden gehouden met de statistische modellen, wat alleen mogelijk was met specifieke strategieën en schaalniveaus. De tweede uitdaging bestond uit het aantonen van de toepasbaarheid van deze strategieën op uiteenlopende niveaus: van de functionele, transnationale ruimte van Luxemburg tot de schaal van stedelijke planning, buurten en boerderijen. Naarmate de schaal groter werd, namen de complexiteit en diversiteit van de narekeningen toe.

In de derde fase, waarvoor zich uiteindelijk vier teams kwalificeerden, moesten voorbeeldige proefprojecten worden ontwikkeld op specifieke locaties. Deze projecten dienden ter verdere uitwerking van de langetermijnplannen op meerdere schaalniveaus, die zowel heel specifiek moesten zijn, maar ook als een gereedschapskist moesten fungeren voor de ontwikkeling van vergelijkbare typologieën op andere locaties. In dit opzicht leek de derde fase meer op een consultatie, waarin bewust geen winnaars werden aangewezen. Het doel was om, in de geest van de Consultation du Grand Paris en naar het voorbeeld van het AIGP, een instituut op te zetten dat proefprojecten zou realiseren, voortvloeiend uit het werk dat in de tweede fase was uitgevoerd, bijvoorbeeld de transformatie van commerciële zones, logistieke centra en tankstationstrips, de aanleg van groene gordels rond steden, de diversificatie van monofunctionele nieuwe

18
Zie: aanbestedingstekst van 15 juni 2020, op. cit. (noot 14), 54.

The second challenge consisted of demonstrating the application of these strategies across different scales: from the functional, transnational space of Luxembourg to the urban planning scale to neighbourhoods and farms. The larger the scale, the more complex the evaluation metrics.

In the third phase, for which four teams finally qualified, exemplary pilot projects were to be developed at specific locations – to deepen the trans-scalar prospective plans, which on the one hand had to be very specific, but on the other needed to be applicable as a toolkit for the development of the same typologies at other locations. In this respect, the third phase was more like a consultation, from which deliberately no winner was to emerge. The intention, in line with the Consultation du Grand Paris and analogous to the AIGP, was to create an institution to implement a large number of pilot projects that had emerged from the diverse work of the second phase, which included the transformation of commercial zones, logistics centres and petrol station strips, the creation of polyvalent green belts around cities and the diversification of monofunctional new development areas, and the introduction of *transferable rights* to transfer building rights from unsustainable development areas to already developed areas.

However, as Claude Turmes was no longer elected as the responsible minister for a further mandate and the new conservative-liberal government could not, or would not, identify sufficiently with the programme, this phase of implementation did not take place. Only two projects are currently still being pursued. The outcome is uncertain. This situation reveals an inherent vulnerability in prospective planning, which by definition is designed for the long term, but relies on political continuity, not least because plans have to be regularly evaluated and adapted, which is at odds with democratically elected politicians who often think and act in the short

Exhibition at the Luxembourg Center for Architecture on the results of Luxembourg in Transition, 2023/ Tentoonstelling in het Luxembourg Center for Architecture over de resultaten van Luxembourg in Transition, 2023

ontwikkelingsgebieden en de introductie van overdraagbare rechten, waarmee bouwrechten van niet-duurzame ontwikkelingsgebieden konden worden overgedragen naar reeds ontwikkelde gebieden.

Omdat Claude Turmes echter niet werd herkozen en dus geen nieuwe ambtstermijn als verantwoordelijke minister kreeg en de nieuwe conservatief-liberale regering zich onvoldoende kon of wilde identificeren met het programma, werd deze implementatiefase niet uitgevoerd. Slechts twee projecten zijn momenteel nog in ontwikkeling, waarvan de uitkomst onzeker is. Deze situatie benadrukt de inherente kwetsbaarheid van langetermijnplanning, die – zoals de naam al aangeeft – is gericht op de lange termijn, maar tegelijkertijd afhankelijk blijft van politieke continuïteit, niet in het minst omdat plannen regelmatig moeten worden geëvalueerd en aangepast, wat vaak haaks staat op het kortetermijndenken en -handelen van democratisch gekozen politici. De komende jaren zal moeten blijken of de toenemende druk van klimaatverandering hierin een kentering teweegbrengt.

Een ander instrument voor kwaliteitsborging zal echter waarschijnlijk een blijvender effect hebben. Naast de oprichting van een wetenschappelijke adviesraad, waarvoor ook vertegenwoordigers van de gemeenten in de grensregio's werden uitgenodigd, werd een burgerberaad met 30 deelnemers ingesteld om het programma proactief te begeleiden. Het is mogelijk dat deze (klimaat)burgerberaden of burgerparlementen in staat blijken om de hierboven beschreven tegenstrijdigheid te overwinnen en duurzame strategieën te waarborgen. In ieder geval presenteerde het burgerberaad van Luxembourg in Transition een catalogus met aanbevelingen die in grote lijnen overeenkwamen met de strategieën van de teams.

In de derde fase, en na een jaar van intensieve arbeid en verschillende tussentijdse presentaties en workshops, werd duidelijk dat de afzonderlijke langetermijnplannen elkaar op veel manieren overlapten. Hoewel ze verschilden qua focus, gingen ze allemaal dezelfde richting op, wat leidde tot de formulering van een gezamenlijk manifest. Het was voor alle teams bijvoorbeeld duidelijk dat er zo snel mogelijk een einde moest komen aan de verharding. Het enige punt van verschil was de vraag of het daarbij om een netto- of bruto ruimtebeslag ging. Naast de transformatie van het mobiliteits-, water- en landbouwbeleid en de bevordering van alternatieve economische en ecologische initiatieven gericht op het algemeen welzijn, bevatte het manifest ook een oproep voor een sterk huisvestingsbeleid zonder winstoogmerk en een beleid voor grondeigendom met het algemeen welzijn als prioriteit.[19] De langetermijnplannen voor een regio als Luxemburg, die een sterke groei moet blijven vertonen om zijn sociale diensten te financieren, gingen zich dus concentreren op de meer fundamentele vraag of (en hoe) groei en ecologie verenigbaar zijn. Verrassend misschien dat alle teams kritisch stonden tegenover de haalbaarheid van een groene, technologisch georiënteerde transformatie van het productiesysteem en dat ze een op toereikendheid en openbaar welzijn gerichte aanpak centraal stelden in hun plannen. Sommige externe waarnemers uitten kritiek op het feit dat geen van de teams zich richtte op de medeplichtigheid en verantwoordelijkheid van de financiële sector, hoewel dit buiten de opdracht van het programma was gebleven.[20]

De meeste teams gingen uit van een gematigde bevolkingsgroei als uitgangspunt of constante (tegenover de vele variabelen) voor de berekeningen en plannen.[21] Alle teams probeerden te laten zien in hoeverre deze groei kon worden opgevangen zonder meer grond te verharden of het

19
2001, AREP, MVRDV, Université du Luxembourg, *Manifeste pour la neutralité carbone du territoire* (2021), luxembourgintransition.lu/fr/la-consultation-internationale/#manifeste (geraadpleegd 29 juni 2024).

20
Iets later lanceerde het Luxemburgse ministerie van Economie een soortgelijk programma, Luxstrategie, onder leiding van Pascale Juncker, die eerder op het ministerie van Planning had gewerkt. Er werd geen poging gedaan om de twee strategische plannen te combineren. De sociaal-democratische minister Franz Fayot, initiatiefnemer van dit programma, maakt momenteel geen deel uit van de regering.

21
Op basis van het scenario voor de middellangetermijn van STATEC dat een demografische groei van 1,5 procent tegen 2050 voorspelt, resulteert dit voor het land Luxemburg in een bevolkingsaantal van 966.000.

term. The next few years will show whether the pressure of climate change will change this.

However, another quality assurance instrument is likely to have a more lasting effect. In addition to the establishment of a scientific and a consultative advisory board, to which representatives of the municipalities in the border regions were also invited, a citizens' council with 30 participants was set up to proactively accompany the programme. It is possible that these (climate) citizens' councils or citizens' parliaments are an instrument for overcoming the contradiction described above and ensuring sustainable strategies. In any case, the Luxembourg in Transition Citizens' Council presented a catalogue of recommendations that essentially coincided with the teams' strategies.

In the third phase and after a year of intensive work with various interim presentations and workshops, it became apparent that there were many overlaps between the individual prospective plans, and that they were all heading in the same direction, albeit with different focal points, which led to the formulation of a joint manifesto. For example, it was clear to all teams that land sealing must be stopped as soon as possible. The only point of divergence was the question of whether this meant net or gross land take. In addition to a transformation of mobility, water and agriculture policy, and the promotion of alternative economic and ecological initiatives orientated towards the common good, the manifesto also includes the call for a strong non-profit housing policy and a common good oriented approach to land ownership.[19] As such, the prospective plans for a region like Luxembourg, which is shackled to strong growth in order to finance its social systems, thus became concerned with the more fundamental question of whether and how growth and ecology are compatible. It may come as a surprise that all the teams took a critical view of the hypothesis of the green, technology-oriented transformation of the productive system and placed sufficiency and public welfare-oriented approaches at the centre of their plans. Some external observers were critical of the fact that none of the teams focused on the complicity and responsibility of the financial industry, although this would have gone beyond the remit of the programme.[20]

Most of the teams assumed moderate population growth as the starting point or constant (compared with the many variables) for the calculations and plans.[21] All teams aimed to demonstrate the extent to which such growth could be accommodated without sealing off more land and without further urban sprawl in the hinterland. The strategies varied from adding storeys to existing buildings and increasing density in certain areas, to utilising vacant land and developing already sealed areas, particularly in commercial and logistics zones, not only to create more usable space but also to systematically diversify existing areas. The fact that these strategies regularly rub up against the constraints of land ownership makes it clear how essential this issue is for the socioecological transition, but also that this is a political project as much as a technological or spatial design challenge. The fact that a minister who at least addressed these controversial and complex issues was ultimately voted out of office does not bode well for the future. Does this mean the end of confidence once again?

The output of Luxembourg in Transition is certainly remarkable: with three extensive reports from each of the four finalists, a joint manifesto, a catalogue of recommendations from the Citizens' Council, many sophisticated pilot projects, a publication and an exhibition. In addition, the findings

19 2001, AREP, MVRDV, Université du Luxembourg, *Manifeste pour la neutralité carbone du territoire* (2021), luxembourgintransition.lu/fr/la-consultation-internationale/#manifeste (accessed 29 June 2024).

20 Somewhat later, the Luxembourg Ministry of the Economy launched a similar programme, Luxstrategie, which was headed by Pascale Juncker, who had previously worked in the national planning ministry. No attempt was made to synthesise the two strategic plans. The social democratic minister Franz Fayot, who initiated this programme, is no longer in the current government.

21 Based on the STATEC medium scenario of demographic growth of 1.5 per cent by 2050, this results in a population of 966,000 for the country of Luxembourg.

Tentoonstelling in het Luxembourg Center for Architecture over de resultaten van Luxembourg in Transition, 2023

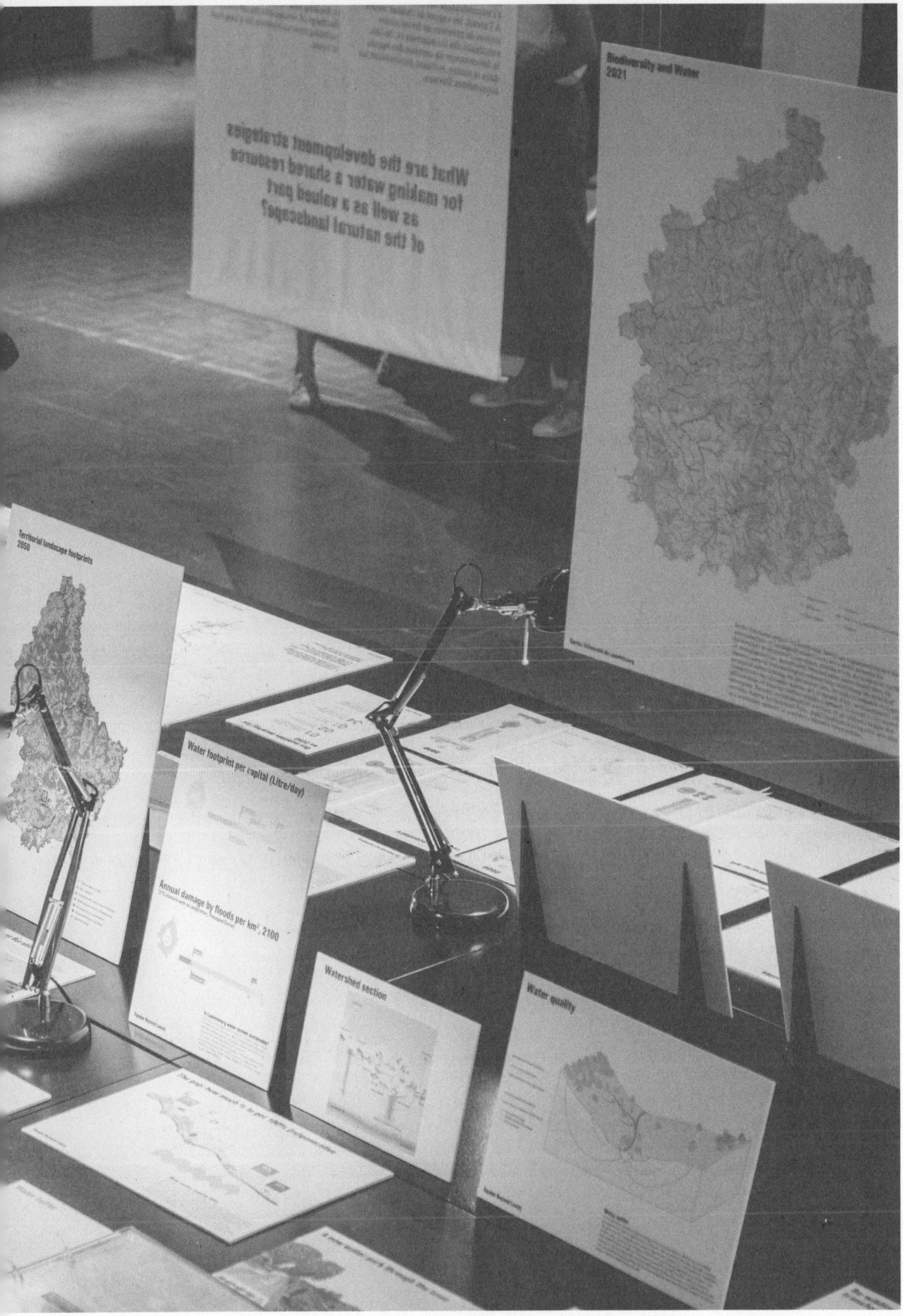

Exhibition at the Luxembourg Center for Architecture on the results of Luxembourg in Transition, 2023

achterland verder te suburbaniseren. Hun strategieën varieerden van de toevoeging van lagen op bestaande gebouwen en grotere dichtheden in bepaalde gebieden, tot de benutting van braakliggend terrein en de ontwikkeling van reeds verharde gebieden, met name commerciële en logistieke terreinen, niet alleen om meer bruikbare ruimte te creëren, maar ook om bestaande gebieden systematisch te diversifiëren. Het feit dat deze strategieën regelmatig botsen met de beperkingen van het grondbezit demonstreert niet alleen hoe essentieel deze kwestie is voor een socio-ecologische transitie, maar ook dat dit net zo goed een politiek project is als een technologische of ruimtelijke ontwerpuitdaging. Het feit dat een minister die deze controversiële en complexe kwesties in elk geval aan de orde stelde, uiteindelijk werd weggestemd, voorspelt niet veel goeds voor de toekomst. Is dit opnieuw een verlies aan vertrouwen?

De resultaten van Luxembourg in Transition zijn zeker opmerkelijk: drie uitgebreide rapporten van elk van de vier finalisten, een gezamenlijk manifest, een catalogus met aanbevelingen van het burgerberaad, een groot aantal geavanceerde proefprojecten, een publicatie en een tentoonstelling. Bovendien hebben de bevindingen en strategieën van Luxembourg in Transition het regionale masterplan van de regering (Plan Directeur de l'Aménagement du Territoire, PDAT) aanzienlijk beïnvloed, hoewel sommige maatregelen, zoals de doelstelling van nul netto grondinname, door andere regeringsafdelingen zijn afgezwakt. Deze rijke en diverse resultaten kunnen worden toegeschreven aan de verschillende kwaliteitsborgingsmaatregelen uit het programma, zoals de uitdaging om kwalitatieve en kwantitatieve methoden en criteria samen te voegen of het belang van iteratieve evaluatieprocessen om doorlopend toezicht op beslissingen en resultaten te houden. De grootste successen waren de strategische combinatie van competitie en consultatie; de prioritering in de eerste fase om data voor decarbonisering en veerkracht te definiëren; de betrokkenheid van zeer verschillende besluitvormers in verschillende commissies en de oprichting van een burgerberaad. Dit burgerberaad was er niet alleen om het programma kritisch en constructief te begeleiden, maar ook om de haalbaarheid ervan te bevorderen. In de toekomst moet de toekomstverkenning, die dringend nodig is, niet alleen voortbouwen op dergelijke benaderingen, maar zelfs nog meer aandacht besteden aan manieren om de meest overtuigende concepten, strategieën en instrumenten uitvoerbaar te krijgen, ongeacht de perioden en cycli van wetgeving en politiek. Niet alleen de strategieën, maar ook de programma's die deze strategieën produceren, moeten tijdig – en in de tijd – worden uitgedacht.

Vertaling: InOtherWords, Maria van Tol

and strategies of Luxembourg in Transition have significantly influenced the government's regional master plan (Plan Directeur de l'Aménagement du Territoire, PDAT), even if some measures, such as the target of zero-net land take, have been watered down by other departments of the government. The rich and diverse outcomes can be linked to various quality assurance measures incorporated into the programme that took up the challenge to integrate qualitative and quantitative methods and criteria, and foregrounded the importance of establishing iterative evaluation processes to enable ongoing monitoring of decisions and outcomes. What were most successful were the strategic combination of competition and consultation processes, the prioritisation in the first phase of establishing the metrics of decarbonisation and resilience, the involvement of very different decision-makers in various commissions, and the constitution of a citizens' council, which was not only intended to critically and constructively accompany the programme, but also to promote its feasibility. Future prospective planning, which is urgently needed, should build on these approaches, and pay even more attention to how the most convincing concepts, strategies and instruments can be implemented, regardless of legislative periods and political cycles. Not only the strategies, but also the programmes that produce these strategies must be thought through in – and on – time.

Hier kan over architectuur gepraat worden: Farrell Centre en Track

Julie Mabilde

Steden zijn voortdurend in verandering. Nieuwe architectuur- en stadsprojecten hebben een grote invloed op de leefomgeving van bewoners, maar niet alle bewoners hebben inzicht en inspraak in hoe die veranderingen aangestuurd worden. Twee initiatieven – het *Farrell Centre* in Groot-Brittannië en *Track* in Brussel – trachten dit te verhelpen, door letterlijk ruimte te bieden voor gesprek. Het Farrell Centre, voortbouwend op het model van *urban rooms* (stadskamers), legt de nadruk op de vergroting van de kennis over stadsontwikkeling; Track werkt aan gemeenschapsvorming, zodat lokale bewoners er beter in slagen voor hun rechten op te komen. Beide willen een breder doelpubliek bereiken en dat publiek een stem geven: de een zet in op emancipatie door verheffing, de ander op emancipatie door vereniging.

Het belang van de plaats

Het ontwerp en de toekomstige ontwikkeling van de stad en de buurt waarin we wonen, gaat iedereen aan, maar stadsplanning wordt vaak gepercipieerd als een top-down en weinig transparant proces van politieke en ambtelijke beslissingen, een zwarte doos waar gewone burgers – in tegenstelling tot ontwikkelaars – geen toegang toe en medezeggenschap over hebben. Daarom moet elke stad een plek hebben waar gesprek over erfgoed, ontwerp en het maken van betekenisvolle plekken (*placemaking*) mogelijk is, waar je kan leren over het verleden en debatteren over de toekomst van steden, en waar ook moeilijk bereikbare groepen hun weg naartoe vinden: een stadskamer (*urban room*).

Dat is althans een van de aanbevelingen van het Farrell Review, waarin een groep experts onder leiding van architect Terry Farrell, en in opdracht van de Britse regering, een onafhankelijke evaluatie maakte van de architectuur en bebouwde omgeving.[1] Het rapport, gepubliceerd in 2014 onder de titel *Our Future in Place*, formuleerde een reeks acties en aanbevelingen om de bebouwde omgeving onder de aandacht te brengen in het onderwijs, en het politieke en publieke debat – niet enkel gericht op beleidsmakers of ontwerpers, maar met de intentie om een bredere betrokkenheid te creëren bij de plekken waar we wonen en werken.

Het begrip 'plaats' stond centraal in de resultaten van het Farrell Review en heeft verschillende betekenissen: PLACE is een acroniem voor de disciplines die betrokken zijn bij het ontwerp van de gebouwde omgeving: *Planning, Landscape, Architecture, Construction & Engineering*, en staat voor de behoefte aan interdisciplinaire uitwisseling en samenwerking tussen deze kennisgebieden. Het centraal stellen van 'plaats' gaf ook aan dat de focus niet beperkt mag blijven tot het ontwerp van individuele gebouwen, maar een meer holistische blik op de bebouwde omgeving als vertrekpunt moet hebben. De nadruk ligt op het belang van plannen op maat van de specifieke plek, haar betekenis, geschiedenis, gebruikers,

1 The Farrell Review of Architecture + the Built Environment, *Our Future in Place* (2014). Het rapport werd besteld nadat de regering in 2011 de Britse Commission for Architecture and the Built Environment (CABE) had opgeheven.

A Place to Talk about Architecture: Farrell Centre and Track

Julie Mabilde

Cities are constantly changing. New architectural and urban projects have a significant impact on the living environment of residents, but not all residents have access to the knowledge or the opportunity to influence these changes. Two initiatives – the Farrell Centre in the UK and Track in Brussels – seek to remedy this by, literally, providing places to talk about architecture. The Farrell Centre, inspired by the 'urban room' concept, focuses on increasing people's knowledge of urban development. Track promotes community building to empower local residents to advocate more effectively for their rights. Both initiatives share the goal of reaching a wider audience and amplifying their voices: one seeks emancipation through education, the other emancipation through collective action.

The Importance of the Place

The design and future development of the cities and neighbourhoods we live in affects us all. Yet urban design is often perceived as a top-down and opaque process of political and bureaucratic decision-making, a black box to which ordinary citizens – unlike developers – have no access and in which they have no say. That is why every city should have a place where people can talk about heritage, design and placemaking, where they can learn about the city's past and discuss its future and to which hard-to-reach groups can find their way: an urban room.

This is one of the recommendations of the Farrell Review, an independent assessment of architecture and the built environment conducted at the request of the UK government by a group of experts led by architect Terry Farrell.[1] The resulting report, *Our Future in Place*, published in 2014, outlined a series of actions and recommendations designed to bring the built environment to the fore in education, policy and public discourse. The proposals were not aimed solely at policymakers or designers, but were also meant to strengthen people's commitment to the places where they live and work.

Central to the findings of the Farrell Review was the concept of 'place', which has several meanings. PLACE is an acronym for the disciplines involved in the design of the built environment: Planning, Landscape, Architecture, Construction & Engineering, and represents the need for interdisciplinary exchange and collaboration between these fields of knowledge. The centrality of 'place' also highlighted the need to move away from a focus on the design of individual buildings to a more holistic view of the built environment. This approach emphasised the importance of planning that is attuned to specific places, including their significance, history, users, residents and local organisations. It also emphasised the importance of placemaking, suggesting that the planning, design and management of public spaces should not be the exclusive domain of professional citymakers, but should involve collaboration with local communities. This is precisely where urban rooms play a crucial role.

1
The Farrell Review of Architecture + the Built Environment, *Our Future in Place* (2014). The Review was commissioned after the government had discontinued the British Commission for Architecture and the Built Environment (CABE) in 2011.

bewoners en lokale organisaties, én op dat van betekenisvolle plekken, ervan uitgaand dat de planning, het ontwerp en het beheer van publieke ruimten niet enkel door professionele stadsmakers, maar in samenwerking met de lokale gemeenschappen dient te gebeuren. En precies dat is waar stadskamers een rol kunnen spelen.

In navolging van het Farrell Review ontstond in 2015 het Urban Rooms Network, waarin goede ervaringen gedeeld worden tussen de vele *urban rooms* die ondertussen in Groot-Brittannië werden opgericht.[2] In werkelijkheid zijn er grote verschillen in de manier waarop, door en voor wie die stadskamers worden ingericht, afhankelijk van de context en de initiatiefnemers. Volgens het Urban Rooms Network kunnen ze nuttig zijn voor lokale gemeenschappen die meer inspraak willen, voor lokale besturen die burgers beter en op andere manieren willen betrekken bij stedenbouw, voor ontwerpers die willen experimenteren hoe ze sociaal engagement inbedden in hun werkwijze, of voor onderzoekers en docenten die samenwerking met burgerorganisaties ambiëren.

Elke *urban room* heeft echter ook een eigen agenda, dus rijst de vraag wie dan – en dit hangt samen met de financiering – het eigenaarschap en de curatorrol op zich neemt. Het Farrell Review formuleert een visie voor een stadskamer, georganiseerd rond een maquette en met veel aandacht voor het stadsverleden, die dicht aanleunt bij klassieke architectuurcentra of stadsmusea met een meer institutionele setting. Het Urban Rooms Network daarentegen benadrukt het belang van een opendeurenbeleid en bottom-up programmering als belangrijke condities, opdat ook bevolkingsgroepen die in planningsprocessen ondervertegenwoordigd zijn, meedoen. De focus ligt nog steeds op de gebouwde omgeving, maar met bijzondere aandacht voor de gedeelde ruimte van straten, buurten en publieke

2 Zie: urbanroomsnetwork.org/. Het Urban Rooms Network wordt gehost door de UCL Bartlett School of Planning en is een van de werkgroepen van Place Alliance, een vrijwillig professioneel netwerk dat eveneens werd opgericht in de nasleep van The Farrell Review.

The Farrell Centre in Newcastle, with a gallery on the ground floor and the urban rooms on the upper level/ Het Farrell Centre in Newcastle, met een galerie op de begane grond en de *urban rooms* op de verdieping

Following the Farrell Review, the Urban Rooms Network was established in 2015 to share good practice between the many urban rooms that have since been established across the UK.[2] On the ground, urban rooms vary widely in how, by whom and for whom they are established, reflecting different contexts and initiators. According to the Urban Rooms Network, they can be valuable for local communities seeking greater participation, for local governments seeking to engage citizens more effectively and innovatively in urban design, for designers exploring ways to integrate social engagement into their work, and for researchers and educators who want to work with community organisations.

2 See: urbanroomsnetwork.org/. The Urban Rooms Network is hosted by the UCL Bartlett School of Planning and is one of the working groups of Place Alliance, a voluntary professional network also established in the wake of The Farrell Review.

However, each urban room also has its own agenda, raising the question of who will take ownership and assume the curatorial role – a question often linked to funding. The Farrell Review envisions urban rooms centred on models, with a strong focus on the city's past, resembling classical architecture centres or urban museums with institutional settings. The Urban Rooms Network, on the other hand, emphasises the importance of open-door policy and bottom-up programming, ensuring that previously underrepresented groups are actively involved in planning processes. While the focus remains on the built environment, the shared spaces of streets, neighbourhoods and public spaces receive special attention and low-threshold creative activities – such as drawing sessions, storytelling, collective mapping, construction kits or interactive models for children, city walks, games, *in-situ* installations – are used to spark curiosity and inspire visitors to look at the future of their neighbourhoods with fresh eyes. Crucially, urban rooms must be situated 'on site', embedded in the places under discussion.

Curatorship and Ownership

The Farrell Review also recommends mixed funding for urban rooms, drawing resources from both the public and private sectors to ensure that neither can claim exclusive ownership. The Farrell Centre in Newcastle is a fascinating example of this approach. Positioned somewhat closer to a cultural institution than other Urban Rooms, the project was initiated by a foundation set up by Terry Farrell himself, who grew up in Newcastle and studied at Newcastle University. The Farrell Centre is located on the edge of the university campus, just north of the city centre, in a former Victorian department store. The building features a gallery for temporary exhibitions on the ground floor, with a display window opening onto the public realm. The upper floors house urban rooms, which are hybrid spaces equipped with various displays – some digital and interactive – that showcase the city's evolution and include historical representations. These spaces can be used by a variety of groups, from schools to local heritage societies, to host activities in line with the Farrell Centre's mission to be a hub for dialogue about the built environment.

The heritage value and the large display window on the ground floor give the Farrell Centre the feel of a museum or art gallery. The active base and the new forecourt are designed to make the building attractive and accessible, drawing visitors inside. The refurbishment has been co-funded by Terry Farrell's own foundation, while Newcastle University's School of Architecture, Planning & Landscape is funding operations and programming. Students and lecturers contribute their knowledge and time, becoming actively involved in the programming of the urban rooms. The Farrell Centre is led by curator, historian and writer Owen Hopkins. He and his

plekken, en laagdrempelige creatieve activiteiten – zoals tekensessies, stadsverhalen breien, *collective mapping*, bouwpakketten of interactieve maquettes voor kinderen, stadswandelingen, spelen, in-situ installaties, enzovoort – worden georganiseerd om de nieuwsgierigheid te prikkelen en bezoekers aan te zetten met een frisse blik naar de toekomst van hun buurt te kijken. Dat de stadskamer 'op locatie' ingericht wordt, middenin de plekken die ter discussie staan, is dan ook essentieel.

3 Mark Tewdwr-Jones, Dhruv Sookhoo en Robert Freestone, 'From Geddes' city museum to Farrell's urban room: past, present, and future at the Newcastle City Futures exhibition', *Planning Perspective*, 35/2 (2020), 277-297.

Curatorschap en eigenaarschap

Het Farrell Review pleit ook voor een gemengde financiering van *urban rooms*, met middelen uit zowel de publieke als de private sector, waarbij geen van beide het exclusieve eigenaarschap kan opeisen. Het Farrell Centre in Newcastle is in dat opzicht een interessant voorbeeld. Het is een (meervoudige) stadskamer die, in vergelijking met andere, wellicht dichter aanleunt bij een culturele instelling. Het project werd geïnitieerd door de stichting van Terry Farrell zelf, die opgroeide in Newcastle en studeerde aan Newcastle University. Het Farrell Centre bevindt zich aan de rand van de universiteitscampus net ten noorden van het stadscentrum, in een voormalig, Victoriaans warenhuis. Het gebouw beschikt op de begane grond over een galerie waar tijdelijke tentoonstellingen plaatsvinden, met een etalage naar de publieke ruimte, en meer vaste inrichtingen op de bovenverdieping. Het zijn hybride vertrekken waar een aantal (soms ook digitale en interactieve) *displays* aanwezig zijn, die tonen hoe de stad geëvolueerd is en hoe ze vroeger werd afgebeeld. De ruimten kunnen verder vrij ingevuld worden door groepen, van scholen tot lokale erfgoedverenigingen, om er activiteiten te organiseren die stroken met de missie van het Farrell Centre om het trefpunt van gesprek rond de bebouwde ruimte te zijn.

De erfgoedwaarde en de grote vitrine op de begane grond geven het Farrell Centre de allure van een museum of kunstgalerie. De actieve plint en een nieuw voorplein moeten het gebouw aantrekkelijk en toegankelijk maken, en bezoekers naar binnen lokken. De verbouwing werd mede gefinancierd door de stichting van Terry Farrell zelf, maar Newcastle University, School of Architecture, Planning & Landscape financiert de werking en programmering. Studenten en docenten investeren kennis en tijd, en zijn op die manier betrokken bij de organisatie van de stadskamers. Farrell Centre wordt geleid door Owen Hopkins: curator, historicus en publicist. Hij en zijn team zijn verbonden aan de universiteit maar geven er geen les, waarbij Hopkins' achtergrond in de sector van de architectuurcultuur uiteraard ook een rol speelt in de programmering. De openingstentoonstelling in mei 2023, waar het silhouet van Michelangelo's David in roze namaakbont werd getoond, en een installatie met mycelium, zwammen en schimmels, had tot doel traditionele methoden en materialen om architectuur te maken ter discussie te stellen, iets waar universiteiten en ontwerpopleidingen vandaag mee experimenteren – al is het wellicht niet het meest evidente thema om een nieuw en breder publiek kennis te laten maken met architectuur.

Farrell's visie op *urban rooms* werd eerder al vergeleken met het pleidooi, meer dan een eeuw oud, van stedenbouwkundige en socioloog Patrick Geddes om civiele musea in te richten waar bewoners een beter idee krijgen van hun relatie tot hun omgeving en hoe die, in al haar gelaagdheid, tot stand is gekomen.[3] Beide gaan uit van het idee dat educatie en informatie een eerste stap naar emancipatie zijn: je moet geïnformeerd

team are affiliated with the university but do not teach there, and Hopkins's background in the field of architecture culture naturally informs the programming. The opening exhibition in May 2023, featuring the silhouette of Michelangelo's David in pink faux fur and an installation with mycelium, fungi and mushrooms, aimed to challenge traditional methods and materials used in architecture. This is an area that universities and design programmes are currently experimenting with – but perhaps not the most obvious theme for introducing architecture to a new and wider audience.

Farrell's vision for urban rooms has previously been compared to urban designer and sociologist Patrick Geddes's century-old call for the creation of civic museums, where residents could better understand their relationship to their surroundings and how this came to be, in all of its complexity.[3] Both start from the idea that education and information are the first steps towards emancipation: people must be informed to be able to participate in a conversation and showing the complexity of urban development in the past, or the many plans that never came to fruition, can be instructive. In his own Outlook Tower in Edinburgh, Geddes combined a museum with an urban laboratory and research, blending a look back at the past with reflection on the future.

However, the idea of having an 'overview' of what is happening in a city and how it is developing, either from a tower or through a model, is insufficient to represent the many, often asymmetrical interests at play – and to counter the imbalance in representation. Citymaking is about much more than building and physically visible activities alone: it is also about the management and use of public spaces, about the question of who gets to appropriate those spaces and about a sense of ownership and belonging.

The fact that the Urban Rooms Network places much greater emphasis on bottom-up programming is therefore refreshing, but likely also necessary to bring discussions about architecture and urban design out of their niche, which is often filled with its own, very hermetic jargon. Urban rooms should not only provide a view of the city from a tower or from a designer's perspective, but also be at eye level, accessible and in the midst of the hustle and bustle of the city and the public space. Many of the urban rooms established in the UK in recent years have stayed far from the model of the classical cultural institution. Some were temporary, or set up in empty buildings or shop windows, without permanent exhibitions or rigid programming. Others have also provided space for a range of activities (yoga, communal cooking, makerspaces) that at first glance may not seem closely related to citymaking, but which help to foster a sense of ownership. There are also urban rooms – such as Live Works in Sheffield – that provide architecture education, forcing educators to adapt the language they use to discuss architecture and quality so that the discourse becomes more accessible to, and better resonates with, the lived experiences of visitors.[4]

The Farrell Centre itself brings together several ambitions: it is a cultural space with its own agenda and programme of exhibitions and lectures, a community space for bottom-up participation in planning processes and, through its association with the university, a knowledge and research centre. The combination of these three ambitions makes it an interesting experiment in how to foster a conversation about urban development from different perspectives – ranging from that of the architecture student or researcher to that of the local resident. However,

3
Mark Tewdwr-Jones, Dhruv Sookhoo and Robert Freestone, 'From Geddes' City Museum to Farrell's Urban Room: Past, Present, and Future at the Newcastle City Futures Exhibition', *Planning Perspective* 35/2 (2020), 277-297.

4
Live Works director Carolyn Butterworth in conversation with Owen Hopkins during the first City Forum organised by the Farrell Centre on 4 May 2023.

zijn om te kunnen meespreken, en het laten zien van de complexiteit van stadsontwikkeling in het verleden, of de vele plannen die het niet gehaald hebben, kan instructief zijn. In zijn eigen Outlook Tower in Edinburgh combineerde Geddes de werking van een museum met die van stedelijk laboratorium en onderzoek, en een terugblik naar het verleden met nadenken over de toekomst.

Het idee 'overzicht' te hebben op wat er gaande is in een stad en hoe die zich ontwikkelt, vanuit een ivoren toren of aan de hand van een maquette, is echter onvoldoende om de vele, vaak asymmetrische, belangen die daarbij spelen in beeld te brengen én die onevenwichtigheid in representativiteit ook te counteren. Stadmaken gaat over veel meer dan louter bouwen en de fysiek zichtbare activiteiten, maar even goed over het beheer en gebruik van publieke ruimten, over wie zich die plekken kan toe-eigenen, over een gevoel van eigenaarschap en erbij horen.

Dat het Urban Rooms Network veel sterker inzet op een programmering van onderop is daarom verfrissend, maar wellicht ook noodzakelijk om gesprekken over architectuur en stedenbouw uit hun niche met een eigen, vaak erg hermetisch jargon te halen. *Urban rooms* moeten de stad niet zozeer of enkel overschouwen vanuit een ivoren toren of met de blik van een planner, maar zich ook op ooghoogte en toegankelijk, middenin het gewoel van de stad en de publieke ruimte plaatsen. Veel stadskamers die de afgelopen jaren in Groot-Brittannië zijn opgericht, strookten niet met het model van de klassieke culturele instelling. Sommige waren tijdelijk, of vestigden zich in leegstaande gebouwen of winkeletalages, zonder permanente tentoonstelling of al te vastgelegde programmering, en soms ook met ruimte voor heel wat andere activiteiten, zoals yoga, samen koken, maakplekken die op het eerste gezicht niet erg veel te maken hebben met stadmaken, maar die helpen om het gevoel van eigenaarschap te vergroten. Er zijn ook *urban rooms*, zoals Live Works in Sheffield, waar architectuurlessen gegeven worden, en dat dwingt docenten om de taal waarin ze over architectuur en kwaliteit praten aan te passen, opdat het discours ook toegankelijk wordt voor en beter aansluit bij de leefwereld van bezoekers.[4]

Het Farrell Centre zelf verenigt verschillende ambities: het is een cultureel centrum met een eigen agenda en programmering van tentoonstellingen en lezingen, een gemeenschapsruimte voor participatie in planningsprocessen van onderop, en door zijn link met de universiteit is het tevens een kennis- en onderzoekscentrum. De combinatie van die drie ambities maakt het tot een interessant experiment in, hoe je vanuit verschillende perspectieven – van architect in opleiding via onderzoeker tot buurtbewoner – een gesprek voert over stadsontwikkeling, maar het is tegelijk ook aartsmoeilijk om het evenwicht tussen die drie te bewaren en een gemeenschappelijke taal te vinden, en onvermijdelijk zal een van de ambities altijd de overhand nemen.

Wat is dan het effect op de bebouwde ruimte, en vereist die niet ook een koppeling met concrete projecten met concrete budgetten, en met de lokale stadsdiensten die de stadsvernieuwingsprojecten aansturen? Terry Farrell gelooft heel erg in het democratische proces, en dat door het belang van de bebouwde omgeving meer in het publieke debat te brengen, dit automatisch ook van invloed zou zijn op de beleidsagenda. Maar, geeft Owen Hopkins aan, zo eenvoudig werkt het niet, en bovendien zijn burgers niet per definitie geïnteresseerd in die holistische blik op de gebouwde omgeving, maar wel in heel particuliere kwesties in hun buurt die hen persoonlijk aangaan.

4 Carolyn Butterworth, directeur van Live Works, in gesprek met Owen Hopkins tijdens het eerste City Forum, georganiseerd door het Farrell Centre, 4 mei 2023.

it is also extremely difficult to maintain a balance between these three ambitions and find a common language and, inevitably, one of the ambitions will always take precedence.

What, then, is their impact on the built environment and does this not also require a connection to concrete projects with specific budgets, as well as with the local city services that drive urban renewal projects? Terry Farrell is a strong believer in the democratic process and also believes that highlighting the importance of the built environment in the public debate will automatically have an impact on the policy agenda. However, as Owen Hopkins points out, it's not that simple and citizens are not necessarily interested in holistic views of the built environment, but rather in very specific issues in their neighbourhood that directly affect them.

This is why, after the startup period that served to put the Farrell Centre on the map, the planning for the coming years will focus more on specific neighbourhoods, both in the city centre and in more suburban areas. Compared with London, Newcastle does not have many large-scale urban regeneration projects, says Hopkins, but rather incremental changes to the built fabric, which can still have a significant impact on neighbourhoods. At the same time, he emphasises the need to look beyond the boundaries of a relatively small city like Newcastle. There is a wider, national or European discussion about the future of cities, with many cities facing the same challenges that the Farrell Centre aims to address.

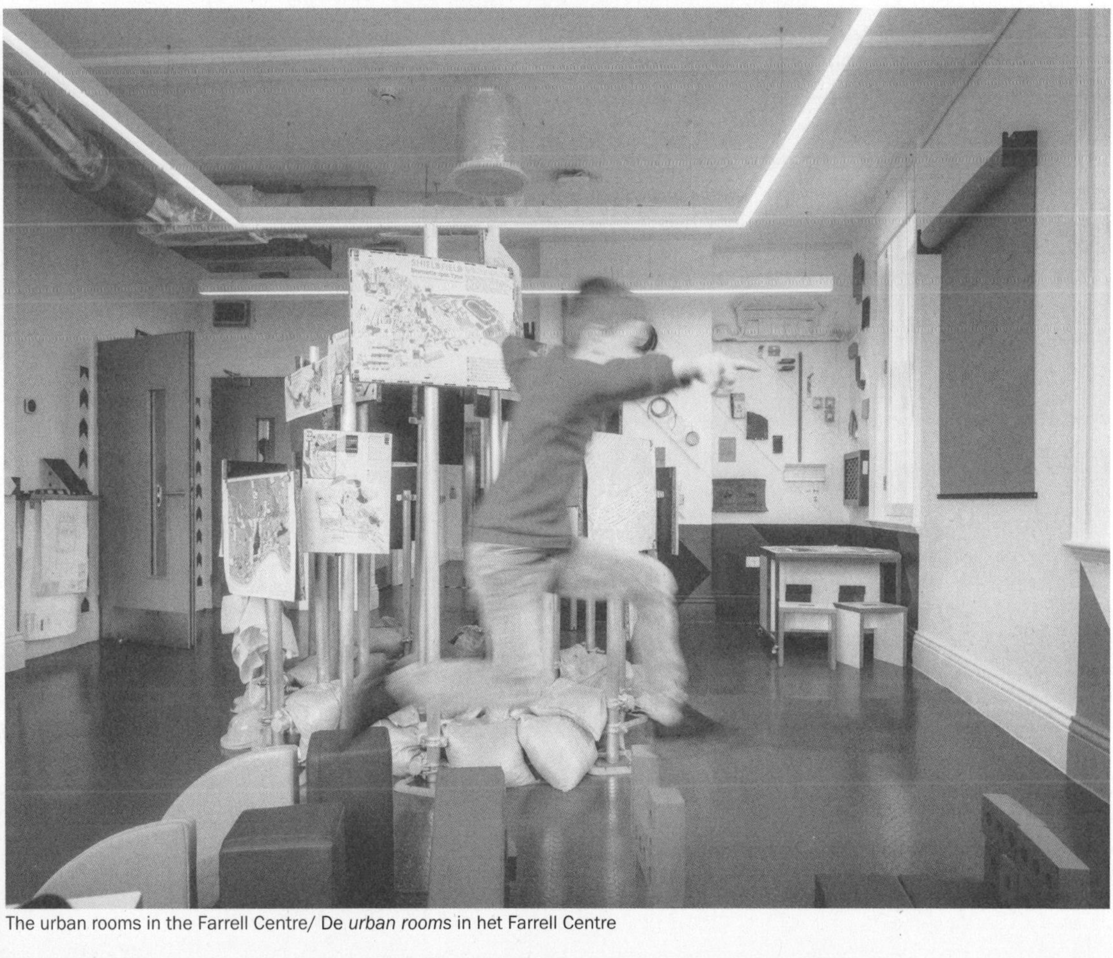

The urban rooms in the Farrell Centre/ De *urban rooms* in het Farrell Centre

In de planning voor de komende jaren komt er daarom, na de opstartperiode die diende om Farrell Centre op de kaart te zetten, meer focus op bepaalde stadsdelen, zowel in het centrum als meer suburbaan. In vergelijking met Londen zijn er in Newcastle niet erg veel grote stadsvernieuwingsprojecten, vertelt Hopkins, eerder stapsgewijze veranderingen in het stedelijk weefsel die niettemin van grote invloed kunnen zijn op de buurt. Maar tegelijk benadrukt hij de noodzaak om voorbij de grenzen van een relatief kleine stad als Newcastle te kijken. Er is een bredere, nationale of Europese discussie gaande over de toekomst van steden; vele steden worden met dezelfde uitdagingen geconfronteerd die het Farrell Centre wil agenderen.

De inbedding in de universiteit biedt mogelijkheden, maar ook verwachtingen. De thema's die curatoren of docenten zelf willen aansnijden, zullen niet altijd overeenstemmen met wat er van onderop leeft, het zijn soms net de thema's – zoals klimaatverandering of mobiliteit – waarover in steden heel verschillende meningen bestaan en die conflict oproepen, maar precies daarom kan het belangrijk zijn om ze op de agenda te zetten, en een universiteit of een onafhankelijke curator kan in dat gesprek een andere, meer bemiddelende rol spelen dan een overheidsdienst.

De twee ambities van *urban rooms*, om invloed te hebben op de kwaliteit van stedelijke ruimten als betekenisvolle plekken (*placemaking*) enerzijds en een verbeterde participatie anderzijds, staan soms op gespannen voet met elkaar. Opdat bezoekers zich betrokken en gehoord voelen, is het van belang dat de ruimte geen institutionele, maar een neutrale plek is zonder een vooraf – door de stad – bepaalde agenda. Maar om werkelijk invloed te hebben op geplande stadsprojecten, is een engagement vanuit de stadsdiensten dan wel noodzakelijk.

Urban rooms on the second floor of the Farrell Centre/ Urban rooms op de derde verdieping van het Farrell Centre

The association with the university creates opportunities, but also expectations. The issues that curators or lecturers want to address do not always match what is felt at the bottom. Sometimes these are the very issues – such as climate change or mobility – about which there are very different opinions in cities and which can cause conflict. But that is precisely why it can be important to put them on the agenda, and a university or an independent curator can play a different, more mediating role in this conversation than a government agency.

The two ambitions of urban rooms – on one hand, to have an impact on the quality of placemaking and, on the other, to improve participation – can sometimes be at odds with each other. For visitors to feel engaged and heard, it is important that urban rooms are not institutional spaces, but rather neutral ones, without a predetermined agenda set by the city. However, to have a real impact on planned urban projects, the involvement of city services is indeed necessary.

Meanwhile Use as an Act of Resistance

There is an initiative in Brussels that bears some similarities to the urban rooms, although the name is not widely known there. In 2018, the temporary use of the soon-to-be-demolished WTC towers by an architecture school, several design offices and artistic practices and the organisation of a spinoff of the Rotterdam Architecture Biennale eventually led to the creation of Track – a space designed to give local residents a voice in the planned urban development. Track builds on and formalises this practice of temporarily occupying transitional spaces.

Track stems from a specific urban regeneration project in the area around Brussels' Noordstation, the Noordwijk district, which faces many challenges: vacant offices, musty apartment blocks, being a gateway neighbourhood where refugees and homeless people seek shelter in the public space, issues with drugs and the trauma associated with the historical demolition of the area. In the 1970s, the working class neighbourhood around Noordstation had to make way for Manhattan Brussels, a modernist district with monofunctional office towers. The WTC towers were the legacy of this 1970s top-down, functionalist planning policy. At the same time, major real estate projects are underway. With demand for office space falling and many of the office towers in need of updating, the question arises what new purpose these buildings can serve and how new spatial needs can be met. The WTC towers were originally slated for demolition, but the final redevelopment strategy shifted the focus to maximising the reuse of materials.[5] After a thorough renovation, the new ZIN project now includes offices, a hotel and dwellings.

During the design process, the WTC towers were temporarily inhabited by stakeholders, functioning as both headquarters and a laboratory for the new project. Dieter Leyssen of architecture office 51N4E – the office also involved in the design of ZIN and one of the initiators of Track – explains how they also learned valuable lessons from this temporary occupation. After all, the temporary occupation also faced criticism: Lietje Bauwens and Wouter De Raeve, themselves temporary residents, made a film highlighting the lack of attention given to social housing residents and local community organisations.[6] The film portrayed the operation as a way of attracting a trendy creative class to Noordwijk, which on the one hand could contribute to a socioartistic project for a more inclusive neighbourhood, but on the other hand ultimately served mainly to legitimise the redevelopment.[7]

5 51N4E & l'AUC (eds.), *How Not to Demolish a Building* (Berlin: Ruby Press, 2022).

6 Lietje Bauwens and Wouter De Raeve, *WTC A Love Story* (2020), *WTC A Never-Ending Love Story* (2023).

7 Julie Mabilde, 'WTC A Never-Ending Love Story', *De Witte Raaf* 226 (2023).

Tijdelijk gebruik als een daad van verzet

Een Brussels initiatief vertoont, hoewel de term er onbekend is, een aantal overeenkomsten met de *urban rooms*. De tijdelijke ingebruikname in 2018 van de tot sloop gedoemde WTC-torens, door een architectuuropleiding, verschillende ontwerpbureaus en artistieke praktijken, en de organisatie van een spin-off van de architectuurbiënnale van Rotterdam, leidden uiteindelijk tot *Track*, een ruimte om buurtbewoners een stem te geven bij de geplande stadsontwikkeling. Track bouwt verder op deze praktijk van tijdelijke bezetting van ruimten in transitie en formaliseert ze.

Track is ontstaan vanuit een concreet stadsvernieuwingsproject, in de wijk rond het Brusselse Noordstation. Deze Noordwijk kampt met heel wat uitdagingen: leegstaande kantoren, verouderde appartementenblokken, een aankomstbuurt waar vluchtelingen en daklozen een slaapplek zoeken in het openbare domein, een drugsproblematiek en trauma's die samenhangen met de historische kaalslag in de wijk. In de jaren 1970 moest de volksbuurt rond het Noordstation wijken voor het Manhattanplan, een modernistische wijk met monofunctionele kantoortorens. De WTC-torens waren de erfenis van dat top-down en functionalistische planningsbeleid uit de jaren 1970. Tegelijkertijd zijn er grote vastgoedprojecten op til. Nu de vraag naar kantoren is gedaald, en vele van de torengebouwen aan een update toe zijn, rijst de vraag welke nieuwe invulling de gebouwen kunnen krijgen, en hoe nieuwe ruimtevragen ingelost kunnen worden. De WTC-torens zouden in eerst instantie gesloopt worden, maar in de uiteindelijke herontwikkelingsstrategie werd gekozen voor maximaal hergebruik van de materialen.[5] Na een grondige renovatie biedt het nieuwe ZIN-project onderdak aan kantoren, een hotel en woningen.

Tijdens het ontwerpproces werden de WTC-torens tijdelijk bewoond, en functioneerden ze ook als hoofdkwartier en laboratorium voor de ontwikkeling van ZIN. Dieter Leyssen van architectuurbureau 51N4E, het bureau dat mede het ontwerp voor ZIN tekende, en een van de initiatiefnemers van Track, vertelt hoe ze ook lessen hebben getrokken uit die tijdelijke bezetting. Op de tijdelijke ingebruikname kwam immers ook kritiek: Lietje Bauwens en Wouter De Raeve, zelf ook tijdelijke bewoners, maakten een film die het gebrek aan aandacht voor de bewoners van de nabijgelegen sociale woningen en de lokale buurtverenigingen aankaartte.[6] De film schilderde de operatie af als een manier om een hippe creatieve klasse naar de Noordwijk te lokken, die wel kon bijdragen aan een sociaal-artistiek project voor een inclusievere buurt, maar uiteindelijk vooral de herontwikkeling moest legitimeren.[7]

Track, een stadslab voor onderzoek naar gedeeld en gemengd ruimtegebruik, opende in februari 2024 de deuren. Dieter Leyssen licht toe hoe het tijdelijk bewonen van de WTC-torens heeft geleerd dat je niet te snel mag gaan, omdat je dan verkeerde verwachtingen schept. In Track is er bewust gekozen om langzaam op te bouwen, om zo vertrouwen te scheppen tussen de partnerorganisaties en de gebruikers van de ruimte. En wat wel goed werkte in de tijdelijke bezetting van de WTC-torens, het delen van tussenruimte door de verschillende organisaties, waardoor gesprekken en nieuwe partnerschappen ontstonden, is ook onderdeel van de organisatie van Track.

De ruimte bevindt zich tussen de sporen en het stationsgebouw van het Noordstation, in een voormalig spoorwegmuseum dat door de spoorwegmaatschappij voor 12 jaar ter beschikking wordt gesteld aan negen organisaties, waaronder architectenbureau 51N4E en Lab North

5 51N4E en l'AUC (red.), *How Not to Demolish a Building* (Berlijn: Ruby Press, 2022).

6 Lietje Bauwens en Wouter De Raeve, *WTC A Love Story* (2020) en *WTC A Never-Ending Love Story* (2023).

7 Julie Mabilde, 'WTC A Never-Ending Love Story', *De Witte Raaf* 226 (2023).

Track, a city lab for research on shared and mixed use spaces, opened its doors in February 2024. Dieter Leyssen explained how the temporary occupation of the WTC towers taught them that haste makes waste, as it can create unrealistic expectations. At Track, there was a conscious decision to build slowly, to build trust between the partner organisations and the users of the space. What worked well in the temporary occupation of the WTC towers – the sharing of intermediate spaces by different organisations, which led to conversations and new partnerships – is also part of the concept of Track.

The space is located near Noordstation, in a former railway museum that the railway company has made available to nine organisations for 12 years. The organisations include architecture office 51N4E and Lab North (an NGO cofunded by the Noordwijk property developers), but most importantly local associations that are involved in some form of citymaking, such as Urban Foxes, a placemaking organisation that involves often overlooked groups in the design of public spaces, Ten Noey, a local community centre and Sew For Life, which offers fashion design training to women from migrant backgrounds. A number of these organisations have fixed workspaces, but the place is large enough to accommodate other activities in line with Track's mission. Track, like the Urban Rooms, aims to increase the involvement of citizens in the changes taking place in their city, but their methods are very different; this is also linked to the way the space is funded and managed. The funding model is based on solidarity: contributions are based on ability to pay, so that nonprofit users pay less

Track is housed in the former railway museum in Brussels North Station/ Track is gehuisvest in het voormalige spoorwegmuseum in het Brusselse Noordstation

(een vzw die mede gefinancierd wordt door de projectontwikkelaars uit de Noordwijk), maar verder vooral lokale verenigingen die op een of andere manier werkzaam zijn rond stadmaken, zoals Urban Foxes, een organisatie van *placemakers* die vaak vergeten groepen betrekt bij het ontwerp van publieke ruimten; Ten Noey, een lokaal gemeenschapscentrum en Sew For Life, dat opleidingen modeontwerp biedt aan vrouwen met een migratieachtergrond. Een aantal van die organisaties heeft er zijn vaste werkplekken, maar de ruimte is groot genoeg om plaats te bieden aan andere activiteiten die in de missie van Track passen. Track heeft, net als de Britse *urban rooms*, de doelstelling om de betrokkenheid van burgers bij de veranderingen in hun stad te vergroten, maar de manier waarop dit gebeurt verschilt, en dat heeft ook te maken met hoe de ruimte gefinancierd én beheerd wordt. Het financieringsmodel is gebaseerd op solidariteit: er wordt bijgedragen naar vermogen, zodat de non-profit gebruikers minder betalen dan de profit-bewoners (waaronder het architectenbureau). Ook wordt de evenementenruimte voor allerlei activiteiten tegen commerciële tarieven verhuurd, zodat precaire sociale groepen er gratis gebruik van kunnen maken.

In de beginfase functioneerde de plek eerder als een open ruimte die vrij ingevuld kon worden, zonder permanente tentoonstellingen. Later kwam er wel een grote kaart van de Noordwijk te hangen waarop de geplande projecten staan en bezoekers ook de voor hen betekenisvolle locaties kunnen duiden, van herkenningsplekken tot goede buurtrestaurants.

Het daadwerkelijk laten samenwonen en samenwerken van die verschillende organisaties en groepen op één plek, is ook een experiment in samenleven en stadmaken op de plek zelf. Stadmaken gaat immers niet louter om de stenen, maar ook om de opbouw van het sociaal weefsel en de programmering van plekken, om gemeenschap creëren, om aandacht voor werkgelegenheid. Om de stem van die lokale organisaties, die elk op hun manier met de stad bezig zijn, meer te laten doorklinken in het debat rond stadsvernieuwing, is het belangrijk dat ze een fysieke plek hebben waar ze ook daadwerkelijk met elkaar in gesprek komen, waar ze een netwerk kunnen vormen, en door zich te verenigen ook een grotere invloed kunnen uitoefenen. Leyssen noemt het 'tussengebruik als een verzetsdaad' omdat het tegengaan van gentrificatie ook gaat over versterking van het sociaal weefsel dat in een buurt al aanwezig is.[8]

In vergelijking met het Farrell Centre is de opzet breder en wendbaarder, en de focus ligt minder op ontwerp per se. Maar die bredere opzet en partnerschap strookt wel met een typisch stedelijke dynamiek en wat een stad tot stad maakt: de menging van verschillende groepen, actoren, belangen, activiteiten. In hoeverre Track een werkelijke invloed kan hebben op de herontwikkeling van de Noordwijk, zal nog moeten blijken, maar ook de meer klassieke, activistische Brusselse burgerverenigingen zoals Bral vinden er vandaag alvast hun weg naartoe, en organiseerden er een discussieavond over het zwartedooskarakter van de Brusselse stedenbouw.

Track heeft de ambitie een neutrale plek te zijn die niet geassocieerd wordt met een overheid, een bedrijf of een ontwikkelaar: Leyssen noemt het een 'witruimte' die gebruikt en geprogrammeerd wordt door een aantal vaste partners maar die ook een veilige ruimte moet zijn voor de meer kwetsbare groepen uit de buurt. Het is een delicate evenwichtsoefening om een publieke ruimte te creëren, zonder het gevoel van onveiligheid dat in sommige delen van de Noordwijk bestaat, binnen te loodsen. Track heeft geen vitrine naar de publieke ruimte (maar wel ramen met zicht op

8 'Tussengebruik' wordt hier begrepen als de tijdelijke ingebruikname van leegstaande of onderbenutte gebouwen in afwachting van herontwikkeling. Het tijdelijk gebruik kan ook van invloed zijn op de beslissingen (van architecten, beleidsmakers of ontwikkelaars) over de toekomstige herbestemming. Een uitvoeriger beschrijving van de lessen uit het tijdelijk gebruik van de WTC-torens is te lezen in: Dieter Leyssen, 'Meanwhile Use as an Act of Resistance', *Joelho – Journal of Architectural Culture* 9, *Reuse of Modernist Buildings: Pedagogy and Profession* (2018).

than forprofit users (including the architecture firm). In addition, the events space is rented for all kinds of activities at commercial rates, allowing marginalised social groups to use it free of charge.

In the initial phase, the space will function more as an open space that can be freely filled, without permanent exhibitions. Later, a large map of Noordwijk will be displayed, showing the planned projects, and visitors will be able to indicate the places that mean something to them, from familiar landmarks to favourite neighbourhood restaurants.

The actual coexistence and collaboration of these different organisations and groups in one space is also an experiment in living together and citymaking *in situ*. After all, citymaking is not just about physical buildings, but also about building the social fabric and programming spaces, creating community and focusing on employment opportunities. To give more weight to the voice of local organisations, each contributing to citymaking in their own way, in the debate on urban regeneration, it is important that they have a physical space where they can actually engage with each other, build networks and, by joining forces, have a greater impact. Leyssen calls this 'meanwhile use as an act of resistance', because resisting gentrification is also about strengthening the social fabric that already exists in a neighbourhood.[8]

Compared with that of the Farrell Centre, the setup of Track is broader and more flexible, with less focus on design per se. However, this broader format and partnership is in keeping with typical urban dynamics and with what makes a city a city: the mix of different groups, actors, interests and activities. Whether Track can have a real impact on the redevelopment of Noordwijk remains to be seen, but even the more traditional, activist Brussels citizens' organisations, such as Bral, have already found their way there and organised a discussion evening on the 'black box' of Brussels urban design.

Track has the ambition to be a neutral space that is not associated with any government, company or developer: Leyssen refers to it as a 'white space' that is used and programmed by a number of core partners, but also serves as a safe space for more vulnerable groups from the neighbourhood. It is a delicate balancing act to create a public space without drawing in the feeling of insecurity that exists in some parts of Noordwijk. Track does not have a display window opening onto the public realm (although it does have windows overlooking the platforms), but during the summer, the organisations move outside to activate the surrounding public space with temporary installations and programmes centred on outdoor play.

Track sees itself as an experiment that can inspire the whole of Noordwijk. After all, the city requires developers to reserve a certain percentage of their buildings for sociocultural programmes. According to Leyssen, developers are also interested in a different kind of public space, to activate the ground floors. The raw design, the unfinished and unpolished space that Track offers to several organisations sharing the space, serves as a demonstration of how things can be done differently. For example, the circular renovation was carried out on a low budget because it did not have to meet the highest standards of finish. Moreover, it was carried out by a social economy partner and thus contributes to local employment in the neighbourhood. Track's aim is not to educate or promote its own agenda, but to strengthen the network among organisations that, unlike developers, have little access to politicians or city services.

8 'Meanwhile use' is understood here as the temporary occupation of vacant or underused buildings pending redevelopment. Temporary use can also have an impact on decisions – by architects, policymakers or developers – about future redevelopment. A more detailed description of the lessons learned from the temporary use of the WTC towers can be found in: Dieter Leyssen, 'Meanwhile Use as an Act of Resistance', *Joelho – Journal of Architectural Culture* 9, *Reuse of Modernist Buildings: Pedagogy and Profession* (2018).

de perrons). Maar in de zomer trekken de organisaties naar buiten om, via tijdelijke installaties en programmering rond bijvoorbeeld 'buiten spelen', de publieke ruimte in de buurt te activeren.

Track ziet zichzelf als een experiment dat inspiratie kan bieden voor de hele Noordwijk. De stad eist immers dat ontwikkelaars een bepaald percentage in hun gebouwen voorbehouden aan sociaal-cultureel programma. Volgens Leyssen hebben ontwikkelaars ook interesse in een ander soort publieke ruimte om de begane grond te activeren, en het ruwe ontwerp, de onaffe, niet gepolijste ruimte die Track deelt met meerdere organisaties, is een demonstratie van hoe het anders kan: een circulaire verbouwing, met een lager budget, omdat het niet aan de hoogste afwerkingsnormen hoefde te voldoen, en die dankzij de verbouwing door een partner in de sociale economie ook bijdraagt aan de werkgelegenheid in de buurt. Het doel van Track ligt minder in het educatieve of het naar buiten brengen van een eigen agenda, maar in de versterking van het netwerk tussen organisaties die (in tegenstelling tot ontwikkelaars) minder toegang hebben tot politici of stadsdiensten.

Architectuursector met een maatschappelijke rol

The Farrell Centre en Track leggen eigen accenten, maar beide zijn een experiment in het opentrekken van het debat rond stadsontwikkeling en architectuur. In het ene is het de universiteit, in het andere een architectenbureau, maar in beide gevallen neemt een actor uit de architectuursector een maatschappelijke rol op zich op de plek waar men gevestigd is, en zet die de eigen positie in om te wegen op beleid of stadsontwikkelingsprojecten. Beide centra illustreren de zoektocht naar nieuwe configuraties

Track: a lab for research into shared and mixed use of urban space/ Track: een stadslabo voor onderzoek naar gedeeld en gemengd ruimtegebruik

An Architecture Sector with a Social Role

The Farrell Centre and Track each emphasise different aspects, yet both serve as experiments in broadening the debate on urban development and architecture. In one it is the university, and in the other an architecture firm, but in both cases actors from the architecture sector assume a social role in the context of their place of business and use their position to influence policy or urban development projects. Both illustrate the search for new configurations of civic action in cities where larger forces and real estate dynamics dominate, leaving citizens with seemingly little control.

The Farrell Centre achieves this by bringing the issues and challenges addressed in design education into the public realm, making them accessible for public engagement. Conversely, students are given the opportunity to engage with the users of the spaces they use for design exercises, or even to participate in engagement processes for concrete public space projects.

Track is an experiment in giving local organisations a voice in neighbourhoods undergoing significant change, by literally providing them with space. This voice will never be as loud as that of the developers at the negotiating table, but it can gain strength through greater visibility in the neighbourhood and through partnerships with more established cultural organisations, design offices or universities.

In both cases, it is vitally important to have a space that can serve as a setting for exchange and discourse development. The long-term impact of these new civic spaces – mediated by universities or design offices – on urban development, and the extent to which they can counter imbalances in power and representation, remains to be seen. The various stakeholders involved often have divergent interests, and there is always the risk that such spaces may elicit or inadvertently contribute to gentrification.

The question of what an effective model for civic engagement in urban development might look like today remains open, as does the role that new initiatives and mediating entities can play. Ultimately, it is the government's responsibility to safeguard the interests of diverse groups in planning processes and construction projects, ensuring that participation is not reduced to a mere pro forma exercise.

My special thanks go to Susan Holden, Maarten Liefooghe and Maarten Van Den Driessche, as well as Owen Hopkins and Dieter Leyssen, whose valuable input and feedback made this text possible.

Translation: InOtherWords, Maria van Toi

voor civiele actie in steden waar grotere machten en vastgoeddynamiek spelen waar burgers weinig vat op lijken te hebben.

In het Farrell Centre gebeurt dit door het naar buiten brengen en toegankelijk maken van de thema's en uitdagingen waar ontwerpopleidingen zich mee bezig houden, om het publiek hierin te betrekken. Maar omgekeerd kunnen studenten kennismaken met de gebruikers van de plekken waarvoor ze hun ontwerpoefeningen maken, of zelfs betrokken worden bij participatieprocessen voor concrete projecten van publieke ruimte.

Track is een experiment in hoe je in buurten in volle verandering aan lokale organisaties een stem kunt geven door hen letterlijk ruimte te bieden. Die stem zal nooit even luid klinken als die van de ontwikkelaars aan de onderhandelingstafel, maar kan aan kracht winnen door hen een grotere zichtbaarheid in de buurt te geven, en door partnerschappen met meer gevestigde culturele organisaties, ontwerpbureaus of universiteiten aan te gaan.

In beide gevallen is het van vitaal belang om over een ruimte te beschikken die kan dienen als setting voor uitwisseling en de opbouw van een discours. Welk effect deze nieuwe civiele ruimten, met universiteiten of ontwerpbureaus als bemiddelende organisaties, op langere termijn kunnen hebben op stadsontwikkeling, en in welke mate ze de onevenwichtigheid in macht en vertegenwoordiging kunnen counteren, zal in de toekomst moeten blijken. De verschillende betrokken partijen hebben niet steeds parallelle belangen, en er bestaat ook altijd het gevaar dat dergelijke locaties gentrificatie in de hand werken.

Het blijft een open vraag wat tegenwoordig een doelmatig model kan zijn voor burgerbetrokkenheid bij stadsontwikkeling, en welke rol nieuwe initiatieven en bemiddelende instanties hierin kunnen spelen. Uiteindelijk blijft het de opdracht van de overheid om in planningsprocessen en bouwprojecten te waken over de belangen van verschillende groepen – ervoor te zorgen dat participatie niet beperkt blijft tot een pro forma oefening.

Veel dank aan Susan Holden, Maarten Liefooghe en Maarten Van Den Driessche, en aan Owen Hopkins en Dieter Leyssen, zonder wiens waardevolle inbreng en terugkoppeling deze tekst niet tot stand had kunnen komen.

Susan Holden and Maarten Liefooghe
Design Quality as a Matter of Governance and Culture: A Diptych

Two parallel articles explore contrasting paradigms that inform contemporary practices and discourses of quality: design quality as a matter of governance versus a matter of culture. Different notions of what is a good place, different rationales for design quality and responsible architectural practice, and different settings for quality assurance correspond to these framings.

Susan Holden en Maarten Liefooghe
Ontwerpkwaliteit als kwestie van bestuur en cultuur: Een tweeluik

Twee parallelle artikelen verkennen contrasterende denkmodellen die in de hedendaagse kwaliteitsdebatten en -praktijken hun neerslag vinden: ontwerpkwaliteit als een kwestie van bestuur (*design governance*) versus een kwestie van cultuur. Daarmee stemmen andere opvattingen overeen over wat een goede plek is, een hoogwaardig ontwerp of een verantwoorde architectuurpraktijk, en ook andere omgevingen voor kwaliteitszorg.

Susan Holden
Quality as a Matter of Governance: Design Review

The idea that design quality is a matter for governing has taken on a new meaning in the wake of neoliberal reforms of government since the 1980s that have dramatically changed the agency of public-sector actors in shaping the built environment. The concept of design governance captures new ways of directing design expertise – such as design review panels – and new socio-political motives for quality. The public interest agendas for quality in contemporary design governance relate to a new 'political economy of place-making', and more recently, to an equitable environmental transition.

Susan Holden
Kwaliteit als een kwestie van *governance*: Ontwerpbeoordeling

Het idee dat ontwerpkwaliteit een zaak is van besturen, heeft in het kielzog van de neoliberale hervormingen van de overheid sinds de jaren 1980 een nieuwe betekenis gekregen, waardoor de rol van actoren in de publieke sector bij het vormgeven van de gebouwde omgeving ingrijpend is veranderd. Het concept *design governance* omvat nieuwe manieren om ontwerpexpertise te stimuleren – zoals kwaliteitspanels – en nieuwe sociaal-politieke redenen om kwaliteit te realiseren. Het huidige ontwerpend besturen is erop gericht om, in het algemeen belang, kwaliteit te realiseren als een nieuwe 'politieke economie van plaats maken' en via een rechtvaardige ecologische transitie.

Maarten Liefooghe
Quality as a Matter of Culture: *Baukultur*

A cultural pillar of architectural quality is sometimes mobilised as a counterbalance to purely technical, economic or energy performance standards. 'Building culture' is one of the concepts that gives specific expression to this. The term aims to extend beyond the culture of architecture and entered European policy frameworks with the Davos Declaration, *Towards a High-Quality* Baukultur *for Europe*, in 2018. Moving between Davos and Zurich, this article explores the notion in relation to various discursive contexts, buildings and traditions of cultural critique, heritage conservation and disciplinary self-reflection within architecture.

Maarten Liefooghe
Kwaliteit als een kwestie van cultuur: *Baukultur*

Een culturele pijler van architectonische kwaliteit wordt soms gemobiliseerd als tegenwicht voor puur bouwtechnische, economische of energieprestatienormen. 'Bouwcultuur' is een van de concepten die daar een specifieke invulling aan geven. De term wil breder reiken dan architectuurcultuur en deed zijn intrede in Europese beleidskaders met de Verklaring van Davos, *Towards a High-Quality* Baukultur *for Europe*, in 2018. Bewegend tussen Davos en Zürich tast dit artikel de notie af in relatie tot verschillende discursieve omgevingen, gebouwen en tradities van cultuurkritiek, erfgoedzorg en architectuurdisciplinaire zelfreflectie.

Maarten Van Den Driessche
Justification, Negotiation and Mediation: Instituting Architectural Quality

In 2012, Agency – an artist initiative founded by Kobe Matthys – presented *Thing 001359 (Chico Mendez Mural Garden)* at the Atelier Bouwmeester in Brussels. Around a concrete scale model, an audience is seated on a scaffold, like a miniature parliament. The audience holds cards that document the controversy and legal proceedings surrounding the demolition of a spontaneously created community garden in Lower Manhattan. This article discusses the analogy between this artistic 'gathering' and the day-to-day institutional functioning of the Flemish Government Architect (*Vlaams Bouwmeester*). This shifts a semantic discussion about the nature of architectural quality to one about the circumstances under which decisions are made. Architectural quality as dispute: Who decides? About what? From which position, and according to which criteria? Maarten Van Den Driessche highlights the acts of accountability, negotiation and mediation, referencing theories by, among others, Luc Boltanski, Bruno Latour, Susan Leigh Star and Chantal Mouffe.

Maarten Van Den Driessche
Verantwoording, Onderhandeling, Bemiddeling: Architectuurkwaliteit instellen

In 2012 voerde Agentschap – een kunstenaarsinitiatief opgericht door Kobe Matthys – 'Ding 001359 (Chico Mendez Mural Garden)' op in het Atelier Bouwmeester in Brussel. Rond een betonnen schaalmodel zit een publiek op een stellage, als een miniatuurparlement. Het publiek houdt fiches vast die de controverse en rechtszaak rondom de sloop van een spontaan geïnstalleerde gemeenschapstuin in Lower Manhattan documenteren. Dit artikel bespreekt de analogie tussen deze artistieke 'samenkomst' en de dagelijkse institutionele werking van de Vlaamse bouwmeester. Dat verlegt een semantische discussie omtrent de aard van architectuurkwaliteit naar een over de omstandigheden waarin beslissingen worden genomen. Architectuurkwaliteit als geschil: Wie beslist? Waarover? Vanuit welke positie en met welke criteria? Maarten Van Den Driessche duidt de acties van verantwoording, onderhandeling en bemiddeling, verwijzend naar theorieën van onder meer Luc Boltanski, Bruno Latour, Susan Leigh Star en Chantal Mouffe.

Kirsten Schipper
Thinking and Acting in a Design-Oriented Way: Interview with Chief Government Architect Francesco Veenstra

The position of the Chief Government Architect has existed in the Netherlands for over two centuries. This independent advisor is concerned with national spatial planning issues, but is also involved in various projects of the Central Government Real Estate Agency, which, through its land and property holdings, exerts considerable influence on our living environment. Since September 2021, Francesco Veenstra has held the position of Chief Government Architect. As the guardian of quality on behalf of the central government, he speaks in this issue of *OASE* about the application of design-led thinking and practice within the largest property organisation in the Netherlands. According to Veenstra, involving designers at an early stage is the most important tool for clearly defining the criteria for quality.

Kirsten Schipper
Ontwerpend denken en handelen: Interview met Rijksbouwmeester Francesco Veenstra

De functie van de Rijksbouwmeester bestaat in Nederland al meer dan twee eeuwen. Deze onafhankelijke adviseur bekommert zich over nationale ruimtelijke inrichtingsvraagstukken, maar is ook betrokken bij diverse projecten van het Rijksvastgoedbedrijf, dat met al zijn grond en vastgoed een invloed heeft op onze leefomgeving. Sinds september 2021 vervult Francesco Veenstra de rol van Rijksbouwmeester. Als kwaliteitsborger van de rijksoverheid spreekt hij zich in dit nummer van *OASE* uit over het inzetten van ontwerpend handelen en denken in het grootste vastgoedbedrijf van Nederland. Het vroegtijdig betrekken van ontwerpers is volgens Veenstra het belangrijkste instrument om de criteria voor kwaliteit scherp te stellen.

Stefan Devoldere
We Need to Talk about Quality: The Urban Workshop in Ostend and the Zilverlaan

In 2016, the Belgian coastal city of Ostend put a plot of land on the suburban city fringe up for sale at a fixed price. This process was overseen by the *Urban Workshop*, a quality review panel composed of external experts and local officials. Private developers were invited to submit proposals featuring a high-quality design not only for the plot itself, but also for the neighbouring sites,

which were occupied by a social housing association and a non-profit organisation providing supported living for people with disabilities. The neighbours joined in the selected design, and a unique collective housing project took shape – founded on shared added value and design quality. Stefan Devoldere, who chaired the *Urban Workshop*, guided the entire process and offers an analysis of how the tools employed influenced the final outcome, assessing their significance in comparison with the personal commitment of the actors involved.

Stefan Devoldere
We moeten het over kwaliteit hebben: Het Stadsatelier in Oostende en de Zilverlaan

De Belgische badplaats Oostende stelde in 2016 een perceel in de suburbane stadsrand te koop voor een vaste prijs. Dat gebeurde onder begeleiding van het Stadsatelier, een kwaliteitskamer met externe experten en lokale ambtenaren. Private ontwikkelaars werd gevraagd een bod te doen met een hoogwaardig ontwerp voor de locatie en voor de percelen van de buren, een sociale woningbouwvereniging en een vereniging zonder winstoogmerk die begeleid wonen aanbiedt voor mensen met een beperking. De buren stapten mee in het gekozen ontwerp en een bijzonder collectief woonproject kreeg vorm, gebaseerd op gedeelde meerwaarde en ontwerpkwaliteit... Stefan Devoldere begeleidde als voorzitter van het Stadsatelier het hele traject en analyseert hoe de gebruikte instrumenten bepalend zijn geweest voor het eindresultaat, en schat in wat ze waard zijn ten opzichte van het persoonlijk engagement van betrokken actoren.

Florian Hertweck
The Return of Confidence? On the Quality Assurance of Prospective Planning: The Example of Luxembourg in Transition

Compelled by the immense need for transformation that we are facing in the context of climate change and resource scarcity, the challenge of upscaling the concepts, strategies and instruments of socioecological transition is more pressing than ever. Prospective planning of cities and regions for future climate neutrality and resilience is one possible approach to upscaling. The international consultation Luxembourg in Transition stands out as a prospective planning programme that sought innovation in its methodology to ensure the quality of both the planning and its realisation. This essay examines the quality assurance mechanisms that were used, but also the obstacles that stood in their way, providing insights into how cities and regions should be strategically planned in the future.

Florian Hertweck
De terugkeer van vertrouwen? Over kwaliteitsborging in langetermijnplanning: Het voorbeeld van Luxembourg in Transition

De enorme noodzaak tot transformatie waarmee we in de context van klimaatverandering en grondstoffenschaarste worden geconfronteerd, dwingt ons meer dan ooit om de concepten, strategieën en instrumenten van socioecologische transitie op te schalen. Langetermijnplanning van steden en regio's voor toekomstige klimaatneutraliteit en veerkracht is een mogelijke opschalingsmethode. Het internationale overleg Luxembourg in Transition onderscheidt zich als een programma dat zocht naar innovatie in zijn methodologie, om de kwaliteit van zowel de langetermijnplanning als de realisatie ervan te waarborgen. Dit essay onderzoekt de mechanismen voor kwaliteitsborging die werden gebruikt, maar ook de obstakels die in de weg stonden, en biedt inzicht in hoe steden en regio's in de toekomst strategisch gepland zouden moeten worden.

Julie Mabilde
A Place to Talk about Architecture: Farrell Centre and Track

Cities are constantly evolving. New architectural and urban projects have a significant impact on residents' living environments, yet not all residents have insight into or a say in how these changes are directed. Two initiatives – the Farrell Centre in the United Kingdom and Track in Brussels – seek to address this by quite literally creating space for dialogue. The Farrell Centre, building on the model of urban rooms, focuses on increasing public knowledge of urban development, while Track works on community building to help local residents more effectively stand up for their rights. Both aim to reach a broader audience and give that audience a voice: the former pursues emancipation through education and uplift, the latter through solidarity and collective action.

Julie Mabilde
Hier kan over architectuur gepraat worden: Farrell Centre en Track

Steden zijn voortdurend in verandering. Nieuwe architectuur en stadsprojecten hebben een grote impact op de leefomgeving van bewoners, maar niet alle bewoners hebben inzicht en inspraak in hoe die veranderingen aangestuurd worden. Twee initiatieven – het Farrell Centre in Groot-Brittannië en Track in Brussel – trachten dit te verhelpen door letterlijk ruimte te bieden voor gesprek. Het Farrell Centre, voortbouwend op het model van urban rooms, legt de nadruk op het vergroten van de kennis over stadsontwikkeling, Track werkt aan gemeenschapsvorming zodat lokale bewoners er beter in slagen voor hun rechten op te komen. Beide willen een breder doelpubliek bereiken en dat publiek een stem geven: de een zet in op emancipatie door verheffing, de ander op emancipatie door vereniging.

Stefan Devoldere is professor and dean of the Faculty of Architecture and Arts at Hasselt University. He was editor-in-chief of the Belgian architectural review *A+*, curated several international art and architecture exhibitions and was involved in the Belgian contribution to the Venice Architecture Biennale in 2008, 2010 and 2012. As deputy and acting Flemish Government Architect, and as president of the Stadsatelier in Ostend and in Hasselt, he directed several projects that used design research as a policy preparation tool, the subject matter of his current research. He is a member of the editorial board of *OASE*.
Stefan Devoldere is hoogleraar en decaan van de faculteit Architectuur en Kunst aan de UHasselt. Hij was hoofdredacteur van het Belgische architectuurtijdschrift *A+*, curator van verschillende internationale kunst- en architectuurtentoonstellingen, en betrokken bij de Belgische bijdrage voor de architectuurbiennale van Venetië in 2008, 2010 en 2012. Als adjunct en waarnemend Vlaams Bouwmeester, en als voorzitter van het Stadsatelier in Oostende en Hasselt, stuurde hij verschillende trajecten aan die ontwerpend onderzoek inzetten als beleidsvoorbereidend instrument, een materie waarnaar hij onderzoek doet. Hij is lid van de redactieraad van *OASE*.

Florian Hertweck is the founder of Less Yellow architecture and urbanism, and professor at the University of Luxembourg. He led a team for the Consultation du Grand Genève with Milica Topalovic, and more recently, for the Consultation Luxembourg in Transition. He curated the Luxembourg Pavillon for the 16th Architecture Biennial in Venice on the land ownership question. More recently, he co-curated the exhibition 'The Great Repair' at the Akademie der Künste in Berlin and at the Pavillon de l'Arsenal in Paris.
Florian Hertweck is de oprichter van Less Yellow architecture and urbanism; hij is hoogleraar aan de Universiteit van Luxemburg. Hij voerde samen met Milica Topalovic een team aan voor de Consultation du Grand Genève, en meer recent voor de Consultation Luxembourg in Transition. Hij cureerde het Luxemburgse paviljoen voor de 16e architectuurbiënnale in Venetië over de kwestie van het grondbezit. Onlangs co-cureerde hij de tentoonstelling 'The Great Repair' in de Akademie der Künste in Berlijn en in het Pavillon de l'Arsenal te Parijs.

Susan Holden is an architect and senior lecturer at the University of Queensland and a member of the ATCH Research Group (Architecture Theory Culture History). Her research links the study of architecture with understanding of its cultural, institutional and governance contexts. Recent areas of focus include cultural policy and heritage, urban design governance and the history of the architecture profession. She has published over 50 articles, book chapters and books and is co-editor of *Fabrications*. She contributes to the professional journal *Architecture Australia* and is a Fellow of the Australian Institute of Architects.
Susan Holden is architect en hoofdocent aan de Universiteit van Queensland; ze is lid van de ATCH Research Group (Architecture Theory Culture History). In haar onderzoek verbindt ze de studie naar architectuur met het begrijpen van de bijbehorende culturele, institutionele en beleidsmatige context. Recente onderwerpen van aandacht zijn cultureel beleid en erfgoed, stedelijk ontwerpbeleid en de geschiedenis van het architectenberoep. Ze heeft meer dan 50 artikelen, hoofdstukken in boeken en boeken gepubliceerd en is mede-uitgever van *Fabrications*. Ze draagt bij aan het vakblad *Architecture Australia*, en is een Fellow van het Australian Institute of Architects.

Maarten Liefooghe is associate professor in Architecture Theory and Criticism at Ghent University. His research revolves around historical and contemporary encounters between objects, practices, institutions and discourses of architecture, art, exhibition making and preservation. His doctoral research was on the architecture of monographic museums, about which he also presented the exhibition 'MONOS. Artist Museums: Shrines and Reflections' in 2024. Together with the ACC research group 'Architecture Culture and the Contemporary', he is currently studying architecture exhibitions and visual culture, competition culture, and notions and policies of 'architectural quality'. He is a member of the editorial board of *OASE*.
Maarten Liefooghe doceert architectuurtheorie en -kritiek aan de Universiteit Gent. Zijn onderzoek betreft historische en hedendaagse interacties tussen architectuur, kunst, erfgoed en tentoonstellingen, als objecten, praktijken, instellingen en discoursen. Zijn promotieonderzoek betrof de architectuur van monografische musea, waarover hij in 2024 ook de tentoonstelling 'MONOS. Kunstenaarsmusea: Schrijnen en spiegelingen' maakte. Samen met de onderzoeksgroep ACC 'Architectuurcultuur en de hedendaagse conditie', doet hij onder meer onderzoek naar architectuurtentoonstellingen, prijsvraagcultuur en architectuur(kwaliteits)beleid. Hij is lid van de redactieraad van *OASE*.

Julie Mabilde was trained as architect-engineer and is an advisor and project director in the Team of the Flemish Government Architect. She coordinates research by design within the platform LABO RUIMTE (space lab) – a collaboration between the Flemish Government architect and the Flemish Department of Environment, to study the impact of societal challenges and long-term evolutions on cities and landscapes. She also advises public authorities on questions regarding space and architecture, and she is a member of the jury evaluating urban renewal projects for Flemish urban policy. Since May 2020 Julie Mabilde is the president of the Quality Chamber of the city of Torhout.
Julie Mabilde, opgeleid als ingenieur-architect, is adviseur en projectleider bij het Team Vlaams Bouwmeester. Ze coördineert er het ontwerpend onderzoek binnen het platform 'LABO RUIMTE' – een samenwerking tussen Team Vlaams Bouwmeester en Departement Omgeving dat via ontwerp onderzoekt welke invloed maatschappelijke vraagstukken en lange termijn evoluties hebben op de organisatie van steden en landschappen. Ze adviseert ook publieke opdrachtgevers bij ruimtelijke en architecturale vraagstukken, en is lid van de jury stadsvernieuwing van het Vlaamse Stedenbeleid. Sinds mei 2020 is ze ook voorzitter van de kwaliteitskamer van de stad Torhout.

Elsbeth Ronner graduated cum laude from the Faculty of Architecture at Delft University of Technology in 2010. Since then, she has been running Lilith Ronner van Hooijdonk, an office for narrative architecture with assignments in research and design. In addition, Ronner contributes texts on architecture to various media, is co-founder of the Dutch architecture podcast *Windoog*, and since 2019 has been involved as a lecturer in the Urban Architecture Chair at Delft University of Technology. She is a member of the editorial board of *OASE*.
Elsbeth Ronner studeerde in 2010 cum laude af aan de faculteit Bouwkunde van de TU Delft. Sindsdien leidt ze Lilith Ronner van Hooijdonk, een bureau voor narratieve architectuur met opgaven in onderzoek en ontwerp. Daarnaast levert Ronner tekstuele bijdragen over architectuur in verschillende media, is ze medeoprichter van de Nederlandse architectuurpodcast *Windoog* en sinds 2019 als docent betrokken bij de leerstoel Urban Architecture aan de TU Delft. Ze is lid van de redactieraad van *OASE*.

Kirsten Schipper obtained a PhD from the University of Groningen in 2023 with a dissertation titled *Architecture as an Act of Culturel: Architecturel-Historical Research into the National Architecture Policy.* She works as an independent researcher, editor and curator for the Dutch College of government advisors and the government architect. Recent publications include 'Architectuur als culturele daad: de bouwkunst tussen politiek verheffingsideaal en neoliberale marktwaarde' *(de Architect*, 2024), 'Gebrek aan culturele ambitie van het Rijk nekt Architectuur Lokaal' (*Archined*, juli 2023) and 'Van metselaar tot filosoof' (*Bouwmeesters*, 2021).
Kirsten Schipper promoveerde in 2023 aan de Rijksuniversiteit Groningen op het onderzoek *Architectuur als culturele daad. Een architectuurhistorisch onderzoek naar het architectuurbeleid van de rijksoverheid.* Kirsten werkt als zelfstandig onderzoeker, redacteur en curator voor onder andere het College van

Rijksbouwmeester en Rijksadviseurs. Recente publicaties zijn 'Architectuur als culturele daad: de bouwkunst tussen politiek verheffingsideaal en neoliberale marktwaarde' (*de Architect*, 2024), 'Gebrek aan culturele ambitie van het Rijk nekt Architectuur Lokaal' (*Archined*, juli 2023) en 'Van metselaar tot filosoof' (*Bouwmeesters*, 2021).

Maarten Van Den Driessche is associate professor at Ghent University. He teaches Theory of Architectural Design, Architecture Theory and History of Contemporary Architecture. He was editor and author of, among others, *Robbrecht and Daem Architects: An Architectural Anthology* (2017), *Living the Exotic Everyday: Bovenbouw architectuur* (2019), *Composite Presence* (2020) and *More Than a Competition* (2021). He is a founding member of labo A and of the ACC research group 'Architecture Culture and the Contemporary'. His research focuses on design methodology, architecture policy, architectural representations and typological thinking in architecture. He is a member of the Ghent Architecture Platform.

Maarten Van Den Driessche is hoofddocent aan de Universiteit Gent. Hij doceert theorie van het architectuurontwerp, architectuurtheorie en geschiedenis van de hedendaagse architectuur. Hij was redacteur en auteur van onder meer *Robbrecht en Daem architecten: An Architectural Anthology* (2017), *Living the Exotic Everyday. Bovenbouw architectuur* (2019), *Composite Presence* (2020), *More than a Competition* (2021). Hij is oprichter/ lid van labo A en van de onderzoeksgroep ACC 'Architectuurcultuur en de hedendaagse conditie'. Zijn onderzoek focust op ontwerpmethodologie, architectuurbeleid, architectuurrepresentaties en het typologische denken in de architectuur. Hij is lid van het Gents Architectuurplatform.

Independent Peer-Reviewed Journal for Architecture, published by the OASE Foundation/ Onafhankelijk peer-reviewed architectuurtijdschrift, uitgegeven door de stichting OASE

OASE is made possible with the support of the Creative Industries Fund NL and the associated universities, institutions and architecture firms.

OASE wordt mede mogelijk gemaakt met de steun van het Stimuleringsfonds Creatieve Industrie en de geassocieerde universiteiten, instellingen en architectenbureaus.

creative industries fund NL

stimuleringsfonds creatieve industrie

OASE foundation/ stichting
p/a Jacquie Grevelink
Veelzigtstraat 7B
3022 DP Rotterdam
the Netherlands
info@oasejournal.nl
www.oasejournal.nl

ISSN 01696238
ISBN 9789462089105

OASE 120 is also available as/ is ook verkrijgbaar als e-book (pdf)
ISSN 01696238
ISBN 9789462089167

OASE editorial board/ redactie
p/a D'Laine Camp
Prins Frederik Hendrikstraat 107
3051 ER Rotterdam
the Netherlands

Associated Universities and Institutions/ Geassocieerde universiteiten en instellingen
Academie van Bouwkunst Amsterdam
Academie van Bouwkunst Groningen
Academie van Bouwkunst Maastricht
ArtEZ Academie van Bouwkunst Tilburg
Bergische Universität Wuppertal
Katholieke Universiteit Leuven campus Brussel
Katholieke Universiteit Leuven campus Gent
Katholieke Universiteit Leuven campus Leuven
Rotterdamse Academie van Bouwkunst
Technische Universiteit Delft
Technische Universiteit Eindhoven
Universiteit Antwerpen
Universiteit Gent
Universiteit Hasselt

Sponsors/ Sponsors
AgwA burgerlijke cvba, Brussel
ANA architecten, Amsterdam
aNNo architecten, Gent
Architectenbureau Bart Dehaene, Gent
ATAMA, Gent
Atelier Quadrat, Rotterdam
BILD, Brussel
Bulk Architecten, Deurne
Carton123 architecten, Brussel
CENTRAL office for architecture and urbanism, Brussel
Collectief Noord, Antwerpen
DaF architecten, Rotterdam
De Nijl Architecten, Rotterdam
De Smet Vermeulen architecten, Gent
De Zwarte Hond Rotterdam, Rotterdam
Diederendirrix architectuur & stedenbouw, Eindhoven
DP6 architectuurstudio, Delft
Frits Palmboom Stedebouwkundige, Amsterdam
Fvww architecten, Antwerpen
GAFPA bureau voor architectuur en stedenbouw, Gent
Geurst & Schulze architecten, Den Haag
Happel Cornelisse Verhoeven Architects, Rotterdam
HBAAT, Lille
HILBERINKBOSCH Architecten, Berlicum
KAAN architecten, Rotterdam
Korteknie Stuhlmacher Architecten, Rotterdam
Korth Tielens Architecten, Amsterdam
LEVS architecten, Amsterdam
M3H Architecten, Amsterdam
MARCEL LOK_ARCHITECT, Amsterdam
martenswillems architecten, Maastricht
MUST Stedebouw, Amsterdam
NL Architects, Amsterdam
Office Winhov, Amsterdam
Prof. ir. Wim van den Bergh Architect, Maastricht
RAPP + RAPP, Amsterdam
Rijnboutt, Amsterdam
Shift Architecture Urbanism, Rotterdam
Stad Antwerpen, Antwerpen
Steenhuis Bukman Architecten, Delft
STUDIO VINCENT Architecture, Amsterdam
Team bouwmeester maître architecte, Brussel
Urbain Architectencollectief, Gent
VVKH, Leiden
West 8, Rotterdam
Ziegler | Branderhorst stedenbouw en architectuur, Rotterdam

Academic Board/ Wetenschappelijk comité
Daniel Barber
Christine Boyer
Maristella Casciato
Adrian Forty
Klaske Havik
Rajesh Heynickx
Michael Müller
Bie Plevoets
Kris Scheerlinck
Lara Schrijver
Pieter Uyttenhove

Illustration credits/ Beeldverantwoording
Opening image/ Opeingsbeeld: Merlin Bauer; BeL Sozietät für Architektur; Veit Landwehr
Second image/ Tweede beeld: Michiel De Cleenep
p. 3 Nico Nelissen en Flip ten Cate*Mooi Europa. Ruimtelijke kwaliteitszorg in Europa* (Nijmegen: Sun, 2009)
p. 10/34 Office of Design and Architecture SA, Government of South Australia. CC BY 3.0 AU
p. 12/36 S AM Swiss Architecture Museum
p. 12/36 Swiss Federal Office of Culture, *The Davos* Baukultur *Quality System* (Bern: Swiss Federal Office of Culture, 2021), 18.
p. 14/38, 18/42, 20/44, 22/46 Maarten Liefooghe
p. 16/17, 40/41 S AM Swiss Architecture Museum, Tom Bisig
p. 16/40 Heimatschutzzentrum Zürich
p. 20/44 Design Council UK
p. 24/25, 48/49 NGV Australia, Melbourne, Peter Bennetts
p. 24/48 Gigon/Guyer, Zürich
p. 26/50 Jules Spinatsch, Zürich
p. 28/52 Office of Design and Architecture SA, Government of South Australia. CC BY 3.0 AU
p. 28/52 Bündner Heimatschutz, *52 beste Bauten*, Ralph Feiner
p. 58/59, 63, 67, 72/73 Filip Dujardin, Team Vlaams Bouwmeester
p. 82, 91 Atelier Rijksbouwmeester
p. 86/87 Absent Matter
p. 97 Archief Stadsatelier Oostende, CONDOR, Bovenbouw Architectuur, CLUSTER
p. 100 Archief Stadsatelier Oostende, ampe.trybou architecten
p. 101 Archief Stadsatelier Oostende
p. 106 Archief Stadsatelier Oostende, Ellen Verbiest
p. 109 Archief Stadsatelier Oostende, Raamwerk, ampe.trybou architecten, Bovenbouw Architectuur, CLUSTER
p. 111 Archief Stadsatelier Oostende, Raamwerk architecten
p. 118/119, 122/123 2001-51N4E-LOLA / Philippe Nathan & Arya Arabshahi & VIVID
p. 125 AREP / Kelissa Cartier & Grégoire Robida
p. 126/127 University of Luxembourg / Florian Hertweck & Céline Zimmer
p. 129 University of Luxembourg / Florian Hertweck & Aristaviva
p. 131,134/135 2023 Luxembourg Center for Architecture (luca) / Pancake
p. 140 Farrell Centre, Jill Tate
p.145,146 Farrell Centre, Jim Stephenson
p. 149, 152 51n4e, Sepideh Farvardin

Design/ Vormgeving
Karel & Aagje Martens

Copy editing/ Tekstredactie
D'Laine Camp, Gerda ten Cate

Printing/ Druk
Wilco Art Books

Paper/ Papier
70 grams Holmen TRND 2.0
400 grams Parelgrijs karton

Font/ Lettertype
Franklin Gothic

Publisher/ Uitgever
OASE foundation/ stichting

Distribution
nai010 publishers/ uitgevers
sales@nai010.com
www.nai010.com

Subscriptions and administration/ Abonnementenadministratie
Abonnementenland
De Trompet 1739
1967 DB Heemskerk
the Netherlands
Tel +31 (0)251 - 257924
www.aboland.nl

Subscriptions/
Abonnementen
OASE is published three times a year. Subscriptions can be taken out via the website of Abonnementenland, see www.aboland.nl. OASE can be found under the 'Art & Culture' category. Students at universities and academies of architecture as well as holders of a *CJP* are entitled to a reduction in the costs of the subscription. For the terms and conditions of the OASE subscription, please consult the website of Abonnementenland.
OASE verschijnt drie keer per jaar. Abonnementen kunnen afgesloten worden via de website van Abonnementenland, zie www.aboland.nl. OASE is te vinden onder de categorie 'Kunst & Cultuur'. Recht op reductie op de abonnementskosten hebben studenten aan universiteiten en academies van bouwkunst, alsmede houders van CJP. Voor de voorwaarden van het OASE-abonnement verwijzen wij u naar de website van Abonnementenland.

Subscriptions for three issues in Europe/
Abonnementsprijs voor drie nummers in Europa
individuals/
particulieren € 77,-
organisations/
instellingen € 125,-
students/
studenten € 55,-

Abonnementsprijs voor drie nummers in Nederland en België
particulieren € 66,-
instellingen € 110,-
studenten € 44,-

Subscriptions for three issues outside Europe/
Abonnementsprijs voor drie nummers buiten Europa
Individuals/
particulieren € 110,-
students/
studenten € 110,-
organisations/
instellingen € 150,-

Subscriptions for three digital issues/
Abonnementsprijs voor drie digitale nummers
individuals/
particulieren € 44,-
students/
studenten € 27,50

For professional and international (business) subscriptions, please send an email to oase@nai010.com/
Stuur voor professionele en internationale (zakelijke) abonnementen een e-mail naar oase@nai010.com.

Books distributed by nai010 are available internationally at selected bookstores and from the following distribution partners:

North, South and Central America – Artbook | D.A.P., New York, USA, dap@dapinc.com

Rest of the world – Idea Books, Amsterdam, the Netherlands, idea@ideabooks.nl

For general questions, please contact the OASE foundation directly at info@oasejournal.nl or visit our website www.oasejournal.nl for further information. For sales information and availability for bookshops, please contact nai010 at sales@nai010.com or visit www.nai010.com

Voor informatie over verkoop en distributie in Nederland en België, stuur een e-mail naar sales@nai010.com of kijk op www.nai010.com.

Printed and bound in the EU/ Gedrukt en gebonden in de EU

AgwA burgerlijke cvba, Brussel—ANA architecten, Amsterdam—aNNo architecten, Gent—Architectenbureau Bart Dehaene, Gent—ATAMA, Gent—Atelier Quadrat, Rotterdam—B-ILD. Brussel—Bulk Architecten, Deurne—Carton123 architecten, Brussel—CENTRAL office for architecture and urbanism, Brussel—Collectief Noord, Antwerpen—Daf architecten, Rotterdam—De Nijl Architecten, Rotterdam—De Smet Vermeulen architecten, Gent—De Zwarte Hond Rotterdam, Rotterdam—Diederendirrix architectuur & stedenbouw, Eindhoven—DP6 architectuurstudio, Delft—Frits Palmboom Stedebouwkundige, Amsterdam—FVWW architecten, Antwerpen—GAFPA bureau voor architectuur en stedenbouw, Gent—Geurst & Schulze architecten, Den Haag—Happel Cornelisse Verhoeven Architects, Rotterdam—HBAAT, Lille—HILBERINKBOSCH Architecten, Berlicum—KAAN architecten, Rotterdam—Korteknie Stuhlmacher Architecten, Rotterdam—Korth Tielens Architecten, Amsterdam—LEVS architecten, Amsterdam—M3H Architecten, Amsterdam—MARCEL LOK_ARCHITECT, Amsterdam—martenswillems architecten, Maastricht—MUST Stedebouw, Amsterdam—NL Architects, Amsterdam—Office Winhov, Amsterdam—Prof. ir. Wim van den Bergh Architect, Maastricht—RAPP + RAPP, Amsterdam—Rijnboutt, Amsterdam—Shift Architecture Urbanism, Rotterdam—Stad Antwerpen, Antwerpen—Steenhuis Bukman Architecten, Delft—STUDIO VINCENT Architecture, Amsterdam—Team bouwmeester maître architecte, Brussel—Urbain Architectencollectief, Gent—VVKH, Leiden—West 8, Rotterdam—Ziegler | Branderhorst stedenbouw en architectuur, Rotterdam

To order back issues of OASE, please visit our website: www.oasejournal.nl, or that of our distrubutor: www.nai010.com/ U kunt eerder verschenen nummers van OASE bestellen via onze website: www.oasejournal.nl, of die van onzedistributeur: www.nai010.com

OASE 119 Rationalism Revisited/ Rationalisme herzien
OASE 118 Book Reviews: From Words to Buildings/ Boekbesprekingen: Van woorden naar gebouwen
OASE 117 Project Village/ Project dorp
OASE 116 The Architect as a Public Intellectual/ De architect als publieke intellectueel
OASE 115 Interferences: Moving across European Architecture Cultures/ Interferenties: Europese architectuurculturen in beweging
OASE 114 Optimism or Bust?/ Optimisme of de ondergang?
OASE 113 Authorship/ Auteurschap
OASE 112 Ecology & Aesthetics/ Ecologie & Esthetiek
OASE 111 Staging the Museum/ Musea in scene gezet
OASE 110 The Project of the Soil/ De grond van de kwestie
OASE 109 Modernities/ Moderniteiten
OASE 108 Ups & Downs: Reception Histories in Architecture/ Receptiegeschiedenissen in de architectuur
OASE 107 The Drawing in Landscape Design and Urbanism/ De tekening in landschapsontwerp en stedenbouw
OASE 106 Table Settings: Reflections on Architecture with Hannah Arendt/ Tafelschikkingen: Reflecties op architectuur met Hannah Arendt
OASE 105 Practices of Drawing/ Tekenpraktijken
OASE 104 The Urban Household of Metabolism/ Het stedelijke huishouden van het metabolisme
OASE 103 Critical Regionalism Revisited
OASE 102 Schools & Teachers: The Education of an Architect in Europe/ Scholen & docenten: De opleiding tot architect in Europa
OASE 101 Microcosm: Searching for the City in Its Interiors/ Microkosmos: Een zoektocht naar de stad in haar interieurs
OASE 100 Karel Martens and the Architecture of the Journal/ Karel Martens en de architectuur van het tijdschrift
OASE 99 The Architecture Museum Effect/ De effecten van architectuurmusea
OASE 98 Narrating Urban Landscapes/ Verhalend stedelijk landschap
OASE 97 Action and Reaction in Architecture/ Actie en reactie in architectuur
OASE 96 Social Poetics: The Architecture of Use and Appropriation/ Sociale Poëtica: De architectuur van gebruik en toe-eigening
OASE 95 Crossing Boundaries: Transcultural Practices in Architecture and Urbanism/ Grenzenloos: Transculturele praktijken in architectuur en stedenbouw
OASE 94 OMA: The First Decade/ OMA: De eerste tien jaar
OASE 93 Making Landscape Public: Making Public Landscape/ Landschap publiek maken: Publiek landschap maken
OASE 92 Codes and Continuities/ Codes en continuïteiten
OASE 91 Building Atmosphere/ Sfeer bouwen, met/ with Juhani Pallasmaa & Peter Zumthor
OASE 90 What is Good Architecture/ Wat is goede architectuur?
OASE 89 Medium: The Mid-Size City as a European Urban Condition and Strategy/ De middelgrote stad als Europese stedelijke conditie en strategie
OASE 88 Exhibitions: Showing and Producing Architecture/ Tentoonstellingen: Architectuur tonen en produceren
OASE 87 Alan Colquhoun: Architect, Historian, Critic/ Architect, Historicus, Criticus
OASE 86 Baroque/ Barok
OASE 85 Productive Uncertainty/ Productieve onzekerheid
OASE 84 Models/ Maquettes
OASE 83 Commissioning Architecture/ Opdrachtgevers in de architectuur
OASE 82 L'Afrique, c'est chic: Architecture and planning in Africa 1950-1970/ Architectuur en planning in Afrika 1950-1970
OASE 81 Constructing Criticism/ Kritiek in opbouw
OASE 80 On Territories/ Over territoria
OASE 79 The Architecture of James Stirling, 1964-1992/ De architectuur van James Sterling, 1964-1992
OASE 78 Immersed: Sound and Architecture/ Architectuur en geluid
OASE 77 Into the Open: Accommodating the Public/ Publieke plaatsen
OASE 76 Context/ Specificity
OASE 75 25 Years of Critical Reflection on Architecture
OASE 74 Invention/ Inventie